Liberty and Law

*Reflections on the Constitution
in American Life and Thought*

Edited and Introduced by

Ronald A. Wells
Thomas A. Askew

William B. Eerdmans Publishing Company
Grand Rapids, Michigan

Copyright © 1987 by Wm. B. Eerdmans Publishing Co.
255 Jefferson Ave. S.E., Grand Rapids, Mich. 49503

Library of Congress Cataloging-in-Publication Data:

Liberty and law.

1. United States—Constitutional history.
2. Freedom of religion—United States—History.
I. Wells, Ronald, 1941–
II. Askew, Thomas A.
KF4541.H2L53 1987   342.73′029   87-24582

ISBN 0-8028-0307-5   347.30229

Contents

Contributors

Thomas A. Askew is Professor of History at Gordon College.

Richard H. Clossman is Professor of History at Judson College.

David E. Maas is Professor of History at Wheaton College (Ill).

Paul Marshall is Senior member in Politics and Vice-President of The Institute for Christian Studies, Toronto.

Richard V. Pierard is Professor of History at Indiana State University.

Richard Pointer is Associate Professor of History at Trinity College (Ill.).

Kathryn J. Pulley is Assistant Professor of Religious Studies at Southwest Missouri State University.

Johan D. van der Vyver is Professor of Law at the University of Witswatersrand.

Ronald A. Wells is Professor of History at Calvin College.

Preface

This book was conceived by the editors four years before its publication. With the bicentennial of the American Constitution four years hence, we hoped to produce a volume in 1987 that would reflect on the Constitution and the constitutional. Moreover, we wanted to find the best writing available by Christian scholars who would bring their Christian commitments to bear in their study. The editors were commissioned by the officers of the Conference on Faith and History to convene the organization's fifteenth annual meeting, focusing on Christian perspectives on the Constitution. With the generous support of the Lilly Endowment we were able to convene and chair a meeting at Gordon College in October 1986. Gordon College also sponsored the conference as one of its centennial colloquia. The chapters in this book originated as papers at that meeting. It should be said, however, that this book is not merely a reprinting of conference proceedings. The authors have worked closely with Ronald Wells in transforming their spoken remarks into carefully constructed literary efforts.

The essays are as diverse as the people who wrote them. Some essays are broadly humanistic while others are more oriented toward the methods of the social sciences. Some are wide ranging while others are more particularly focused. Five of the authors are historians while the others are professors of law, politics, and religious studies. Six of the authors are United States citizens while one is a Canadian and another a South African.

What the essays share is a common aspiration of thinking Christianly about the American frame of government, the Constitution. Within that common aspiration there is no party line or unified set of political beliefs. While some of the essays are notably laudatory of the beneficial effects of the Constitution in American life and thought, others are more critical of that ideology and practice. The diversity of views is the hallmark of this effort, because we believe that the study of history is an on-going process in which there are many honorable views.

There are certain persons whose contribution to this volume must be acknowledged publicly. Thomas Askew's colleagues in the Gordon

College history department, especially Russel Bishop, were of great help in organizing the conference from which this book comes. Robert Lynn, Vice-President of the Lilly Endowment, worked closely with Ronald Wells in providing financial support for the conference. Calvin College deserves thanks for giving logistical support to Ronald Wells. Jacqueline de Vries, research assistant in Calvin's history department, contributed significantly in bringing these essays to their current form.

We hope and trust that readers will find it worthy of their time to join us in reflecting on both the Constitution and American liberty and law.

February 1987   RONALD A. WELLS,
                                        Grand Rapids, Michigan

                                        THOMAS A. ASKEW,
                                        Wenham, Massachusetts

Foreword

Congressman Paul B. Henry

Nineteen eighty-seven marks the two hundredth anniversary of the drafting of the Constitution of the United States of America. Despite the relative youth of the nation, the Constitution survives as the longest-serving national legal charter in the history of mankind.

When the fifty-five delegates to the Constitutional convention gathered in Philadelphia, they were responding to a breakdown of governmental institutions under the Articles of Confederation. They were motivated not by philosophical or academic or religious visions of some grand scheme of human governance. They were responding to the practical problems of the young American republic.

But as they proceeded in their deliberations, they drew from a shared tradition of moral and intellectual assumptions from which the practical questions of the new national charter would find their answers. A joining of Judeo-Christian values, eighteenth-century Enlightenment rationalism, and the classical history of ancient Greece and Rome provided the soil from which the Constitution received its nourishment.

One cannot, for example, fully appreciate the Constitution's guarantees of human rights without acknowledging the presumed belief its authors shared concerning the divinely rooted origins of human existence—despite the fact that the Constitution remarkably makes no direct reference to the Divine Being. One cannot fully appreciate the Constitution's protections for free expression without acknowledging the presumed belief its authors shared regarding the substantive nature of truth. The First Amendment freedoms were championed not as ends in themselves, but as the most secure path to truth itself. One cannot fully appreciate the Constitution's elaborate system of political checks and balances without acknowledging its authors' deep suspicion of human nature.

The Constitution is the meeting place between belief in man's capacity for good and practical insights about his penchant for evil. It demonstrates that prudence and practical experience in human affairs are necessary correlates to abstract philosophy and religion. And it demonstrates, with equal intensity, that philosophic and religious values underlie that which is deemed prudent and practical.

Americans, in particular, tend to forget that the Constitution was not a "perfect" document. Its ratification was secured only with advance commitment to adoption of what we now know as the "Bill of Rights," the first ten amendments to the Constitution. It fundamentally compromised its own moral assumptions and foundations in forging a political accord on the slavery issue. But even in its failures, we can learn lessons on the frailty of human governmental institutions and procedures which can inform and strengthen the constitutional tradition in subsequent generations.

The impact and significance of the United States Constitution extends well beyond the borders of the people whose life it governs. It served as the inspiration for the Latin American constitutions of the eighteenth century, it brought forth European constitutions in the nineteenth century, and it strongly informed the constitutional charters of the postcolonial world in the twentieth century. And it has beguiled many into equating the presence of a written constitution with the practice of constitutional government.

We need to be reminded that the concept of "constitutional" government is a separate question from the existence of a written constitutional charter. The English tradition of constitutional government preceded and strongly informed our own Constitution, despite the fact that the United Kingdom has never relied on a written charter. And until only recently, our neighbor to the north, Canada, had no document of truly constitutional standing. Indeed, it is the unwritten moral and intellectual assumptions about man and society which truly guide the political behavior of nations. There are numerous examples today of nations with splendid written constitutional charters whose actual behavior is far removed from anything which most of the community would regard as "constitutional" government.

Thus, we return to the beginning assumption of this brief introduction, and the underlying thesis of the essays which follow. Ideas have consequences. There were certain underlying ideas and concepts which informed the authors of our Constitution and which are reflected in that document. The question remains: Can the document continue to exercise its authority if and when the moral and intellectual assumptions upon which it is based are called into question?

Introduction

In 1878, in respect of the Constitution's centennial, British Prime Minister William Gladstone described the American Constitution as "the most wonderful work ever struck off at a given time by the brain and purpose of man." While surely hyperbole, the remark lends point to the suggestion that the young republic's frame of government was—and is—a remarkable achievement. Even though the United States is a relatively new nation, it is governed by the oldest and most durable written constitution.

Adopted by a nation of about 4 million citizens scattered thinly across the thirteen original states, the Constitution now governs the lives of 250 million persons in fifty states. Despite the nation's evolution from rural republic to industrial giant, the Constitution as basic law has been amended a mere twenty-six times.

The Constitution, however, is not an artifact, a parchment to be revered like an icon. It is an amalgam of ideals, principles, compromises, and authorizations for action that embody the spirit and determination that shaped the American experiment in its formative years. Composed at the end of a quarter century marked by conflict with Britain and a search for effective government at home in the new nation, the document of 1787 was built on experience as much as theory, on concrete interests as much as ideals. Once fashioned and ratified, the Constitution became a dynamic instrument whose meaning and application could evolve with America's history, politics, economy, and society.

The longer-term success of the Constitution derives from the insights and good sense of the fifty-five convention delegates, thirty-nine of whom finally signed it. By today's standards they were strikingly youthful. Five were still in their twenties. A number, including Alexander Hamilton and James Madison, were in their early or mid-thirties. Another group clustered in the early forties. George Washington, along with two others, was fifty-five. Only four exceeded sixty, the oldest being Benjamin Franklin at eighty-one. In addition they reflected a cross-section of leadership within the infant state. Twenty-eight had

served in the Confederation Congress; most of the others had state
legislative experience. Several had been college professors and two
were college presidents. At least twenty-eight held baccalaureate
degrees. Nine were born abroad; four others learned law in London at
the Inns of Court. Many developed a sense of national loyalty and identity while serving in the Continental Army. With the exception of John
Adams and Thomas Jefferson who were in Europe and John Jay attending to foreign policy, the Federal Convention gathered the greater share
of political thinkers available to the young country.

The debates reflected the plethora of historical allusions, philosophic arguments, British legal precedents, and Christian theology that
animated political discussions during the Revolutionary period. Most
delegates were familiar with the natural-law essays of Enlightenment
thinkers, the common-law writings of English jurists, and the contents
of Scripture. Whether trinitarian, unitarian, or deist, they all affirmed a
moral order established by a transcendent deity. Even the most devout
Christian believers, in typical eighteenth-century fashion, felt little tension in blending classical antiquity, Enlightenment rationality, and
empiricism with Christian theology, a synthesis that would unravel in
the following century. Confident that men, like nature, answered to the
precepts of universal laws, these founders sought to discern what John
Adams had earlier termed "the divine science of politics."

At the same time the framers were realists about both the task to
be achieved and human nature itself. Two centuries of colonial politics
coupled with two decades of state making provided ample experience
on which to draw. They were committed to the possible, not the ideal.
Men were accountable moral agents whose baser side must be checked.
Somehow, the tendency toward self-centeredness needed counter-
balancing. Thus, unrestricted power and authority could not be lodged
in one social group, department of government, or region. Interests
must be balanced by competing interests. Yet to these designers of the
nation, politics was not irretrievably egoistic and individualistic. There
was need for community, covenant, and civic virtue; a virile and force-
ful federal government would prove an antidote to instability within and
among the states and to demeaning treatment from governments
abroad. In this sense the Constitution writers should be termed nascent
nationalists in a society still characterized by extensive localism.

The salient features of the Federal Convention's recommendations
are well known. The national government, like the respective state
governments, was to draw its powers directly from the citizens, a con-

cept that became known as dual federalism or divided sovereignty. "We the people" assigned distinct functions to national and state levels and in turn were directly responsible to both spheres of authority. Good republicans that they were, the framers labored hard to erect a mechanism of representation that would be workable yet avoid the rashness of direct, unicameral majoritarianism. Also, any scheme of representation had to reflect the uneven distribution of persons and property in the populace at large yet allow for state interests to be heard. A two-house legislature, the House of Representatives and the Senate, provided the answer. Balance and prudence would be built into the law-making process. Finally, the separation of functions among executive, judicial, and legislative branches avoided unchecked, arbitrary power flowing from any one sector of governance.

The Constitution framers wrote in general concepts, leaving later interpreters to work out the specific applications. This ensured longevity by permitting future generations to debate and apply its principles in changing circumstances. Almost immediately a continuing dialogue began over the nature of national policy the fundamental law would support. Within these debates the Constitution proved expansive. A broadening electorate and the rise of parties rapidly set aside the writers' original elitist priorities in favor of democratic participation. Energized by the ideals of the Declaration of Independence, females and minorities eventually and belatedly joined the body politic. The empowerment of the "necessary and proper" clause in legislation, coupled with court decisions and executive precedents, undergirded the emergence of a national government able to meet its responsibilities. Along the way, especially after the thirteenth, fourteenth, and fifteenth amendments, the Constitution and Bill of Rights gradually became the avenue for gaining civil liberties against local injustices. Never fully attained, the quest for human rights and equality before the law continue as ideals to be realized. Also, Christianity and the churches came to flourish under the First Amendment promise that "Congress shall make no law respecting an establishment of religion, or prohibiting the free exercise thereof."

In retrospect the Constitution was a venture in republicanism unprecedented in history for its scale of operation and breadth of vision. Nowhere previously had the social contract brought together such diverse peoples and local sovereignties into a national whole. It truly is a gift from the founding generation to our own. Thoughtful observers recognize that parliamentary governments have their particular advantages, and inefficient anachronisms are surely evident in the 1787 document. Yet it remains difficult to envision a more apt framework of fundamental law fitting the two-hundred-year saga of the United States of America.

The essays in this book center on three themes: the impact of the constitutional form of government on the early republic; the American Constitution in comparison to other nations' constitutions; the implications of constitutional thinking for life in the twentieth century.

David Maas's essay begins the book with a study of the context of ideology—localism versus nationalism—which must be understood in light of religious dialogue in the eighteenth century. Richard Pointer's work, also on the ideology of the founding generation, builds on current scholarship (notably that of Forrest McDonald) regarding the heritage of Lockean thinking. The founders were unafraid of truth because of their largely unspoken conviction about the nature of social truth and about what a free people could, or would, do with that truth. Richard Clossman sees the connection between the republican ideology of virtue and the Protestant idea of social righteousness.

The next group of essays compares the American Constitution with other constitutions, specifically the parliamentary systems of Canada, West Germany, and South Africa. Here is one of the most significantly Christian contributions of this book. Christians are firstly citizens of the kingdom of God, and only secondarily citizens of nation-states. American Christians can learn more about themselves and their form of society and law when compared with other constitutional experiences. Paul Marshall begins this section with a critique of American progressivist assumptions in respect of conservative Canadian thinking. Richard Pierard centers his work on the relationship of church and state in the American and West German constitutions. Johan van der Vyver, in a theoretically demanding essay, contrasts the nature of law and social obligation in the United States and the Republic of South Africa.

In the final section, Kathryn Pulley and Ronald Wells discuss some twentieth-century concerns. Pulley describes the pluralist intentions of the founders and the way in which pluralism places strains on social cohesion in our time. Wells, in the final essay of the book, reviews the pattern of thought and behavior that lies behind the Constitution, and then discusses the paradoxical erosion of community in America in respect of America's greatest quality—liberty. He discusses whether or not it

is possible to recover the mind of republican virtue, the world we have
lost.

The Philosophical and Theological Roots of the Religious Clause in the Constitution

David E. Maas

America had already begun to drift toward "unbelief" by 1787. So concluded a prominent contemporary scholar after comparing the text of the Declaration of Independence with the text of the Constitution.[1] The Declaration acknowledges God the "Creator" as author of our liberties, appeals to the "Supreme Judge of the World" for justice, and trusts in the protection of "divine Providence."[2] Furthermore, its text reflected basic Christian values.[3] But the federal Constitution does not contain even so much as a deistic reference to God. The Constitution's sole religious reference, one that might be interpreted as even antireligious, appears in Article 6, Clause 3: federal and state officials "shall be bound by Oath or Affirmation, to support this Constitution; but no religious test shall ever be required as a qualification to any office or public trust under the United States."[4]

Since the minutes of the Constitutional Convention were first published in 1819, over three decades later, most contemporaries based their evaluations solely on the text of the Constitution. For example, in 1788 a Connecticut citizen condemned the framers for following secular rather than spiritual wisdom, lamenting that their Constitution wore "marks of art, ambiguity, and the properties of worldly wisdom." He was certain it was drawn not from the "wisdom which is from above," but from "natural, or worldly wisdom." Moreover, he concluded, it must have been drafted by godless men for "surely neglect of God, breach of solemn covenants, do not indicate purity of heart or life."[5]

Should a contemporary right-wing pastor preach a thundering sermon against the decline of Christian America from 1776 to 1787? A title like "The Drift to Secularism" may make a powerful message, but would be misleading if based solely on a comparison of the two texts. Use of the Constitution as litmus paper to indicate unbelief or secularism seems problematical for several reasons. First, the Constitution, apart from other documents, neither proves nor disproves secularism.[6]

Second, Thomas Jefferson, the leading American proponent of the Enlightenment, wrote the more religiously phrased Declaration of Independence. He was in France when the Constitutional Convention met and so had little ideological impact on the Constitution. Third, deists such as Jefferson write wishfully about a future enlightened age.[7] Finally, an interpretation based on silence, or upon a single clause, violates the principle of context. The framers met in Philadelphia not to chart the religious course of four million Americans but to draft a political document.

In this chapter I will attempt a systematic examination of Article Six's prohibition of religious oaths within the context of the framers' earlier experiences, namely the colonial days, the Revolution, the formulation of state constitutions, and legislative debates at the Constitutional Convention. Scholars from Henry Baxter Adams to Frederick Jackson Turner have often sought an illusive thread to hold together the rich tapestry of American history. No doubt, all such helpful integrative attempts are guilty of oversimplification. Nevertheless, the tension between localism and nationalism, or regionalism and centralism, contextualizes much of American history from colonial times down to the Civil War. The prescience of the framers allowed them to devise a government based on *both* nationalism and regionalism.

We enter the labyrinth of the framers' world, not blindly, nor plucking single Constitutional clauses out of context, but guided by the creative tensions of localism versus nationalism. Then, although our exploration involves circumvolutions, turning through colonial history, the American Revolution, early state constitutions, and finally into the Constitutional Convention, we will emerge with a new paradigm. The Constitution's prohibition on religious oaths was a sugar-coated pill for localists, who at the convention lost to the nationalists.

From the first charter to Virginia in 1606 to the last charter to Georgia in 1732, England faced a problem of authority. How could England maintain effective political and economic control over British America some three thousand miles away? At first, England's efforts at centralism were restricted to ineffective clauses in the early charters. Until the 1660s, the crown let local assemblies have a large measure of self-government. Following the Restoration, England increased its control by refusing to establish any more charter colonies; henceforth, England only created proprietary or royal colonies. Then in 1685 came the Dominion of New England, an abortive and short-lived unification under one royal governor of all the governments north of Pennsylvania. These colonies, after three years of no representative government and taxes by executive decree, revolted during the Glorious Revolution of 1688. After the accession of William and Mary, the crown restored local power to colonial legislatures. There were occasional efforts by the Board of Trade, especially under the leadership of the Earl of Halifax, but America fed well on British neglect. The primary reminder of the colonies' subordination to British authority were the symbolic oaths— oaths that the framers would also later replicate in the Constitution to achieve loyalty to a national government.

Since the Middle Ages land owners took oaths of "fealty," similar to an "oath of allegiance" to their lord. After 1066, every English male over twelve took an oath of allegiance to the king.[8] Because the 1688 Glorious Revolution established Protestant dominance over the Roman Catholic religion, additional oaths were required. All English office-holders took the oath of adjuration, promising to support the king and the Revolution against "the descendants of the late pretender."[9] English males also took a third oath, the oath of supremacy, which renounced the pope's authority.[10] These oaths were appointed by statute "for better securing the government"[11] Finally, all officers, civil and military, had to take the Test, an oath denying transubstantiation, and within six months of taking office, partake of the Lord's Supper, following Anglican forms.[12]

England insisted that the colonists incorporate these civil and religious oaths into colonial charters and practices. Connecticut, by its charter of 1662, required the freemen of the colony to take the oath of allegiance and the oath of fidelity.[13] As soon as the British captured New York from the Dutch, the people had to take an oath of allegiance to the crown.[14] No Virginian in the eighteenth century became a justice or militia officer without taking all the oaths in open court. Periodically, each local Virginia court reconstituted itself by the junior justice administering all the oaths to the senior justice, who would then swear in the rest of the court.[15] Such extensive oath taking symbolically reminded the colonists of their subordination to the crown.

Turning our attention to the American Revolution, it is important to understand that nationalism versus localism lay at its epicenter. Bernard Bailyn, the foremost historian of the American Revolution, argues that all the revolutionary "agitation was to confine the use of power; to protect the population against the threat of unrestrained coercion."[16] Colonial leaders such as John Adams, Thomas Jefferson, and Alexander Hamilton read the works of English Commonwealth writers

who warned that powerful governments always were destructive of individual rights. For these writers, history was a constant struggle between power and liberty. Upper-class Americans embraced this Commonwealth Whig ideology since it reinforced their own conservative
attitudes.[17] Displaying elitist ideology, which simplified the whole war
into a struggle over authority, Edmund Quincy claimed England had a
"Lust of Despotism" and greatly feared any "Democratical power."[18]
Or in the words of a Boston minister, "what misery doth Pride & a Lust
of Dominion bring on mankind." England, he argued, could save
money by not sending an army to force American submission, but "she
must assert her Authority & her supreme Power must be owned."[19] The
Reverend Stephen Johnson, a twenty-year-old American preacher, carried the argument against one supreme authority to ridiculous extremes
when he argued that if Parliament could pass a stamp tax, why not "a
poll tax, a land tax, a malt tax, a cider tax, a window tax, a smoke tax,
and why not tax us for the light of the sun, or the air we breathe, and
the ground we are buried in?"[20]

Colonial elites soon rejected the British concept that members of
Parliament represented the whole empire. They wanted a governmental representative to reflect local self-interests. When a town in New
England elected a member to the Popular Assembly, he should mirror
the "individuality of their interests." Such a "sense of articularity"
prompted colonial assemblies to argue they had the right to govern their
own internal affairs, without outside interference from Parliament.[21]
American revolutionists also drew heavily on the medieval concepts of
natural law and natural rights. Natural law advocates in America argued
that man had God-given rights—such as freedom from arbitrary authority and of life, liberty, and property—that were antecedent to positive
law. Citing Sir Edward Coke, a preeminent English jurist, the Americans argued neither king nor Parliament could violate natural law. The
idea that individual rights were superior to the decrees of a centralized
authority in England struck a responsive chord among lower-class
Americans. Many of them liked Adam Smith's economic liberalism
with its stress on aggressive individualism. Why should England hinder
their pursuit of economic self-interest[22]—especially when 40-55 percent of all colonists lived at subsistence levels and in urban centers un-
employment was a serious problem. As one historian concluded, "once
disorder was rampant, control became difficult and in the tumultuous
excitement anti-authoritarianism spread."[23]

What functions did oaths serve? First, oaths were used in revolutionary times as a method to prevent the lower class from anarchy and as a check against leveling ideology. Upper-class leaders feared arbitrary centralized British rule, but even more frightening to them was the thought of arbitrary mob rule. For example, Gouverneur Morris, a twenty-three-year-old American aristocrat, in 1774 observed a mass meeting of tradesmen in New York City. He then wrote that if the mob, the "poor reptiles," get power "we shall be under the domination of a riotous mob."[24] In August 1765, after a mob inflicted £3,000 damage on Lt. Governor Thomas Hutchinson's home, Josiah Quincy, a young patriot lawyer, wrote in his journal, "who, that sees the *Fury and Instability* of the Populace, but would seek Protection under the ARM OF POWER? Who that beholds the *Tyranny and Oppression* of arbitrary Power, but would lose his Life in Defence of His LIBERTY?"[25]

The revolutionary patriots believed, second, that oaths were a social and civil obligation. Even without an oath, citizens owed allegiance, because it was "written by the finger of the law in their hearts." However, "the sanction of an oath . . . strengthens the *social* tie by uniting it with that of religion."[26] As trouble heated up between England and America in 1774, British officials vainly tried to administer the required oaths as a method to maintain British loyalty.[27] Patriots countered by adjuring oaths renouncing the king. As early as 1775, mobs in Massachusetts assembled and forced magistrates "to bind themselves by oaths" not to obey the recent acts of Parliament.[28] When Maryland legislators met in June 1776, they voted to abolish altogether "oaths of allegiance" to the crown. Pennsylvania's 1776 assembly admitted members to their seats "without taking the Oath of Allegiance, and dispensed with that oath upon all other occasions."[29]

However, the colonies did not stop at dispensing with oaths to the crown; rather, they began establishing oaths of their own. Again this movement began at the local level in most colonies. For example, in April 1775 officials in Essex County, Massachusetts, arrested twenty-nine citizens suspected of Toryism. The patriots demanded a confession of past disloyalty and a promise of future good behavior. When these Tories acted obstinate, their captors marched them off to the dreaded mines in Simsbury, Connecticut. Only fourteen miles into the trip, all recanted and signed loyalty oaths.[30] In May 1775 the Massachusetts Provincial Congress recommended that each town's committee of correspondence inquire into principles of suspected persons and disarm all those not pledging to defend America against British tyranny.[31] In response to this suggestion, Medway forced its suspicious citizens to

sign two papers of loyalty.[32] Tories also used oaths as a method of securing loyalty. In areas protected by the British army, Tories took oaths
to support each other and to "promote, encourage, and . . . enforce obedience" to George III.[33]

In May 1775, the Continental Congress recommended that each
colony form a new government. The preamble to this famous resolve
pointed out that it was "irreconcilable to reason and good conscience"
any longer to take "the oaths and affirmations" to the crown.[34] Then in
the spring of 1777, Congress proposed that states should use oaths as a
method to distinguish loyal from disloyal citizens. Some states already
required oaths of their military officers and state officeholders, but internal enemies, such as men loyal to the crown, it was thought, were
more dangerous and should also be required to take oaths.[35] Connecticut, Virginia, and Massachusetts delegates in the Congress urged their
states to pass test oaths to "distinguish previously the Whigs from the
Tories."[36] John Adams suggested Massachusetts draft an oath that
would "outlaw all who will not take it—that is suffer them to hold no
Office, to take out no Execution."[37] Gradually, each state passed laws
requiring citizens suspected of disloyalty to take oaths of allegiance to
the state. In May 1778 Delaware denied political rights to any citizen
refusing to take oaths of allegiance to the state.[38] New York in June
1778 passed an act requiring all suspected citizens to take an oath acknowledging New York "to be of right a free and independent State."[39]
Eventually every state required loyalty oaths.[40]

Third, oaths had moral and spiritual implications for the revolutionary generation.[41] Private citizens suspected of disloyalty realized
their solemnity. Loyalists like Peter Van Schaack spent years in exile
because his conscience would not permit him to take the oath of allegiance to the state of New York.[42] Both the loyalists and patriots were
critical of turncoats like Benedict Arnold or Jacob Duche, who would
take an oath and then desert—traitors who "Oath & Conscience cannot
bind."[43] According to John Adams, armies often lacked both "Religion
or Morality." The "one Principle of Religion" that worked wondrously
in both the Roman and British armies was the "Sacred obligation of
oaths." Adams urged General Nathaniel Greene to encourage his chaplains to adopt as their "favourite Subject . . . the Solemn Nature and
Sacred Obligations of oaths."[44] James Wilson of Pennsylvania argued
oaths were major pillars maintaining order and authority in government. If oaths cease "the people will be instantly in a state of nature."[45]

A fourth character of oaths was that only sovereign powers could require them. This viewpoint came sharply into focus in 1776 when American general Charles Lee, on his own initiative, required Rhode Island and New York Tories to take an oath of allegiance to America. This upset localists in the Continental Congress who argued that "to impose a Test is a sovereign Act of Legislation—and when the army becomes our Legislators, the People that Moment become Slaves."[46] The following year George Washington issued a proclamation declaring that all Americans were to swear an oath of allegiance to the United States.[47] This action prompted legislative complaints about usurpation of civilian powers.[48]

Finally, oaths of allegiance were sworn to state or local committees, not to the national government. During the whole Confederation period, Congress never endorsed a single national loyalty program. There never were any oaths, tests, or declarations required of delegates to the Continental Congress. Localism or state supremacy dominated during the Confederation period.[49] The Articles of Confederation carefully defined its structure as a loose confederation of sovereign states. Article II stated, "Each state retains its sovereignty, freedom and independence, and every Power, Jurisdiction and right, which is not by this confederation expressly delegated to the United States, in Congress assembled."[50] Therefore, Congress left it up to each state to define oaths of loyalty and to draft state constitutions, which determined both oaths and the religious beliefs of voters and state officials.

I want to suggest that each delegate's understanding of religious freedom and oaths crystallized when his state drafted its new constitution. If we ever hope to understand the Constitution's prohibition of religious oaths, we must look into the treatment of both religion and oaths in the first state constitutions. These state constitutions rehearsed and conditioned the national delegates' perceptions at the Federal Convention. One half of its members had previously served on their states' constitutional conventions. Furthermore, most of the formal provisions of the national constitution, including oaths, already existed in one or more of the state constitutions.[51]

In eight brief years from 1776 to 1783, before the British signed the peace treaty granting American independence, twelve different states wrote fifteen full-bodied constitutions.[52] Many of these constitutions were contradictory, often containing both a liberal clause disestablishing religion and later a clause mandating religious oaths for officeholders. One example is New Jersey's constitution, which contained the first specific disestablishment of religion: "there shall be

no establishment of any one religious sect in this Province, in preference to another." In addition, it promised one freedom of worship of
"Almighty God in a manner agreeable to the dictates of his own conscience," with tithes or taxes for ministers or church buildings on a voluntary basis. Yet despite these progressive clauses, New Jersey's constitution still required all state officials to be "Protestants" and an oath
of all legislators that they would never attempt to repeal the articles on
religious freedom.[53]

The South Carolina 1776 constitution also required oaths. The very
day the legislators finished drafting it, they prepared an oath for the new
governor that contained a strong religious provision, requiring him and
all governors thereafter to defend the "Laws of God, the Protestant Religion, and the Liberties of America. So HELP ME GOD."[54] By 1778,
South Carolina's second constitution required all state officials to be
"of the Protestant religion."[55] It went on to define the voter as a "free
white man . . . who acknowledges the being of a God, and believes in
a future state of rewards and punishments."[56]

Another bell-weather constitution, Virginia's 1776 constitution,
established numerous precedents and became the most frequently
copied model. Its bill of rights endorsed religious freedom: "That religion, or the duty which we owe to our Creator, and the manner of dis-
charging it, can be directed only by reason and conviction, not by force
or violence; and therefore all men are equally entitled to the free exercise of religion, according to the dictates of conscience; and that it is
the mutual duty of all to practise Christian forbearance, love, and char-
ity towards each other." However, apart from this one deistic reference
to the "Creator," the Virginia constitution refrained from mentioning
God by name. For example, Section 1 echoes phrases used later in the
Declaration of Independence about inherent rights, but stops short of
calling them endowments from God. Furthermore, in the body of the
constitution ministers were barred from political office: "all ministers
of the gospel, of every denomination, be incapable of being elected
members of either House of Assembly or the Privy Council."[57] Clearly
such provisions foreshadowed Virginia's disestablishment of religion
in January 1786.[58]

Delaware borrowed heavily from its neighbors, New Jersey and
Virginia. Aping Virginia's constitution, Delaware's started out with a
separate bill of rights, which included an article "That all Men have a
natural and unalienable Right to worship Almighty God according to
the Dictates of their own Conscience and Understandings; and that no

Man ought or of Right can be compelled to attend any religious Worship or maintain any Ministry contrary to or against his own free Will and Consent, and that no Authority can or ought to be vested in, or assumed by any manner control the Right of Conscience."[59] A later article exempted Quakers from bearing arms provided they paid for a replacement.[60] Copying words from New Jersey's constitution, Delaware's asserted "there shall be no establishment of any one religious sect in this State in preference to another." It also mandated that "no clergyman or preacher of the gospel, of any denomination, shall be capable of holding any civil office in this State, or of being a member of either of the branches of the legislature, while they continue in the exercise of the pastoral function." However, in Article 29 Delaware added a new religious wrinkle by requiring all members of their House to take a religious oath: "I, _____ , do profess faith in God the Father, and in Jesus Christ His only Son, and in the Holy Ghost, one God, blessed for evermore; and I do acknowledge the holy scriptures of the Old and New Testament to be given by divine inspiration."[61] Such an oath, with explicit doctrinal belief, went beyond the governor of South Carolina's oath.

Pennsylvania, which had no established church in colonial days, reflecting either its colonial heritage or the religious freedom clauses of Virginia and Delaware, banned any religious establishment in the future. Article II stated: "That all men have a natural and unalienable right to worship Almighty God according to the dictates of their own consciences and understanding: And that no man ought or of right can be compelled to attend any religious worship, or erect or support any place of worship, or maintain any ministry, contrary to or against, his own free will and consent." Perhaps because Pennsylvania had such a diversity of religious sects, it did not hesitate to sprinkle its constitution with references to God. For example, in the preface it referred to "their natural rights, and the other blessings which the Author of existence has bestowed upon man." In another section, it stated that the convention had met for the express purpose of drafting a constitution, "confessing the goodness of the great Governor of the universe (who alone knows to what degree of earthly happiness mankind may attain, by perfecting arts of government)." All members of the Pennsylvania Assembly had to take a Protestant religious oath: "I do believe in one God, the creator and governor of the universe, the rewarder of the good and the punisher of the wicked. And I do acknowledge the Scriptures of the Old and New Testament to be given by Divine inspiration." Then came a very significant phrase: "and no further or other religious test shall ever hereafter be required of any civil officer or magistrate in this state."[62]

Maryland's 1776 constitution also included religious provisions. In its bill of rights it provided for freedom of religion for all "professing the Christian religion" and banned future religious preferential taxes. However, it guaranteed that Anglican ministers who had remained in their parish during the war would still receive financial support. Furthermore, the legislature, at their discretion, could levy a general tax for the "support of the Christian religion," with each taxpayer designating the church or minister to receive his tax money. Article 34 voided all gifts or sales of lands to ministers, without the prior consent of the legislature. However, grants of under two acres of land for a church or burial ground were valid without prior consent of the legislature. Maryland required all officeholders to take both an oath of fidelity to the state and a separate "declaration of a belief in the Christian religion." The body of the constitution followed the increasingly popular ban on any minister "or preacher of the gospel, of any denomination" holding a seat in the General Assembly or the Council of State.[63]

North Carolina's bill of rights contained a simple statement that religious freedom was a "natural and unalienable right." In Article 34 of its constitution it disestablished religion on a preferential basis—"no establishment of any one religious church or denomination in this State, in preference to any other." Furthermore, it prohibited religious taxes and dropped its colonial requirement of church attendance. However, officeholders were expected to hold to a strict Protestant theology. Article 32 denied political offices to any "person, who shall deny the being of God or the truth of the Protestant religion, or the divine authority either of the Old or New Testaments, or who shall hold religious principles incompatible with the freedom and safety of the State."[64]

Georgia's constitution of 1777 followed the norm of prohibiting clergymen from seats in the legislature. It also required assemblymen to be of "the Protestant religion." Finally, it established freedom of worship: "All persons whatever shall have the free exercise of their religion; provided it be not repugnant to the peace and safety of the State; and shall not, unless by consent, support any teacher or teachers except those of their own profession."[65]

New York's constitution of 1777 guaranteed the "free exercise and enjoyment of religious profession and worship, without discrimination or preference." Freedom of religion was notably granted to Quakers by allowing them to take an affirmation rather than an oath of allegiance. Article 35 disestablished religion as it "abrogated and rejected" any common law, or laws of the colony that might have been interpreted to establish any "particular denomination of Christians." Finally, it prohibited ministers or priests from holding any civil or military office.[66]

The most novel of New York's religious clauses required new immigrants to disavow allegiance to the pope. This clause reflected the attitudes of John Jay, who led a movement in the convention to exclude Roman Catholics from religious liberty. His first rejected amendment would have denied religious liberty to any Christians who taught doctrines dangerous to the state. Most delegates saw through this veiled anti-Catholic reference and disliked the idea that the state should regulate and rule on private religious belief. Jay, therefore, withdrew his motion and immediately proposed an amendment to exclude from religious toleration, citizenship, and ownership of land all Roman Catholics until such "professors of the religion of the church of Rome" swore before the supreme court of New York that they believed "that no Pope, priest, or foreign authority on earth, hath power to absolve the subjects of this State from their allegiance to the same." After "long debates" the proposal was defeated 19 to 10. For four more days, Jay persisted in suggesting various amendments, until finally the convention agreed to his suggestion of an oath before naturalization of those "born in parts beyond the sea."[67] As finally drafted, Article 42, dealing with foreign immigrants, attempted to keep Roman Catholics from becoming citizens of New York by requiring all new foreign immigrants to "abjure and renounce all allegiance and subjection to all and every foreign King, Prince, Potentate and State, in all matters ecclesiastical as well as civil.[68]

Vermont's 1777 constitution required all members of its House of Representatives to take both an oath of allegiance to the state and a religious oath. The religious oath, full of doctrinal statements, stated: "I do believe in one God, the Creator and Governor of the universe, the rewarder of the good and punisher of the wicked. And I do acknowledge the scriptures of the old and new testament to be given by divine inspiration, and own and profess the protestant religion." And "no further or other religious test shall ever, hereafter, be required of any civil officer or magistrate in this State."[69]

If we could put ourselves into the shoes of the framers, we would arrive at the convention shaped by some of the philosophical and historical events of the Confederation period. Most delegates came to the

Constitutional Convention with a commitment that oaths should be required of officeholders and a belief that oaths stabilized governments. Many believed that religious diversity was so widespread that religion should be left up to the states. Finally, all were mildly nationalistic—men who desired to strengthen the national government, but with a minimum of interference with state sovereignty. None of the delegates were such radical localists as Samuel Adams or Patrick Henry, "old patriots [who] wish to see a form established on the pure principles of republicanism."[70]

A legislative study of Article Six's prohibition of religious tests not surprisingly reveals this clause grew out of a conflict between nationalism and localism. Any scholar who has traced a clause in our federal Constitution through its numerous permutations knows that the final text reflects a compromise of competing interest groups. During the Constitutional Convention there were a number of competing factions—large population states versus small states and northern states versus southern states, just to name two. Important as these fights were, they were side attractions to the main event: the debate of nationalists versus localists. As the Confederation Congress increasingly proved itself inept, early nationalists gained converts.[71] Failures to increase Congress's power by amending the Articles, a weak international reputation, and interstate tariff barriers ultimately led to a Constitutional Convention in Philadelphia from 25 May to 17 September 1787.

Virginia delegates arrived in Philadelphia early and drafted fifteen resolutions, presented the fourth day of the convention by the governor of Virginia, Edmund Randolph.[72] At its heart, these resolutions—called the Virginia Plan—proposed a drastic shift in power from a confederation of thirteen sovereign states to one national government. For the first two months the fifty-five delegates sat as a committee of the whole and debated six days a week, five to six hours each day, on general principles—primarily issues raised by Randolph's Virginia Plan. Resolution fourteen of the Plan proposed "that the Legislative, Executive, & Judicial powers within the several States ought of be bound by oath to support the articles of Union,"[73] making obvious where ultimate loyalty, obedience, and authority resided. Randolph clearly told his fellow delegates that his resolutions proposed "a strong *consolidated* union, in which the idea of states should be nearly annihilated."[74]

Initially delegates favoring state power successfully tabled the resolutions on oaths, but within a week the nationalists brought it back up for debate.[75] Williamson argued it was "unnecessary, as the union will become the law of the land." But Governor Randolph defended the necessity of oaths, saying that "if the state judges are not sworn to the observance of the new government, will they not judicially determine in favor of their state laws. We are erecting a supreme national government; ought it not to be supported, and can we give it too many sinews?"[76]

Luther Martin of Maryland proposed dropping the words "within the several states," so the oath would be required only of national officials. This radical amendment failed when only four states supported it. Next Roger Sherman opposed the oaths as "unnecessary intruding into the state jurisdiction." Randolph again defended them as necessary because there was already too much "competition" between state and national authority. He pointed out that all state officials are already under "oath to the States. To preserve a due impartiality they ought to be equally bound to the Natl. Govt." Without such an oath, state officials will "always lean too much to the State systems, whenever a contest arises between the two."[77] Elbridge Gerry, a consistent localist who ultimately refused to sign the Constitution, countered by proposing an amendment "that the national legislation ought to be sworn to preserve the state constitutions, as they will run the greater risk to be annihilated." This amendment passed 7 to 4.[78]

The proposed section on oaths, now renumbered resolution 18, came up a second time for extensive debate on July 23, 1787. By this date both the nationalists and localists seemed to agree that both federal and state officers should swear to support the Constitution. James Wilson doubted the value of oaths, declaring them "a left handed security only. A good Govt. did not need them and a bad one could not or ought not to be supported." He was fearful that an oath to support the Constitution might imply the document could never be altered. Gorham reassured Wilson that altering a constitution would not violate the oath.[79]

The agreed-upon text sent to the five-member Committee of Detail states: "Resolved that the legislative, executive and judiciary Powers, within the several States, and of the national Government, ought to be bound by Oath to support the Articles of Union."[80] The convention adjourned for ten days while the committee worked on the first printed text of the Constitution. Since the delegates had accepted in principle the idea of oaths, the Committee of Detail went beyond their assigned task and inserted a proposed form of oath for the President and members of the Supreme Court.[81]

The full convention reconvened on August 6 and for the next month debated from a printed copy of the Constitution, the finished work submitted by the Committee of Detail.[82] During this debate Charles Pinckey suggested adding to the clause the words, "but no religious Test shall ever be required as a Qualification." Pickney justified this proposal on the grounds of religious toleration, calling it "a provision the world will expect from you, in the establishment of a System founded on Republican Principles, and in an age so liberal and enlightened as the present."[83] There was only mild opposition to his suggestion. Roger Sherman "thought it unnecessary, the prevailing liberality being a sufficient security against such tests."[84] A few delegates suggested adding a general religious requirement to distinguish between "the professors of Christianity and downright infidelity or paganism." Since America was a "Christian country" perhaps words should be required indicating a "belief of the existence of a Deity, and of a state of future rewards and punishments."[85] Luther Martin argued against such religious oaths as being "unfashionable," and his argument carried the day.[86]

A number of delegates understood Pickney's prohibition deliberately to defer to state authority over oaths. In fact, Roger Sherman later argued that the clerk had made a simple clerical error, and the correct wording of the prohibition was "no other Religious test."[87] Hence, since most states had religious oaths, Congress simply pledged that it would not meddle with state authority by adding any *additional* religious requirements. This probably seemed wise in view of the diversity of religious positions taken in the various state constitutions, especially since two constitutions explicitly opposed any *additional* religious oaths. Delegates also may have been influenced by petitions against any doctrinal religious oaths.[88] Clearly the delegates were very nervous about the reaction of state legislatures to the whole document. In too many other clauses the nationalists had subordinated and curtailed state powers. At least in the area of oaths the convention could give the appearance of retaining some state authority.[89]

In the months that followed the convention, nationalists (who took the name Federalists) and localists (who took the name Antifederalists) both propagandized on the merits and demerits of the proposed Constitution.[90] While most critics attacked the lack of a bill of rights, some did criticize the oath section in Article Six.[91] Opponents of a constitutional oath decried the dilution of state authority, not the religious test portion. William Findley, a delegate at the Pennsylvania Ratification

Convention, complained that oaths to support the Constitution would destroy state power. "Was it ever known that *judges* took an oath to be bound by the laws of two sovereign *states?*"[92] John Smilie further argued that existing state bills of rights, including religious clauses, had been destroyed by the clause claiming the Constitution was "the supreme Law of the land." This section in Article Six "sweeps away all the rights we have under states' governments."[93] James Wilson, a supporter of the Constitution at the Pennsylvania Convention, jotted down thirty-four Antifederalist objections. He summed up the opposition to oaths by noting, "There is a dependence of the state officers on the general government; they must swear to support it."[94]

During the ratification process, Federalists agreed with Antifederalists that the controversial portion of the oath clause was centralism versus federalism, not the prohibition of religious oaths. The archnationalist Alexander Hamilton in Federalist no. 27 argued that the primary purpose of the required oath was to instill loyalty to the national government. Thus state legislators, state judges, and state officials "will be incorporated into the operations of the national government . . . will be rendered auxiliary to the enforcement of its laws."[95] In its totality, the Constitution represents a resounding victory for centralization. After the Constitution, a British official observed that it would be difficult to find a more stunning reversal in authority. As he saw it, a rare example of "so general a resumption of authority has taken place without violence in so short a time."[96] Defeated Antifederalists lamented the loss of true "Revolution principles" and the defeat of the "old Whigg Interest" to the "self Created Nobility."[97]

It is curious that Antifederalists should criticize the religious prohibition on oaths because it was one of the few victories for localists. By this prohibitory clause the federal government left standing existing state religious test oaths. Furthermore, it limited the powers of Congress, which had the power to describe the words of an oath, but denied itself the right to include required religious belief. James Madison, the father of the Constitution, explained the necessity of a prohibition on religious oaths for officeholders: it meant "nothing more than that without that exception, a power would have been given to impose an oath involving a religious test."

Let us return to our original query. What does the Constitution's silence on religion indicate about America: Was the new nation on the slippery slope of secularism? Or did a different factor shape the clause prohibiting religious oaths? I have suggested here that the history of

America to the Civil War can be understood as a struggle betweeen advocates for nationalism and the champions of localism. During the American Revolution, colonial elites temporarily lost control to lower-class, democratic localists. These localists wrote the Declaration of Independence and state constitutions, which freed the individual from central control and unleashed the energies and chaos of self-interest. The Constitution represents a reactionary document in which conservatives again reasserted the need for a balanced but strong central government. But not wishing totally to destroy local options and power, the Philadelphia Convention wisely preferred to leave religion and oaths up to each state. James Madison defended the absence of any major clause on religion by stating, "there is not a shadow of right in the general government to intermeddle with religion." A fellow Virginia delegate agreed that "no power is given expressly to Congress over religion."[98] The famous jurist Joseph Story argued the prohibition on religious tests was "to cut off forever every pretence of any alliance between church and state in the national government."[99] Too often in past history, nations such as England had misused oaths with "pains and penalties of non-conformity written in no equivocal language, and enforced with a stern and vindictive jealousy."[100] England failed to allow for a growing diversity of local religious preferences. The first colonies were intolerant of religious dissenters, but by the 1740s religious and cultural pluralism within each local community dictated toleration. The framers of the Constitution were silent on religion because this question had been decided previously during the state constitution drafting period. Some states voted for religious pluralism; others retained established churches. The framers had no desire to meddle with regional differences or preferences. It would have been impossible for the national government to prescribe religious oaths without violating clauses in at least one state constitution. Since the nationalists had won most of the battles over localists at the convention, it seemed expedient to allow localists to win a minor skirmish over religious oaths.

NOTES

1. Robert N. Bellah, *Religion and the University: The Crisis of Unbelief. The William Belden Noble Lectures—1982.* In sharp contrast to Bellah, Martin Diamond argues the two documents are "indissolubly linked," with the Constitution preserving ideals of the Declaration, including religious qualities. Martin Diamond, "The Revolution of Sober Expectations," in *The American Revolution: Three Views* (New York: American Brands, 1975), 57-85.

2. The Declaration of Independence, in Merrill Jensen, ed., *The Documentary History of the Ratification of the Constitution,* 14 vols. (Madison, Wis.: State Historical Society, 1976–1983), 1:62; hereafter cited as DHR.

3. For further expansion of this thesis see David E. Maas, "The Watchwords of 1774," *Fides et Historia,* Oct. 1986.

4. Henry Commager, ed., *Documents of American History,* 6th ed. (New York: Appleton-Century-Crofts, 1958), 145.

5. Christian Farmer, *Connecticut Gazette* (New London), 29 Aug. 1788, in Gordon DenBoer, ed., *The Documentary History of the First Federal Elections, 1788–1790* (Madison, Wis.: Univ. of Wisconsin Press, 1984), 2:11-12; ibid., 23 Oct. 1788, 13-14.

6. There is no doubt that Americans were heavily influenced by the intellectual concepts of European Enlightenment theorists, who increasingly argued that rational thinking would bring liberal progress to civilization. Such an emphasis on belief in reason led many American Enlightenment thinkers to view religion as almost synonymous with the superstitious practices of primitive peoples. The best book on the Enlightenment is still Henry May, *The Enlightenment in America* (Oxford: Oxford Univ. Press, 1976).

John Adams as early as 1755 recorded in his diary that deism was gaining ground in Worcester, a frontier town in Massachusetts. He wrote, with dissatisfaction, that "The Principles of Deism had made a considerable progress among several Persons." He then listed as deists some important community members—the town's most prominent lawyer, a merchant, and the registrar of deeds. Lyman H. Butterfield, ed., *The Adams Papers: Diary and Autobiography of John Adams,* 4 vols. (Cambridge, Mass.: Harvard Univ. Press, 1961–1962), 3:263-66. The fifteen state constitutions reflect this growing liberalism. Several states provided for separation of church and state; five excluded ministers of the gospel from holding public office; and several constitutions liberalized religious qualifications for officeholders. Forrest McDonald, *Novus Ordo Seclorum: The Intellectual Origins of the Constitution* (Lawrence, Kans.: Univ. Press of Kansas, 1985), 43n.

7. Liberals like Thomas Jefferson praised Connecticut's efforts toward religious disestablishment by lamenting that Massachusetts was now "the last retreat of Monkish darkness, bigotry, and abhorrence of those advances of the mind which had carried the other states a century ahead of them." However, in Connecticut "a protestant popedom is no longer to disgrace the American history and character." Jefferson to John Adams, 5 May 1817, in Lester J. Cappon, ed., *The Adams-Jefferson Letters: The Complete Correspondence between Thomas Jefferson and Abigail and John Adams,* 2 vols. (Chapel Hill, N.C.: Univ. of North Carolina Press, 1959), 2:512.

Moreover, when John Adams in 1820 at the Massachusetts Constitutional Convention proposed an amendment to abolish state support of religion, Jefferson praised such efforts as proving "the advance of liberalism in the intervening period," for if America could give the world "the example of physical liberty," did it not also have to provide a model of "moral emancipation"? Thomas Jefferson to John Adams, 22 Jan. 1821, ibid., 2:569.

Deists such as Maine's George Thacher, who served in the First Congress, longed for the day when the "mystical nonsense" of religion would die and Americans would "let reason be the guide." Crazy Jonathan [George Thatcher], *Cumberland Gazette,* 18 Dec. 1788, in Merrill Jensen, ed., *The Documentary History of the First Elections, 1788–1790* (Madison, Wis.: Univ. of Wisconsin Press, 1976), 1:578. Another deist agreed that soon "frantic enthusiasts, and virulent bigots" would give way to "the rational, the liberal . . . philosophy and liberality of sentiment will overspread America." Daniel Cony to George Thatcher, Hallowell, 12 March 1789, in Jensen, *First Elections,* 1:578.

8. William Blackstone, *Commentaries on the Laws of England,* 12th ed., 4 vols. (Dublin: L. White, William Jones, and John Rice, 1794), 1:386-88.

9. Ibid., 388-89.

10. Ibid. Failure to take this oath carried stiff penalties—loss of a seat in Parliament, suspension of the right to keep weapons in your house, and a ban on keeping a horse above the value of five pounds. Ibid., 4:56-57.

11. Ibid., 116-24.

12. Ibid., 59.

13. Charles M. Andrews, ed., *The Colonial Period of American History,* 4 vols. (New Haven, Conn.: Yale Univ. Press), 2:137-38.

14. Ibid., 3:98.

15. Rhys Isaac, *The Transformation of Virginia, 1740–1790* (Chapel Hill, N.C.: Univ. of North Carolina Press, 1982), 91.

16. Bernard Bailyn, "Lines of Force in Recent Writings on the American Revolution," *Reports,* International Congress of Historical Sciences 14 (1975): 27-28; see also Bernard Bailyn, *The Ideological Origins of the American Revolution* (Cambridge, Mass.: Harvard Univ. Press, 1967), 407.

17. For amplification see Robert E. Shalhope, "Republicanism and Early American Historiography," *The William and Mary Quarterly,* 3d ser., 39 (April 1982): 334-56; Joyce Appleby, "The Social Origins of American Revolutionary Ideology," *The Journal of American History* 64 (March 1978): 935-37.

18. Edmund Quincy IV to Edmund Quincy, Jr., 1 March 1775, Quincy Papers, Box 9A, Massachusetts Historical Society.

19. Andrew Eliot to Thomas B. Hollis, 25 April 1775, MS. 1071, Boston Public Library.

20. Cited in Bernard Bailyn, "Religion and Revolution: Three Biographical Studies," *Perspectives in American History* 4 (1970): 128-30.

21. Gordon S. Wood, *Revolution and the Political Integration of the Enslaved and Disenfranchised* (Washington, D.C.: American Enterprise Institute, 1974), 6. For an essay on why the colonists rejected virtual representation see Cecelia Kenyon, "Ideological Origins of the First Continental Congress," *Commemoration Ceremony in Honor of the Two Hundredth Anniversary of the First Continental Congress* (Washington, D.C.: Government Printing Office, 1975), 8-10. Another helpful essay is Paul G. Kauper, *The Higher Law and the Rights of Man in a Revolutionary Society* (Washington, D.C.: American Enterprise Institute, 1974).

22. Appleby, "Social Origins," 935-37.

23. Comment by Bernard Bailyn, "Lines of Force," 13-17. For studies on the poor see Jesse Lemisch, "The American Revolution Seen From the Bottom Up," in *Towards a New Past: Dissenting Essays in American History,* ed. Barton Berstein (New York: Pantheon Books, 1968), 7-8; Jackson Turner Main, *The Social Structure of Revolutionary America* (Princeton, N.J.: Princeton Univ. Press, 1965), 156; Aubrey Land, "Economic Base and Social Structure: The Northern Chesapeake in the Eighteenth Century," *Journal of Economic History* 25 (Dec. 1965): 639-54.

24. Gouverneur Morris to John Penn, 20 May 1774, cited by Alfred F. Young, "Con-

servatives, the Constitution, and the 'Spirit of Accommodation,'" in *How Democratic is the Constitution,* ed. Robert E. Goldwin and William A. Schambra (Washington, D.C.: American Enterprise Institute for Public Policy Research, 1982), 118-19.

25. Cited in Hiller B. Zobel, *The Boston Massacre* (New York: W. W. Norton & Co., 1970), 39.

26. Blackstone, *Commentaries,* 1:388-89. The legislature of New Jersey, as it debated whether to ratify the proposed Articles, pointed out to the delegates in Congress this flaw in the Articles. Since the United States also has a collective interest, New Jersey proposed a national oath as an amendment to the Articles. At least an oath "to assert to no Vote or Proceeding which may violate the general Confederation, is necessary. The Laws and Usages of all civilized Nations envince the Propriety of an Oath on such Occasions; and the more solemn and important the Despote, the more strong and explicit ought the Obligation to be." Congress rejected this proposed amendment, on the grounds that since each state required an oath of its citizens, an additional oath of allegiance was unnecessary. The only member of Congress who took any national oath was the clerk of the Confederation Congress, who took an oath of secrecy and fidelity. 23, 25 June 1778, DHR, 113.

27. Mercy Warren, *History of the Rise, Progress and Termination of the American Revolution: Interpresed with Biographical, Political and Moral Observations,* 3 vols. (Boston: Manning and Loring, 1850), 1:38.

28. Ibid., 145.

29. John Adams to Richard Henry Lee, 4 June 1776, in Paul H. Smith, ed., *Letters of Delegates to Congress, 1774-1789,* 10 vols. (Washington, D.C.: Government Printing Office, 1976-1983), 4:135-36, hereafter cited as LDC; James Wilson to William Thompson, 23-24 June 1776, LDC, 4:301-3.

30. *Essex Gazette,* 17 April 1775.

31. 8 May 1775 resolve, Massachusetts Provincial Congress, Massachusetts Archives, vol. 206:9, Boston, Massachusetts.

32. Medway Committee of Correspondence, 14 June 1775, CH.B.12.21, Boston Public Library.

33. E.g., see Duchess County, New York Association, 18 Jan. 1775, in Peter Force, ed., *American Archives: Fourth Series, Containing a Documentary History of the English Colonies in North America from the King's Message to Parliament, of March 7, 1774, to the Declaration of Independence by the United States,* 6 vols. (Washington, D.C.: M. St. Clair Clarke and Peter Force, 1837-1846), 1:1164.

34. 15 May 1776, in Worthington Chauncey Ford, ed., *Journals of the Continental Congress, 1774-1789,* 34 vols. (Washington, D.C., 1904-1937), 4:358; hereafter cited as JCC.

35. Delegate Roger Sherman to Jonathan Trumbull, Sr., 9 April 1777, LDC 4:560-61.

36. Richard Henry Lee to Patrick Henry, 13 May 1777, LDC 7:75.

37. John Adams to Abigail Adams, 16 June 1777, LDC 7:347-48.

38. DHR 3:39.

39. Gouverneur Morris to George Clinton, 6 Sept. 1778, LDC 10:590.

40. Abraham Clark to Elias Dayton, 7 March 1777, LDC 6:411-14.

41. The famous jurist Joseph Story, commenting on oaths, said, "Oaths have a solemn obligation upon the minds of all reflecting men, and especially upon those, who feel a deep sense of accountability to a Supreme being." Joseph Story, *Commentaries on the Constitution . . .* (Cambridge, Mass.: Brown, Slattuck, 1833), 688.

42. Gouverneur Morris to Peter Van Schaack, 8 Sept. 1778, LDC 10:605-6.

43. Samuel Peters to Samuel Parker, 15 Nov. 1787, Rev. Samuel Parker Papers, Diocesan Library, Boston.

44. John Adams to Nathaniel Greene, 2 June 1777, LDC 7:162-64.

45. 13-15 May 1776, John Adams notes of Debate, LDC 3:669-70.

46. John Jay to Alexander McDougall, 13 March 1776, LDC 3:373-74.

47. George Washington did this as a counter to Lord Howe's 30 Nov. 1776 proclamation calling for Americans to take oaths to the crown. Richard Stockton, the New Jersey delegate to the Continental Congress and a signer of the Declaration of Independence, was captured by the British army and in early December 1776 took the oath of allegiance offered by Howe. Stockton then repudiated this oath after his release and on 2 Dec. 1777 signed the oaths of adjuration and allegiance prescribed by the New Jersey legislature. John Witherspoon to David Witherspoon, 17 March 1777, LDC 6:xxvi, 454-56.

Daniel Huger of South Carolina in 1780 took the oath of loyalty to England, but after the war stayed in the United States and gradually came back into political favor. He served as a delegate in 1786 to 1788 in the Confederation Congress and was elected to the First Congress in 1789. Jensen, *First Elections,* 1:221.

48. Abraham Clark to John Hart, Speaker of New Jersey Assembly, 8 Feb. 1777, LDC 6:240-41. Congress deferred to the state governments' loyalty programs. Thus when three New Jersey prisoners petitioned Congress for release, their cases were sent to the Council of Safety of New Jersey, which then administered the oath of allegiance to the state. New Jersey Delegates to William Livingston, 31 March 1777, LDC 6:515.

49. Symbolically a bill on oaths was the *first* law passed by our new government and signed by President Washington on 1 June 1789. This law, one of 143 laws passed by the First Congress, fulfilled the third section of the sixth article of the new Constitution by describing the form of oath and prescribing when it should be taken. Linda Grant DePauw, ed., *Documentary History of the First Federal Congress of the United States of America, March 4, 1789–March 3, 1791* (Baltimore, Md.: Johns Hopkins Univ. Press, 1972), 1:723, 740; 15 April 1789, Senate Journal, in ibid., 1:16.

50. Articles of Confederation, 15 Nov. 1777, DHR 1:79.

51. William C. Webster, "Comparative study of the state constitutions of the American Revolution," *Annals,* American Academy of Political and Social Science 9 (May 1897): 103. As each colony rebelled against royal officials, the patriots maintained an air of legality. Thus citizens constituted committees of correspondence, elected delegates in the spring of 1774 to a Continental Congress, and finally formed provincial congresses as replacements for the colonial assemblies. Merrill Jensen, *The Founding of a Nation* (New York: Oxford Univ. Press, 1968), provides a good description of this process.

Bailyn states that some seven thousand individuals participated in the hundreds of committees of correspondence, safety, inspection, and provincial congresses. Bailyn, "Lines of Force," 47n. After several colonies asked the Continental Congress's advice as to whether it was wise to form a new government, Congress on 15 May 1776 advised all the colonies to form new constitutions. New Hampshire asked first on 18 Oct. 1775 (JCC 3:298). Congress on 3 Nov. 1775 advised New Hampshire to form a new government (3 Nov. 1775, JCC 3:319; 15 May 1776, JCC 4:358).

In response to this recommendation, eight colonies (N.H., S.C., Va., N.J., Del., Penn., Md., and N.C.) drafted new constitutions in 1776. Georgia, New York, and Vermont wrote new constitutions in 1777. South Carolina drafted a second constitution in 1778 and Massachusetts in the same year drafted a constitution that the voters rejected 5-1, with a vote of 9,972 to 2,083. Allan Nevins, *The American States During and After the Revolution* (New York: Macmillan, 1924), 177. Massachusetts finally drafted an acceptable document in 1780. When New Hampshire attempted to expand its skeletal constitution the voters rejected the 1778 revision, but finally approved the new draft in 1784.

Only the colonies of Rhode Island and Connecticut, each with a large measure of self-government under their colonial charters, failed to alter their governments.

52. Excluded from this number is the New Hampshire constitution of 1776, which was so defective that it took the state six distinct later constitutions and fourteen sessions of conventions to create a satisfactory document in 1784. Lynn Warren Turner, *The Ninth State: New Hampshire's Formative Years* (Chapel Hill, N.C.: Univ. of North Carolina Press, 1983), 13.

The constitution of New Hampshire, the first new state constitution, had little impact. It is a document of only two pages, so brief and make-shift that its framers did not even number its paragraphs. Possibly because of its brevity, New Hampshire's 1776 constitution had no direct or indirect reference to God, nor any religious clauses. New Hampshire Constitution, in Francis N. Thorpe, comp., *The Federal and State Constitutions . . .* , 7 vols. (Washington, D.C.: Government Printing Office, 1909), 4:2451-53.

53. New Jersey Constitution, in Thorpe, *State Constitutions*, 5:2594-98.

54. [South Carolina], *An Ordinance for Establishing an Oath of Office* (Charleston, 1776), Evans 43168. For the action of the legislature in appointing the first officials and the committee to draft the oath see [South Carolina] *Provincial Congress Journal* (Charleston, 1776), Evans 15091.

55. South Carolina 1778 Constitution, in Thorpe, *State Constitutions*, 6:3249, 3252.

56. South Carolina 1778 Constitution, ibid., 3251-52.

57. Virginia Constitution, ibid., 7:3812-19.

58. Nevins, *American States*, 435-36.

59. Thorpe fails to include the Delaware bill of rights. For this see [Delaware] *Convention, 1776 and New Castle* (Wilmington, Del.: James Adams, 1776), Evans 14732.

60. Ibid.

61. Delaware Constitution, in Thorpe, *State Constitutions*, 1:562-68.

62. For the radical nature of Pennsylvania's constitution see Young, "Conservatives, the Constitution, and the 'Spirit of Accommodation,'" 121-22; Pennsylvania Constitution, in Thorpe, *State Constitutions*, 6:3085.

63. Maryland Constitution, in Thorpe, *State Constitutions*, 3:1686-1701.

64. North Carolina Constitution, ibid., 5:2787-94.

65. Georgia Constitution, ibid., 2:777-85.

66. *New York Constitution 1777*, Evans 15472-73.

67. 20 March 1777, [New York State] *Journals of the Provincial Congress, Provincial Convention, Committee of Safety and Council of Safety of the State of New York, 1775–1776–1777*, 2 vols. (Albany, N.Y.: Thurlow Weed, 1842), 1:843-54.

68. 1 April 1777, ibid., 1:860-61. John Jay's anti-Catholic position was a commonly held prejudice in the eighteenth century. Ever since some Catholics tried to blow up Parliament on 5 Nov. 1745, the day was a national holiday in England and its colonies. In Boston Guy Fawkes Day or Gunpowder Plot Day became an annual anti-Catholic and anti-Stuart day, with parades and effigies of the pope, climaxing in a fist fight between the North End and South End gangs. Alfred F. Young, "English Plebian Culture and Eighteenth-Century American Radicalism," in *The Origins of Anglo-American Radicalism,* ed. Margaret and James Jacobs (London: Allen & Unwin, 1984), 198.

In addition, two other clauses reflect Jay's anti-Catholic campaign. One stated that "rational liberty" required the state "to guard against that spiritual oppression and intolerance, wherewith the bigotry and ambition of weak and wicked priests and princes have scourged mankind." Furthermore, it exempted liberty of conscience from excusing "acts of licentiousness, or justify practices inconsistent with the peace and safety of the State." *New York Constitution 1777*, Evans 15472-73.

This law really did not keep out many Catholics, for by 1787 the federal Constitution controlled naturalization and only required a simple oath to uphold the Constitution. Perhaps because of federal naturalization procedures, John Jay in 1788 persuaded the New York legislature to require all state officeholders to take a prescribed oath that stated: "I renounce and adjure all allegiance and subjection to all and every foreign king, prince and State, in all matters, ecclesiastical as well as civil." For this story see John Webb Pratt, *Religion, Politics, and Diversity: The Church-State Theme in New York History* (Ithaca, N.Y.: Cornell Univ. Press, 1967), 107-8.

69. Thorpe, *State Constitutions*, 7:3743.

70. Mercy Warren to Catharine Macaulay, 2 Aug. 1787, Mercy Warren Letterbook, 22-23, Massachusetts Historical Society.

71. The Continental Congress itself formed a committee as early as 1781 to draft amendments giving more power to Congress. Most scholars are familiar with the abortive impost amendment in 1781 and 1783, while less well known are suggestions of a national oath. In July 1781 Congress discussed twenty-one amendments to the Articles. Suggestion eight called for an oath taken by all "the officers of the U.S. or any of them against presents, Emoluments, office or title of any kind from a king, prince, or foreign State." These ideas were discussed, but no action was taken. Committee report, Continental Congress, 20 July 1781, DHR 1:143-44.

72. 29 May 1787, ibid., 232.

73. Virginia Resolution, 29 May 1787, ibid., 245. The best minutes of the Federal Convention were taken by James Madison of Virginia, but James McHenry of Maryland, Rufus King of New York, William Paterson of New Jersey, and Robert Yates of New York also took notes. William Jackson, the official secretary, took sloppy, inaccurate notes. Paterson's notes refer to this first proposal on oath as "That the legislature, executive and judiciary officers should be bound by oath to observe the Union." Paterson notes, 29 May 1787, in Max Farrand, ed., *The Records of the Federal Convention of 1787*, 4 vols. (New Haven, Conn.: Yale Univ. Press, 1911-1937), 1:28.

74. Edmund Randolph speech, 29 May 1787, DHR 1:233.

75. 5 June, 11 June 1787, in Farrand, *Records*, 1:117, 119, 207.

76. 11 June 1787, Yates notes, ibid., 207.

77. For this debate see 11 June 1787, Madison notes, ibid., 203-4.

78. 11 June 1787, Yates notes, ibid., 207.

79. 23 July 1787, Madison notes, ibid. 2:87-88.

80. 23 July 1787, Committee of Detail, ibid. 133; 23 July 1787, Committee of Detail, VIII, ibid., 159-60.

81. 23 July 1787, Committee of Detail, IX, ibid., 172.

82. For details on the daily working of the convention see Farrand, *Records*, 1:xxii-xxv and DHR 1:232.

83. 28 May 1787, Charles Pickney, "Observations on the plan of government," in Farrand, *Records*, 3:122.

84. 20, 30 Aug. 1787, Madison notes, ibid., 342, 460-61, 468.

85. 29 Nov. 1787, Luther Martin, "The Genuine Information," to the legislature of Maryland, cited in Farrand, ibid., 3:277 appendix CLVIII.

86. 29 Nov. 1787, Luther Martin, ibid.

87. A Citizen of New Haven [Roger Sherman], *New Haven Gazette*, 18 Dec. 1788, in DenBoer, *First Elections*, 2:15-17.

88. For an example of a petition from a Jew see Jonas Phillips, a Jew, to President and members of Constitutional Convention, 7 Sept. 1787, cited in Farrand, *Records*, 3:78-80.

89. The delegates became so worried about state legislatures rejecting the document that it was never submitted to them for their ratification. Instead the Constitution called

for state conventions in each state to ratify or reject the Constitution. For a foreigner who saw the Constitution subverting state authority see comments of Antoine de la Forest, the French Consul for New York, in Antoine de la Forest to Comte de Montmorin, 28 Sept. 1788, DHR 1:349-50.

90. It is beyond the scope of this chapter to trace from 1787 to 1790 the ratification debates. During this time period some 150 newspapers were published in the United States containing nearly forty thousand items on the Constitution. In addition, both Federalists and Antifederalists wrote pamphlets. *The Federalist Papers* was the most important Federalist pamphlet, and *Letters from the Federal Farmer* the widest distributed Antifederalist pamphlet. In addition, thirteen state legislatures called ratification conventions consisting of 1,700 delegates. Obviously it is impossible to know all of their feelings about oaths. DHR 1:25, 36-38.

91. Over six thousand Pennsylvanians signed petitions urging nonratification of the Constitution. Their major objection was the lack of religious freedom—a bill of rights. Petition against confirmation of the Ratification of the Constitution to the Pennsylvania Assembly, Jan. 1788, DHR 2:709-11.

92. Speech by William Findley, Pennsylvania Convention, 1 Dec. 1787, ibid., 446.

93. 28 Nov. 1787, John Smilie speech, Pennsylvania Ratification Convention, in Jensen, ibid., 386, 391-92.

94. James Wilson notes, 4 Dec. 1787, ibid., 467-69. The newspapers were full of comments that the Constitution was really a plan by the "ARISTOCRACY" to regain power from the average citizen. *Massachusetts Centinel,* 29 Sept. 1787, 3. A British spy, Major Beckwith, reported that the ablest men supported the Constitution as the first step on the road to monarchy. Dorchester to Lord Sydney, 14 Oct. 1788, in Brymner, ed., *Report on Canadian Archives* (Ottawa: MacLean, Rogert & Co., 1891), 100-102.

95. Alexander Hamilton, Federalist no. 27, cited in Edward S. Corwin, ed., *The Constitution of the United States of America: Analysis and Interpretation* (Washington, D.C.: Government Printing Office, 1953), 736.

96. Dorchester to Lord Sydney, 14 Oct. 1788, in Brymner, *Report,* 100-102.

97. James Warren to Elbridge Gerry, 1 Feb. 1789, in C. Harvey Gardiner, ed., *A Study in Dissent: The Warren-Gerry Correspondence, 1776–1792* (Carbondale, Ill.: Southern Illinois Univ. Press, 1968), 212-14.

98. Cited in Leonard W. Levy, *Judgments: Essays on American Constitutional History* (Chicago: Quadrangle Books, 1972), 172-73, 219.

99. Story, *Commentaries,* 690.

100. Ibid.

Freedom, Truth, and American Thought, 1760–1810

Richard W. Pointer

Truth is great and will prevail if left to herself; . . . she is the proper and sufficient antagonist to error, and has nothing to fear from conflict unless by human interposition disarmed of her natural weapons, free argument and debate."[1] So proclaimed the 1777 Virginia Bill for Establishing Religious Freedom. Considered by its author, Thomas Jefferson, to be one of his three greatest public achievements, the Virginia Bill sounded a confidence in the greatness of truth and the beneficence of free discussion that was echoed, at least implicitly, fourteen years later in the passage of the first amendment to the United States Constitution. Both documents reflect the Founders' deep-rooted assurance that truth would prosper, not suffer, amid open inquiry. Jefferson, Madison, and a host of other Americans in the 1770s and after readily maintained that where truth and falsehood were given free rein, the former would inevitably win out.

Although only one of a number of convictions late eighteenth-century Americans held about the relationship of freedom and truth, the "truth triumphant" notion (as I shall refer to it) stands out as the most historically intriguing because of what it reveals about the fusion of Christian and Enlightenment elements in the American mind of the early republic. Rooted in the political and religious writings of English libertarians such as John Milton and John Locke, and affirmed by a diverse set of American ministers, lawyers, and politicians in the critical years from 1770 to 1810, belief in truth's ultimate triumph embodied both biblical and rationalist concepts about the nature of man, the character of truth, the role of government, and the course of human history. Few ideas bespoke either the intellectual heritage or the prevailing mindset of the constitutional period more clearly. For this reason, it is worth investigating where this idea came from, who promoted it and why, and what it can tell us about the state of American thought, particularly American Christian thought, in the post-Revolutionary era.

In recent years, historians of colonial America have dispelled the once firmly held notion that patriot political ideology depended largely, if not exclusively, on the writing of John Locke. Bernard Bailyn, Gordon Wood, and J. G. A. Pocock have overseen a reinterpretation of colonial political thought that highlights its various sources ranging from the classical republicanism of Cicero to the English "country party" opposition of Lord Bolingbroke.[2] Their collective work has laid to rest any argument that the Founders gained their political wisdom from a narrow set of Enlightenment treatises.[3] Yet it would be a mistake to deduce from this historiography any suggestion that Lockean political theory played no role in fomenting the Revolution or forming the new republic. On the contrary, as Forrest MacDonald points out in his new book on the intellectual origins of the Constitution, natural law theory, as explicated principally by John Locke, was one of the major philosophical wells from which the minds of America's Revolutionary elite drank.[4] It comes as no affront to current scholarship, then, to suggest that in the case of the truth triumphant notion, Locke's influence was paramount.

While addressing it in several places, Locke gave greatest attention to the relationship of freedom and truth in his four *Letters Concerning Toleration*.[5] Locke's aim in these letters was to defend religious toleration for England's Protestant dissenters. He tailored his arguments to meet the objections of those who feared that wider religious freedom would endanger religious truth. Specifically, Locke concentrated on proving two points: first, that the use of state force on behalf of the church had had only ill consequences for true religion, and second, that true religion (by which he and most other Englishmen meant Protestant Christianity) had nothing to fear from religious toleration. Locke, simply, was suggesting that present policy harmed religion whereas toleration would aid it.

Locke looked to history to demonstrate both points. Recent and ancient history, he insisted, were replete with examples of the damage done to true religion when men were coerced to believe or practice a religious faith against their wills. State-imposed restrictions on popular religious freedom had driven men away from rather than toward the national church. In contrast, Christianity had flourished when free from the "help" of state force. The experience of the early church under Roman rule illustrated how well Christianity could do apart from state aid and amid competing religious beliefs. There was no reason to believe that the present church could not fare equally well under similar circumstances, for the same assets that had allowed Christianity to prevail then still existed now, specifically its own truth and light.[6]

Locke supported his historical arguments with appeals to Scripture. Men could only use evangelistic means that were enjoined by the Bible and force was not one of these. Furthermore, Christ promised no other assistance to his church than that of the Holy Spirit; therefore, Christians should not think that any other power was necessary for religious truth to prevail. Instead, they should rest confidently in the Savior's promises to build his church on the truth that he was God's Son and that no evil would triumph against that truth.[7]

In Locke's view, the innate strength of Christian truth was sufficient to ensure its prevalence. "The inventions of men in religion," he wrote, "need the force and helps of men to support them. A religion that is of God wants not the assistance of human authority to make it prevail."[8] Locke carried the argument one step further when he claimed that religious toleration could enhance the likelihood of truth's triumph. Toleration would afford the most congenial environment for people to see and hear the truth, because truth was likeliest to prevail "when strong arguments and good reason" were joined with "the softness of civility and good usage."[9] In other words, warm but charitable debate among rational men of good will held the greatest promise of advancing the cause of truth. Such was Locke's vision of freedom's beneficent consequences.

In the hands of eighteenth-century English libertarians, Locke's arguments were enlarged and broadened to support disestablishment and complete religious liberty in the 1780s. Before sampling their views, however, it is worth pausing to note that a half century before Locke's letters on toleration, English Puritan John Milton had advanced many similar opinions in his defense of a free press. In his pamphlet *Areopagitica: A Speech for the Liberty of Unlicensed Printing*, Milton boldly attacked a Parliamentary statute that required a state license for all printed matter. The law smacked of the Catholic Inquisition, he charged, and hindered the discovery of "religious and civil Wisdom."[10] A free press was essential to the search for truth, for truth needed freedom not protection:

> Let her [truth] and Falsehood grapple; who ever knew Truth put to the worse, in a free and open encounter? . . . She needs no policies, nor strategems, nor licensings to make her victorious; those are the shifts and the defences that error uses against her power. Give her but room, and do not bind her when she sleeps. . . .[11]

Why would truth fare so well when openly wrestling with error? Milton's answer presaged Locke's: the innate greatness of truth ensured its success. Milton rhetorically queried, "Who knows not that Truth is strong, next to the Almighty?"[12] That strength guaranteed that truth of all kinds would only be polished and brightened by free debate. In addition, freedom would persuade truth to reveal herself more quickly: "See the ingenuity of Truth, who, when she gets a free and willing hand, opens herself faster than the pace of method and discourse can overtake her."[13] Thus, for Milton, as for Locke, freedom was an asset, not a liability, to truth. Their respective treatises were, in essence, similar attempts to persuade the English state of this simple but profound premise. Leonard Levy and other historians of Anglo-American civil liberties have warned against exaggerating the progressive character of Milton and Locke's views. After all, neither advocated granting political and religious freedoms to non-Protestants.[14] However, it seems that these men laid the groundwork for the more radical positions on civil liberties adopted in Anglo-America a century later; and, more specifically, bequeathed to the Revolutionary generation the truth triumphant notion.

That legacy reached American patriots largely through the essays, sermons, and broadsides of eighteenth-century English libertarians. Throughout the 1700s but especially after the outbreak of the American Revolution, colonists borrowed from English proponents of wider political and religious freedoms. While many examples could be cited, two noteworthy English propagandists of the 1780s were the ministers Richard Price and Robert Hall.[15] Price was one of those rationalist Dissenters who exemplified the link between theological and political radicalism. In denouncing state interference in religious matters, he and other liberal nonconformists contended that freedom of inquiry was necessary for the pursuit of new religious truth and the progress of general knowledge. Price's close associate, Philip Furneaux, claimed in 1771 that "truth is so far from suffering from free examination, that this is the only method in which she can be effectually supported and propagated."[16] Writing in the next decade to an American audience, Price insisted that "the cause of truth will certainly be served" by fair and open examination. He was convinced that all truth, including that of Christianity, would always triumph from a free exchange of ideas, for "nothing reasonable can suffer by discussion." In fact, Price argued that this was the best test of truth. "All doctrines *really* sacred," he wrote, "must be clear and incapable of being opposed with success."

Christianity had proved itself in its first few centuries by becoming "the religion of the world . . . by evidence only in opposition to the strongest exertions of civil power." For Price, there could not be "a more striking proof, that nothing but fair discussion is necessary to suppress error and propagate truth."[17] Like Locke, he found the experience of the early church a powerful example of truth prospering apart from state support and used it to bolster his case for disestablishment and complete religious liberty.

Evangelical Baptist minister Robert Hall did not share Richard Price's theological views but did sympathize with his convictions about freedom and truth. Hall charged that church establishments had often sanctioned false religious opinions and then refused to alter them "in spite of superior light and improvement."[18] Principles of freedom, including the separation of church and state, ought to be cherished by Christians because those principles alone could secure the liberty of conscience and freedom of inquiry essential for the proper fulfillment of religious duties. Furthermore, every advance toward freedom in the government of nations represented "not only a barrier to the encroachments of tyranny, but a security to the diffusion and establishment of truth."[19] In Hall's mind, such advances included not only religious disestablishment but also wider political liberties. He insisted that free expression (i.e., free speech and free press) was to be cherished as an essential step to the discovery of truth. Since most opinions were a mixture of truth and error, society as a whole, and not the magistrate, was responsible for sifting out what was of social value.[20] The state's role, Hall concluded, was to be the protector of freedom, not the arbiter of political or religious truth.

From the ranks of both British evangelicalism and liberalism in the late eighteenth century, then, came voices praising civil and religious liberty as benefits to the cause of truth. These sounds amplified and sometimes varied the melody sung a century earlier by Milton and Locke. Nevertheless, a sufficient harmony was struck to produce a clear tune for Americans to hear: truth had nothing to fear from freedom.

In the decades surrounding the writing of the American Constitution, the truth triumphant notion became a familiar refrain in the rhetoric of the new nation's political and religious elites. While far from gaining universal adherence, it enlisted support from a wide variety of prominent Americans ranging from Yale president Ezra Stiles to Catholic bishop John Carroll and republican lawyer Tunis Wortman. The truth triumphant idea gained its wide appeal from its usefulness in arguments for broad religious and political freedoms. Not surprisingly, it was in the contexts of debates over religious pluralism, disestablishment, and a free press that this notion found greatest utterance in the half century from 1760 to 1810.

In his 1761 discourse on Christian union, Ezra Stiles extolled the advantages of "free inquiry and universal liberty" for Christianity in general and Congregationalism in particular. As historian Edmund Morgan has described, Stiles believed that all religious opinions should be given "free play." In the competitive market of ideas, truth and error would be distinguished from each other, and "truth in its greatness would prevail." For Stiles, free discussion was the means given by God for truth to make itself known.[21] Consequently, a diversity of sects within Protestantism and a multiplicity of views within Congregationalism were to be tolerated so that through the mutual exchange of ideas, truth would be allowed to make its way and "terminate the whole in universal harmony."[22] Furthermore, since people would recognize and accept truth "because of its self-evident excellence and superiority," truth required no help from outside force or creeds to sustain it.[23]

Many of the same themes run through the letters and sermons of John Carroll in the 1780s. As part of his "republican blueprint" for American Catholicism, Bishop Carroll endorsed the separation of church and state and convinced many American Catholics that religious pluralism would have positive results. He was persuaded that if the state protected the free flow of ideas, the causes of Christian unity and truth would be well served: "If we have the wisdom and temper to preserve civil and religious liberty, America may come to exhibit a proof to the world, that general and equal toleration, by giving a free circulation to fair argument, is the most effectual method to bring all denominations of Christians to an unity of faith."[24]

In the next decade the same kind of confidence in free inquiry and truth characterized the writings of such Protestant ministers as William Linn and John Leland. A Dutch Reformed pastor in New York City and an arch anti-Jeffersonian, Linn nonetheless sounded like his Virginia foe when he declared, "If men were left to judge for themselves, and act according to their light, there would be less error and greater uniformity among Christians. The great doctrines of religion," Linn continued, "would ever support themselves by their own evidence. Truth needs only an equal advantage with error, to gain an eternal victory over it."[25] Meanwhile, Virginia Baptist John Leland attacked Connecticut's religious establishment on the grounds that "Truth disdains the aid of law for its defense—it will stand upon its own merits." He insisted that true religion would prosper best when "left entirely to Christ."[26]

Linn and Leland were not alone in the 1790s in holding such views. Dedicated to the proposition that "candid inquiry after truth is the proper employment of mankind," *The Theological Magazine,* published in New York between 1785 and 1798, contained numerous articles and letters defending free theological discussion as the best means to obtain "the knowledge of truth." To those who questioned the wisdom of giving free voice to error, the editor replied that "truth has greatly the advantage of error on equal ground; and therefore, if the defenders of the former are as bold and active as the propagators of the latter, there is no reason to fear the consequences of a fair contest—for great is truth and will prevail."[27] Another contributor justified free inquiry on the grounds that it promoted intellectual humility and provided an opportunity to win over "infidels." In addition, he insisted that the suppression of some theological opinions might, in effect, mean the suppression of the truth, as well as encourage a curtailment of free speech and free press.[28]

The truth triumphant notion was employed to discredit religious establishments and creeds, to legitimate religious liberty and pluralism, and to defend theological dialogue and disputation. At the heart of all of these uses was a firm and seemingly unlimited confidence in the greatness of truth. Among orthodox Protestants like Stiles, Linn, and Leland, as well as for Catholics like Carroll, that confidence resided in the truths of historic Christianity. Thus, for example, when Leland's Baptist colleague, Isaac Backus, preached on the theme "Truth is Great, and Will Prevail," there is no doubt that he was referring to the ultimate victory of God's revealed doctrine of grace.[29] There is also no doubt that when Thomas Jefferson wrote of truth's prevalence in the Virginia Bill of 1777, he meant something quite different by "truth."[30] Yet, in the quest to end religious establishments and ensure religious liberty, different definitions of the substance of truth meant very little compared to the more fundamental consensus among some evangelicals, Catholics, and rationalists that truth's excellence assured its inevitable triumph in a free environment.

Among those who campaigned for complete freedom of the press in the 1780s and 1790s a similar argument existed that truth would rise to the surface and make itself known in a society where all opinions were guaranteed an equal right to be voiced. The debate over a free press culminated in the early republic in the clash over the Sedition Act of 1798. In that battle, democratic-republican supporters of Thomas Jefferson developed a libertarian interpretation of the first amendment rooted in the assumption that when ideas compete freely true opinions always triumph.[31] In their minds, all political views, and not simply those of the dominant elite, were to be allowed free expression. Out of the interchange of conflicting perspectives a consensus would emerge that would represent not only reliable political wisdom but, in fact, truth itself.[32] According to Gordon Wood, this republican belief that an aggregation of opinions would lead to the truth rested upon a faith in something similar to Adam Smith's invisible hand. The same beneficent results produced in the free marketplace of goods seemed plausible in the free marketplace of ideas.[33]

Federalist defenders of the Sedition Act did not share this faith, however. Pennsylvania judge Alexander Addison rejected the republicans' theory as an unrealistic view of the process of political debate. Toleration of obvious libels and slanderous falsehoods within the public arena seemed to him a "strange way to discover truth." While defending the legitimacy of political dissent, Addison repeatedly argued that "a proper view of free expression rejected a blind faith in any unregulated, essentially self-correcting marketplace of ideas."[34]

Despite this opposition, in both the short run and the long run the libertarian interpretation of freedom of speech and press won out in America. And with its victory came a growing confidence that open political discussion served the interests of truth very well. Americans in the early republic increasingly began to believe that the state, if popularly selected and supported, had nothing to fear from free expression.[35] Equally important, they concluded that the public rather than the state was to determine what was political truth.

Parallel conclusions were being reached regarding the respective roles of the public and the state in defining religious truth for the new nation. Between 1776 and 1791, lawmakers at both the state and national levels moved America away from religious establishments and toward complete religious liberty. In the process, they made it clear that in this republic, the magistrate would not be called upon to judge religious truth. Instead, that task would be left to the people themselves.

Americans in the "critical" decades after the Revolution thus rejected traditional conceptions of the state and demanded their governments to espouse policies of religious neutrality and political tolerance. At the same time, they legally and psychologically committed their society to the tenet that public opinion alone was the arbiter of truth—

political, religious, and every other kind. "Public opinion" was increasingly understood to be the collective product of all individual sentiments and not simply the wisdom of a few learned gentlemen. So whether the issue was the embargo against Great Britain and France or the limits of Christ's atonement, truth was now equated with what won general acceptance among the general populace as a result of free discussion.[36]

We cannot fully know what exact role the truth triumphant notion played in persuading Americans to adopt these views in the early republic. It is known, however, that whenever this notion was invoked by Englishmen or Americans in the late 1700s it was always used to push the new nation's thinking in precisely the way that thinking ended up going. Herein, then, lies much of the significance of the truth triumphant notion for the constitutional era. One will search in vain to find this idea being expressed among the delegates to Philadelphia or in the debates over ratification.[37] Likewise its importance to constitution writing at the state level was probably very limited.[38] But in encouraging a general mindset among the framers and other Americans that allowed public opinion to replace the state as (in Gordon Wood's apt phrase) the "resolving force" of all truth, the truth triumphant notion may be seen as making a substantial contribution to the new kind of political and intellectual order that emerged in the United States at the end of the eighteenth century.

From a modern vantage point, the dangers of equating truth with the popular will seem readily evident. Within this scheme, for example, belief in popular sovereignty over the determination of truth largely replaces any assertion of divine sovereignty over truth. Likewise, the fallen and corrupted character of human reason is obscured in the claim that the fruits of free debate among reasonable people may always be regarded as truth. In light of such problems it would be easy to suppose that Christians in the early republic played little role in promoting these ideas. Close examination reveals in fact that there were Presbyterians, Baptists, Methodists, Quakers, Catholics, and members of other religious groups who remained skeptical of public opinion. At the same time, however, as has already been shown, a wide spectrum of sincere believers were active advocates of the truth triumphant notion. Consequently, we must ask why some Christians accepted this notion in the first place and what resulted from their doing so.

The explanation seems to lie partly in the supreme faith they had in the ultimate triumph of their own perceptions of truth.[39] Such faith derived principally from their convictions about the direction in which history was headed. Persuaded that the course of human events was moving inexorably toward God's victory over Satan, these believers viewed the future as a time in which *their* understanding of truth would come to be shared by more and more people. In different circumstances, this view of the coming ages may have had little impact upon attitudes toward the present. But in the early republic, it proved to have a profound influence because it was linked to strong postmillennial hopes that the future was now.

Throughout this era but particularly from 1790 to 1810, American Protestant Christians pointed to numerous signs that indicated (in their minds) the imminence of Christ's millennial reign.[40] Chief among them was the expansion of civil and religious liberties in America, France, and other parts of the world. Nathan Hatch has described how postmillennialists understood the destruction of political and ecclesiastical tyranny to be opening the way for the spread of the gospel and ultimately the establishment of the kingdom of God on earth. They made liberty a sacred cause and used its advance to measure how swiftly the world was moving toward the millennium.[41] In the process, they made the triumph of Christian truth virtually dependent upon the progress of human freedom.

It is not hard to see in light of such millennialist convictions why the truth triumphant notion found wide acceptance. If world history was quickly moving toward its culmination in the advent of Christ's kingdom, and if the expansion of liberty was largely responsible for spurring movement in that direction, then it was eminently reasonable to suppose that truth would not suffer at the hands of free discussion but instead would triumph both now and in the future. Each small victory truth won in the present, in effect, would be a step toward its more complete victory in the coming millennium.

Two other factors made all this even more persuasive. One was the overwhelming religious dominance of Protestantism in America. From a practical standpoint, Protestants' numerical superiority was a virtual guarantee that if truth was determined by majority rule, their version would always win out. The other factor was the early republican view of truth as perspicuous. Influenced by Scottish Common Sense Realism and Baconianism, many American Christians in the late eighteenth and early nineteenth centuries embraced the idea that the truths of God's special and general revelations were plain for men and women to apprehend. No special learning was required to understand God's

Word or creation; people only needed to exercise their "common sense."[42] Therefore, in an open debate where all opinions were given free voice, truth by its very nature would be plainly visible to common folk and intellectuals alike. Truth's inherent clarity, in other words, provided reassurance that the American public would recognize it.

If postmillennialism, the perspicuity of truth, and Protestant dominance were not powerful enough by themselves to persuade early republican Christians to accept the truth triumphant notion, they became convincing when combined with a desire to counteract the radical Enlightenment. Thoughtful Christians at the turn of the nineteenth century were rightfully concerned with the attacks French *philosophes* had made upon Christianity. In particular, they felt compelled to respond to the vehement denunciations of Christianity (and religion in general) as an obstacle and restraint to free inquiry. Such denunciations, according to Peter Gay, were at the very heart of a French Enlightenment that sought to divorce inquiry and science from religion.[43] As might be expected (as Dwight Bozeman has explained), Protestant churchmen responded by arguing that Christianity was an aid, not a barrier, to free inquiry.[44]

Nowhere was this more clearly argued than in Samuel Miller's *A Brief Retrospect of the Eighteenth Century,* published in 1803. A Presbyterian pastor in New York City, Miller gave a long overview of the accomplishments of the previous century and concluded that it was preeminently an age of free inquiry. He then boldly countered the *philosophes'* thesis:

> It has been often objected to Christianity, that it is unfavourable to the progress of knowledge; that it discourages scientific enterprize; that it is inimical to free inquiry, and has a tendency to keep the minds of men in blindness and thraldom. The history of the last concurs with that of many preceding centuries, in demonstrating that the very reverse of what the objection states is the truth.[45]

Miller did not stop there, however. To emphasize his point about the harmony of Christianity and the search for new knowledge, he insisted that the scientific discoveries of the 1700s had individually and collectively confirmed many of the claims of the Bible.[46] Miller's argument, then, was twofold: first, that Christianity had stimulated, not retarded, the discovery of new truth, and second, that the discovery of new truth corroborated the doctrines of the Christian faith.

Arguments like Miller's extolling the compatibility of Christianity and scientific inquiry undoubtedly made it easier for Christians in the early republic to adopt the truth triumphant notion. For believers to affirm the legitimacy and value of open investigation into any issue was for them to question Enlightenment claims of religion's intellectual backwardness. And to know that the new findings of science supported age-old biblical tenets made it all the more plausible to think that free inquiry would always produce additions to, or confirmations of, Christian truth. On the other hand, the belief that truth would triumph helped quell any residual fears that science or learning might threaten the faith.

Many Protestant Christians in the last quarter of the eighteenth century embraced the truth triumphant notion in the confidence that the ultimate victory of God's truth was at hand. They were determined to confute Enlightenment opposition to religion precisely because they believed that millennial truth would triumph. These beliefs and actions had three important historical consequences.

First, by placing trust in whatever output flowed from a free debate, Christians contributed to the democratization of the American mind. Gordon Wood and Nathan Hatch have described how the early republic's newfound faith in the common man and public opinion opened up intellectual realms such as political theory and theology to the educated and untrained alike. The net result was a more egalitarian culture, but one in which there was little support or perceived need for the extraordinary man of ideas.[47]

Additionally, Protestantism was left open to attacks that it was a slave to public opinion. Catholic convert Orestes Brownson condemned Protestantism as helplessly bound to the "popular will, passion, interest, ignorance, prejudice, or caprice."[48] At the same time, belief that their version of the truth would inevitably win out eventually left Protestant believers ill prepared to deal with the far more radical brand of religious and intellectual pluralism that characterized American society by the late nineteenth century. In the face of massive Catholic and Jewish immigration, not to mention higher criticism and evolutionary naturalism, it became increasingly difficult for Protestants to rest comfortably with the idea that truth's innate greatness was alone sufficient to ensure Protestantism's dominance. Some nevertheless kept the faith. So, for example, certain liberal Protestants at the turn of the twentieth century supported nonsectarian public schools on the grounds that Christianity would naturally prevail in such a setting because of its innate superiority.[49] Others had more severe doubts. They periodically resorted to state force to assure continued Protestant supremacy over

American culture. In retrospect, neither of these responses to the nation's growing diversity served the interests of Christianity or truth very well. Both kept believers from developing a workable approach to the problem of how Christians fit into a pluralistic society. Neither response allowed Christians to recognize the value of cultural pluralism.

The truth triumphant notion *had* allowed, in the nineteenth century, a close identification of Protestant Christianity with the interests of the republic. The story of the amalgamation of Protestantism and American civilization in the 1800s needs no rehearsing here. Suffice it to say that the truth triumphant idea suggested that Christianity had nothing to fear from freedom and freedom had nothing to fear from Christianity. This meant that at least in theory, the church could champion itself as a liberating rather than a confining force in society. Regrettably, however, it also meant that the fusion of Christianity and American culture could go on unabated with little thought given to the consequences of either.

Amid the turmoil of the 1640s in England John Milton had written that

> when God shakes a Kingdom with strong and healthful commotions to a general reforming . . . [He] raises to His own work men of rare abilities, and more than common industry, not only to look back and revise what hath been taught heretofore, but to gain further and go on some new enlightened steps in the discovery of truth. For such is the order of God's enlightening His Church, to dispense and deal out by degrees His beam, so as our earthly eyes may best sustain it.[50]

Whether Milton would have thought that any American Christians were fulfilling this high calling amid the commotions of the early republic is difficult to speculate. But the judgments he would have reached about Christian acceptance of the truth triumphant notion in the constitutional era may likely have been similar to the ones we can make with two hundred years of historical hindsight. I think we can applaud those believers who insisted that Christianity could foster human inquiry and learning without compromising itself. Likewise, we should be impressed with those who overturned efforts to impose political and religious uniformity and committed American society instead to a respect for diversity. Perhaps we should be most stirred by those Christians who celebrated the greatness of truth because they, like Milton, had imbibed a sense of truth's power and wonder, traits clearly derived from its eternal source.

These positive observations must be balanced, however, by recognizing the ways the truth triumphant idea hurt Christian thought. It left believers, for instance, with the naive assumption that the fortunes of truth, and more specifically the fortunes of Christianity, depended principally upon the presence of freedom. In the process, it obscured the fact that the real determinant of truth's fate was how well American Christians did at thinking and acting Christianly. The truth triumphant notion also obscured the limits of human rationality. In encouraging believers to place their faith in public opinion as the arbiter of truth, it not only challenged divine sovereignty but overlooked reason's need for grace. Both these examples exemplify the strong Enlightenment roots of the truth triumphant notion and reveal the irony of its Christian acceptance. In embracing this idea in the early republic, believers showed just how vulnerable Christian thought was to the influx of unbiblical presuppositions amid the free exchange of ideas. If truth was to prosper amid open inquiry in America, something more than freedom itself was required to make it do so.

NOTES

1. As printed in William Lee Miller, *The First Liberty: Religion and the American Republic* (New York: Alfred A. Knopf, 1986), 357-58.

2. Bernard Bailyn, *The Ideological Origins of the American Revolution* (Cambridge, Mass.: Harvard Univ. Press, 1967); Gordon S. Wood, *The Creation of the American Republic* (Chapel Hill, N.C.: Univ. of North Carolina Press, 1969); J. G. A. Pocock, *The Machiavellian Moment: Florentine Political Thought and the Atlantic Republican Tradition* (Princeton, N.J.: Princeton Univ. Press, 1975).

3. Forrest McDonald, *Novus Ordo Seclorum: The Intellectual Origins of the Constitution* (Lawrence, Kans.: Univ. Press of Kansas, 1985), 57-96, describes the various systems of political theory familiar to the Founders.

4. Ibid., 57-70. Will Morrisey, "The Moral Foundations of the American Republic: An Introduction," in Robert H. Horwitz, ed., *The Moral Foundations of the American Republic,* 3d ed. (Charlottesville, Va.: Univ. Press of Virginia, 1986), 12, calls Locke "the political philosopher who most influenced the Founders."

5. John Locke, *The Works of John Locke,* 10 vols. (London, 1823; repr., Germany, 1963), vol. 6.

6. Ibid., 62-63, 71-72.

7. Ibid., 81-82, 484-85.

8. Ibid., 64.

9. Ibid., 20.

10. John Milton, *Areopagitica: A Speech for the Liberty of Unlicensed Printing, To the Parliament of England,* in Robert Maynard Hutchins, ed., *Great Books of the Western World,* 54 vols. (Chicago: Encyclopoedia Britannica, 1948), 32:381-87.

11. Ibid., 409.

12. Ibid.

13. Ibid., 393.

14. Among Leonard Levy's many works see *Legacy of Suppression: Freedom of Speech and Press in Early American History* (Cambridge, Mass.: Harvard Univ. Press, 1960) and *Constitutional Opinions: Aspects of the Bill of Rights* (New York: Oxford Univ. Press, 1986).

15. The best work on Price is David O. Thomas, *The Honest Mind: The Thought and Work of Richard Price* (Oxford: Clarendon Press, 1977). I am not aware of any extended scholarly treatment of Robert Hall.

16. Philip Furneaux, *Letters to the Honourable Mr. Justice Blackstone,* 2d ed. (Philadelphia: Robert Bell, 1773), 28.

17. Richard Price, *Observations on the Importance of the American Revolution* (Boston: Powers & Willis, 1784), 25-26.

18. Robert Hall, "On Dissenters," in *The Works of Robert Hall,* 6 vols. (London: Henry G. Bohn, 1845), 3:143-46.

19. Robert Hall, "Christianity Consistent with a Love of Freedom," in *Works,* 3:12-14.

20. Levy, *Legacy of Suppression,* 254-56.

21. Edmund S. Morgan, *The Gentle Puritan: A Life of Ezra Stiles, 1727–1795* (New Haven, Conn.: Yale Univ. Press, 1962), 178.

22. Ezra Stiles, *A Discourse on the Christian Union* (Boston: Edes & Gill, 1761), 96.

23. Morgan, *The Gentle Puritan,* 178-79.

24. As quoted in Jay P. Dolan, *The American Catholic Experience* (Garden City, N.Y.: Doubleday & Co., 1985), 109.

25. William Linn, *Discourses on the Signs of the Times* (New York: Greenleaf, 1794), 110.

26. John Leland, "The Connecticut Dissenters' Strong Box: No. 1," in Charles S. Hyneman and David S. Lutz, eds., *American Political Writing during the Founding Era*, 2 vols. (Indianapolis: Liberty Press, 1983), 2:1196, 1205.

27. *The Theological Magazine* 1 (1795): 1-3.

28. *The Theological Magazine* 2 (1796): 69-72, 142-43.

29. Isaac Backus, *Truth is Great and Will Prevail* (Boston: Freeman, [1781]).

30. Miller, *The First Liberty*, 214.

31. Richard Buel, Jr., "Freedom of the Press in Revolutionary America: The Evolution of Libertarianism, 1769–1820," in Bernard Bailyn and John B. Hench, eds., *The Press & the American Revolution* (Worcester, Mass.: American Antiquarian Society, 1980), 90.

32. Tunis Wortman, *A Treatise Concerning Political Enquiry, and the Liberty of the Press* (New York: George Forman, 1800), 30-69, 119-23. Also of interest is [Tunis Wortman], *A Solemn Address to Christians & Patriots, upon the approaching election of a President of the United States* (New York: David Denniston, 1800).

33. Gordon S. Wood, "The Democratization of Mind in the American Revolution," in Horwitz, ed., *Moral Foundations*, 133-34.

34. Norman Rosenberg, "Alexander Addison and the Pennsylvania Origins of Federalist First-Amendment Thought," *Pennsylvania Magazine of History and Biography* 108 (Oct. 1984): 403-14.

35. Buel, "Evolution of Libertarianism," 96.

36. Wood, "Democratization of Mind," 133; Buel, "Evolution of Libertarianism," 90.

37. I surveyed the Constitutional Convention debates and the Federalist Papers and found no mention of this idea. See Max Farrand, ed., *The Records of the Federal Convention of 1787*, rev. ed., 4 vols. (New Haven, Conn.: Yale Univ. Press, 1937; repr., 1966), and James Madison, Alexander Hamilton, and John Jay, *The Federalist Papers* (New Rochelle, N.Y.: Arlington House, 1966).

38. Some suggestions on the role of this idea in shaping constitution writing in New York in the 1770s are contained in Richard W. Pointer, *Protestant Pluralism and the New York Experience: A Study of Eighteenth-Century Religious Diversity* (Bloomington, Ind.: Indiana Univ. Press, 1987), chap. five.

39. Fred Hood, *Reformed America: The Middle and Southern States, 1783–1837* (University, Ala.: Univ. of Alabama Press, 1980), 127, finds this idea particularly strong among Reformed Christians in the early republic.

40. Among the signs Protestants pointed to were the decline of Roman Catholicism in France, the rise of missionary organizations throughout Europe, and the American and French revolutions. For one example of postmillennial literature from the 1790s, see Linn, *Discourses on the Signs of the Times*.

41. Nathan O. Hatch, *The Sacred Cause of Liberty* (New Haven, Conn.: Yale Univ. Press, 1977), 96-175.

42. Among the many works detailing these influences see Mark A. Noll, "Common Sense Traditions and American Evangelical Thought," *American Quarterly* 37 (Summer 1985): 216-38, and Theodore D. Bozeman, *Protestants in an Age of Science: The Baconian Ideal and Antebellum American Religious Thought* (Chapel Hill, N.C.: Univ. of North Carolina Press, 1977).

43. Peter Gay, *The Enlightenment: An Interpretation,* 2 vols. (New York: Alfred A. Knopf, 1967–1969), 1:212-422.

44. Bozeman, *Protestants in an Age of Science,* 45-48.

45. Samuel Miller, *A Brief Retrospect of the Eighteenth Century,* 2 vols. (New York: T. & J. Swords, 1803), 2:433.

46. Ibid., 434.

47. Wood, "Democratization of Mind," 109-10, 131-35; Nathan O. Hatch, "Evangelicalism as a Democratic Movement," in George Marsden, ed., *Evangelicalism and Modern America* (Grand Rapids: Wm. B. Eerdmans, 1984), 75-76; Nathan O. Hatch, "The Christian Movement and the Demand for a Theology of the People," *Journal of American History* 67 (Dec. 1980): 545-67.

48. Edwin S. Gaustad, ed., *A Documentary History of Religion in America,* 2 vols. (Grand Rapids: Wm. B. Eerdmans, 1982–1983), 1:443-44.

49. Gary Scott Smith, *The Seeds of Secularization: Calvinism, Culture, and Pluralism in America 1870–1915* (Grand Rapids: Wm. B. Eerdmans, Christian Univ. Press, 1985), 83-84.

50. Milton, *Areopagitica,* 410-11.

The Constitution and
the Benevolent Empire

Richard H. Clossman

In the north transept of the Washington Cathedral, inscribed in stone, is a dedication that reads: "To the Glory of God and in honor to the Signers of the Constitution of the United States of America." The signers are listed, headed by George Washington, "President and Deputy from Virginia." The inscription eloquently expresses the allegiance with which Christian churches in America have acclaimed a Constitution wedded to a republican form of government. Drawn to this principle of governance by the promises of liberty and justice, American church leaders have voiced, through the past two centuries, a consistent determination to guard and sustain the Constitution.

The Founding Fathers had this kind of relationship in mind when they were drafting the Constitution, at least to the extent that the churches felt encouraged to nourish the flowering of civic morality needed to maintain the republican structures of government. It was an underlying axiom of the day: public virtue was necessary for a republic. If righteousness among the citizens declined, the republic declined. If the citizens were virtuous, the republic flourished.[1]

The remarkable increase in humanitarian and religious energy that flowed through American society in the early nineteenth century was, in part, a strategy designed by Christian groups to provide the personal and corporate righteousness necessary to protect the republic and its Constitution from failure, and to implement the moral vigor that a written document could not deliver. The Constitution offered the potential for righteousness; the Christian faith among a dedicated citizenry supplied its actualization. The Constitution was religion-neutral; Christian churches were sectarian advocates of particular viewpoints who were free to address matters relating to their own vision of God's kingdom on earth. The Benevolent Empire, that is, the many reform societies, educational institutions, and missionary agencies, operated, in large part, to fulfill that vision of Christ's emerging kingdom that was now possible under the American Constitution. There was, consequently, a linkage between the Constitution and the Benevolent Empire. Religious reformers had a vested interest in the success of the Constitution; and political leaders depended upon that kind of civic integrity which flourished within religious societies.

This civic integrity was particularly important to the life of the new nation because the Constitution was compromised, even flawed, from the very beginning. It was in need of a strong company of persons who, committed to an ideal of Christian commonwealth, or at least of moral progress, would labor to fulfill the reforms and visions that were beyond the capacity of fundamental law to infuse into a society. The most notable deficiency within the Constitution was the enigma ensconced in the antislave trade clause in Article I, Section 9, a compromise adjustment that all agreed was mandatory to effect an adequate federal union.

The story of slavery provides us the best opportunity to investigate the linkage between the Constitution and the reforming movement of the next few decades. The Founding Fathers, while constructing a Constitution, were forced to translate their moral and religious views of slavery into a workable, though imperfect, system of government. This system, then, became the context in which the new humanitarianism emerged. The story of slavery continues through this entire period, revealing changes in attitudes among the founding statesmen and religious reformers, and the attempts to implement reform. In studying such a linkage, the problem of slavery becomes the axiological linchpin around which the Founding Fathers struggled to join morally disparate views into a Constitution, and reformers labored to rid a nation of the curse of slaveholding. The government, at the same time, rested upon a moral citizenry and an amoral, or at least religion-neutral, Constitution. The slavery debate, therefore, presents a strong case study as to how moral and religious motivations and strategies were translated into societal and national structures.

Perhaps *linkage* is too strong a word, since it suggests some demonstrable connection between the Constitution and the humanitarian reforms. There is, however, something resembling a choreography of themes and rhetoric on the national stage that sets both statesman and reformer in motion. The dance is, at times, a minuet, done with the polite etiquette of the genteel rhetoric of the Founding Fathers at the convention of 1787. At other times, the movement is more a country reel, with the zealous and confrontational forms of regional argument espoused by preacher and politician alike.

No greater moral issue faced the delegates in Philadelphia at the Constitutional Convention in 1787 than that of the slave issue. The problem cut across several of the major questions facing the delegates. There was the question of equitable representation among the states within a national legislature, an issue that raised the predicament of whether the African slave was a person, three-fifths of a person, or property. The question of taxation presented the same dilemma: How does one count the slave, as person or property? In addition, there was the debate over control of exports and imports, a power that, a few years later, could have eliminated the profitability of the slave trade and of slavery itself. Another contingent issue was defense, which raised the question whether tax monies could be expended to put down slave insurrections, or whether the entire nation would be vulnerable in time of war because of its numerous enslaved and dangerous residents. The debates, as they are represented in James Madison's journal, are predominantly economic and political in nature. Religious and moral dimensions, however, are not absent, even though earlier usage of biblical idiom and Christian authority had long since been muted into more secular terminology. When the final draft of the Constitution was completed, the outcome was an accommodation that sustained the right of individual states to retain the practice of slavery, viewing slaves as three-fifths persons, and also disallowing the importation of slaves from outside the nation after a twenty-year grace period. It was a compromise that largely divided the southern states from the "eastern" ones, as the northern states commonly referred to themselves. The two regions, southern and eastern, had already drifted far apart in economic and social treatment. By 1787 it was, in political realities, too late to effect any policy other than compromise regarding slavery and the slave trade.

The South had become dependent upon tobacco, rice, and sugar profits, all of which utilized large numbers of slaves. In particular South Carolina and Georgia needed larger numbers of plantation laborers. Virginia, North Carolina, and Maryland appeared far less insistent on importing slaves. The animus against Africans entering the social order was no doubt deeper among the southern states than in the North, but only because there were more slaves to control and, consequently, more to fear.[2]

The eastern colonies to the north were affected far more by the events in England regarding the legal status of resident slaves than were the southern states. The most famous case in England was in 1772 regarding James Somersett, a slave living in England. Somersett, with the sponsorship of Granville Sharp, obtained a ruling from Lord Mansfield, Chief Justice of the King's Bench, that he be set free. The ruling was soon interpreted to mean that "as soon as any person whatever set his foot in their country, he came under the protection of the British laws, and was consequently free."[3] The case was quickly publicized in the colonies and became popular, particularly in the eastern colonies, since the Mansfield ruling tended to reinforce Quaker and Methodist feelings and also was viewed as corroborating the natural law rhetoric fashionable at the time. The Somersett case accelerated a number of "freedom suits" that developed in Massachusetts and in other colonial court systems. More radical leadership began to assert that slavery should not exist at all in the colonies since it was unconstitutional.[4]

A year after the Somersett case the Massachusetts royal charter of 1691 came under attack by the antislave leadership, who argued that all migrants or natives in America "shall have and enjoy all Liberties and Immunities of free and natural subjects . . . as if they . . . were born within this Our Realm of England."[5] During the revolutionary period, freedom suits multiplied in the Massachusetts court system, bringing freedom to individual black slaves. The argument between "Liberty" and "Property" was consistently settled in favor of Liberty as the more important of the two, since it agreed with the Law of Nature principle. In 1780, the Massachusetts Supreme Judicial Court declared slavery to be ended.[6] Other New England states in the 1780s drafted statutes for gradual abolition, giving visible evidence of the "withering away" of slavery in that region of the country.[7]

In addition to local precedents, some decisions were made by the Congress of the Confederation and became landmark rulings for later constitutional determinations. In 1774, the First Continental Congress signaled an intent to remove the American colonies from the British slave trade commerce, although the pronouncement was more of a protest of Britain's continued insistence that the American slave trade proceed without any colonial duties levied upon it than an attempt actually to prohibit the trade. The ruling was never effective. Nevertheless, the congressional affirmation did imply the moral bankruptcy of the commerce, leading individual states to pass resolutions prohibiting the foreign trade. Another significant precedent occurred on July 16, 1783, when a compromise was reached on an aspect of a revenue amendment. The compromise allowed for the counting of a slave as three-fifths of a person in enumerating the population. The policy became, as Rufus King described it not long after, "the language of all America," and thus was a principle that influenced the 1787 Constitutional Convention debates.[8]

One other precedent must be mentioned. The Ordinance of 1787 included a sentence excluding slavery from the Northwest Territory, again burdening the slave institution with the onus of moral stigma. The ordinance was almost concurrent with the Philadelphia Convention, leading one to wonder how the first decision could have been so humanitarian and sagacious and the second such an ill-drafted concession. However, we should not praise the Northwest Ordinance prohibition too highly. William Grayson of Virginia wrote to James Monroe some three weeks after the ordinance was completed, saying:

> The clause respecting slavery was agreed to by the southern members for the purpose of preventing tobacco and indigo from being made on the northwest side of the Ohio, as well as for several other political reasons.[9]

More typical of the real dichotomy of feelings was the result of Thomas Jefferson's attempt to include in his original draft of the Ordinance of 1784 the phrase, "the abolition of slavery in the new States after the year 1800." Congress rejected the clause.[10]

All of the changes in political and judicial policies in large part rested upon an underlying corpora of ideological and religious currents of the day. The origins of these eighteenth-century ideas were more European than homegrown; it is doubtful that the American conscience, by itself, could have generated the momentum for the attacks on slavery or the slave trade. Both the French *philosophes,* with their ideas of freedom and equality, and the British evangelical and nonconformist leadership, contributed to the American momentum toward the anti-slave feelings, but the British appear to have been more directly influential to the New England mind. The Quakers and Wesleyans were driving forces among the religious groups in England; political voices, such as those of William Wilberforce, Granville Sharp, Thomas Clarkson, and the other members of the Clapham Sect, also raised the cause of antislavery, as Howard Temperley phrased it, "almost to the status of a religion in England."[11] The idea of progress and the eschatological expectancy in the Christian faith bound each other, both in Britain and in the American colonies, until they were inextricably entangled.

The effects of England's swelling moral crusade was especially obvious in the northern states. For instance, in 1783, both the Pennsylvania Quaker and Presbyterian Synod leadership in Philadelphia appeared "on the floor of congress" in order to "procure eventually the final abolition of slavery in America."[12] The southern states were less successful in struggling with the moral implications of slavery and the slave trade. The Virginians, one contemporary observed, "are forever talking of abolishing slavery, and falling upon some other mode of improving their lands, etc."[13]

These attitudes and precedents, then, set the stage for the Philadelphia deliberations of 1787, revealing two opposing positions already firmly in place. The heated debates over slavery soon threatened to permanently dismantle any agreement. The only hope of a resolution, after two particularly stormy periods of verbal controversy, was the acceptance of a bitterly fought-over paragraph (Art. I, Sec. 9) in which the southern states, most notably South Carolina, relinquished their demand for control of the "passing of navigation acts" by requiring a two-thirds vote of both houses and, in return, insisted upon a twenty-year delay in the discontinuance of the slave trade for any state wishing to permit it. The agreement was hailed at the time as a very necessary compromise that halted the advance of slavery and saved the nation through an accommodation so delicately balanced that the union of North and South depended upon it.[14]

The framers of the Constitution were dealing here with moral and humanitarian issues in which the sensibilities of several of the delegates were deeply offended both by slavery and the slave trade. Their arguments, however, as revealed in Madison's journal, were predominantly economic and political rather than religious or humanitarian. Religious remarks were typically disregarded or neglected.[15] "Religion and humanity had nothing to do with this question," retorted John Rutledge of South Carolina in response to Maryland antislave delegate Luther Martin's opening barrage in the August debate. "Interest alone," Rutledge argued, was "the governing principle with nations."[16] Self-interest, however, was not necessarily the antithesis of humanitarian concern, in the South's point of view. Embracing nine-tenths of the approximately 650,000 slaves in the United States, the southern states raised the question of humanitarian concern for its own white citizens if slaves, given their freedom, were to seek their revenge. The southerner viewed his humanitarianism through the lens of law and order rather than through a troubled conscience over the inhumanity of slavery.[17] Gouverneur Morris of Pennsylvania, another outspoken anti-slave delegate, expressed his dismay by admitting the standoff as a "dilemma of doing injustice to the Southern States, or to human nature."[18]

The Constitution that, though perhaps not going far enough, embraced a modicum of justice for human nature by outlawing the slave trade, was also used by reformers as a tactic employed to promote righteousness in the nation. Church leaders and others recognized the Constitution as a vehicle capable of instigating moral reform and social change to the nation. The document guaranteed a political voice in civic affairs to strong, grassroots majorities who would demand moral decorum and social righteousness. The republican political structure was thus easily wedded to the harbinger voices of millennial expectation. It was a new way to envision civic order and the commonweal.

Benjamin Franklin's remarks on the day the Constitution was signed (Sept. 17) gained wide dissemination in years afterward. Franklin had watched the proceedings as the delegates of the eleven states present recorded their unanimous assent to the document. He had also scrutinized, from time to time over the long summer, the design of a sun "blazoned" on the backrest of Washington's chair. After the vote was complete, Franklin remarked to his colleagues nearby, "In the vicissitudes of hope and fear I was not able to tell whether it was rising or setting; now I know that it is the rising sun."[19]

Franklin's optimism in America's future characterized the dominant mood of his fellow countrymen. The homey imagery of the rising sun is like the coming new age of the millennial kingdom, or, in a more secular tone, like the transcendent purpose in history as espoused by those who were certain of the idea of progress in human affairs. The Constitution was the actual embodiment of much of the progress John Adams wrote about in his book of that year, *Defence of the Constitution of the United States of America*. In his preface, Adams rapturously announces his era as displaying such wonders as "a regular course of progressive improvement," "the advancement of civilization and humanity," "considerable improvements," "reformation in manners and improvement in knowledge," to list but a few of his euphemisms.[20] Christians, especially, were able to integrate this rising sun of republicanism into a new commitment for righteousness and benevolence; and this Constitution opened up new vistas of work and ministry for them.[21]

Many persons in the North assumed that the prohibition of the importation of slaves implied the approaching decline of slavery. One

such speaker, Mr. Davis, in Massachusetts, during the debates for the
ratification of the Constitution in 1788, commented, "although slavery
is not smitten by an apoplexy, yet it has received a mortal wound, and
will die of a consumption."[22] Others were not so sure. In the ratification debate in New Hampshire the Hon. Joshua Atherton spoke regarding Art. I, Sec. 9, and warned:

> We do not behold in it . . . that an end is then to be put to slavery. Con-
> gress may be as much, or more, puzzled to put a stop to it then, than we
> are now. The clause has not secured its abolition.[23]

Pointing out that acceptance of the Constitution would allow an
"implicit approval of slavery," a substantial number of northerners
viewed the document as unworthy and flawed. This was Atherton's
position:

> . . . we do not esteem ourselves under any necessity to go . . . to abolish
> the detestable custom of enslaving the African; but, sir, we will not lend
> the aid of our ratification to this cruel and inhuman merchandise, not
> even for a day.[24]

Luther Martin, who opposed the Constitution he helped to draft,
cogently disclosed to his Maryland constituents the profound incon-
sistency within the document. On one hand, there was a "government
over free people—a government formed pretendedly on the principles
of liberty, and for its preservation." On the other hand, there were contained in the government no powers "to restrain and prevent the slave
trade" but rather a circumstance "encouraging that most infamous traf-
fic."[25]

Other voices honored the necessity of a compromise, no matter
how ignominious it appeared. "The federal Convention went as far as
they could," defended General Heath in the Massachusetts debate. He
explained:

> . . . it is not in our power to do any thing for or against those who are in
> slavery in the Southern states. . . . We have no right to compel them. . . .
> We are not, in this case, partakers of other men's sins; for in nothing do
> we voluntarily encourage the slavery of our fellowmen.[26]

The complicity of antislave citizens with the southern slave-
holders, however, was indeed apparent, and made for a circumstance in
which individual states held legitimate authority to sustain slavery if
they desired. All agreed that the federal government could not abolish
the peculiar institution by any peaceful means. William Wiecek in his

book *The Sources of Antislavery Constitutionalism in America, 1760–1848*, describes the arrangement by the term *federal consensus.*[27]

The flaw that marred the Constitution from its beginnings was a "federal consensus" run riot without the moral anchorage of adequate sensibilities of heart and mind. Hailed on the one hand as a God-given masterpiece of the American people, the document also carried this significant blemish, and was eventually to be interpreted as a proslavery instrument. Henry Thoreau soon would zealously contrast the Constitution of 1787 with "that eternal and only just CONSTITUTION, which He [the Lord God] and not Jefferson or Adams, has written in your being."[28] William E. Channing would echo the same argument:

> There is, however, a constitution which precedes all of men's making, and after which all others are to be formed; a constitution, the great lines of which are drawn in our very nature; a primitive law of justice, rectitude, and philanthropy, which all other laws are bound to enforce, and from which all others derive their validity and worth.[29]

The comments of Thoreau and Channing point out the ideational concepts of the Constitution that emerged almost immediately after its ratification. There were, in fact, at least two Constitutions, that is, two forms that existed side by side in the American mind. One was nearly perfect in conceptual jurisprudence with the role of religious institutions to defend and acclaim the superiority of this faultless mode of government. The second was blemished and insufficient to spur a nation on to civic virtue. In this view the task of churches, reform societies, educational institutions, home mission agencies—indeed, the whole assemblage of what has come to be called the Benevolent Empire—was to fashion a people whose righteousness could sustain a republican government, and thus rescue the Constitution from the many failures of past republican endeavors of ancient Greece and renaissance Italy.

The Constitution as an ideal form had more fundamental penetration into American society in earlier years than the other form. It became nothing less than a sacred guide. Many of the early forms and voices of the birth of the republic gained levels of veneration akin to religious reverence. For example, in *The Bonds of Wickedness: American Evangelicals Against Slavery, 1770–1808*, James Essig describes the epic poem *Avenia,* written by the antislave preacher Thomas Branagan in 1805.[30] In addition to portraying the cruelties of slave trading, Branagan pictured a scene in which Gabriel was with some of the heavenly saints, namely, George Whitefield, John Wesley, and George Washington. Today, Washington's prominence in heavenly places seems strangely inappropriate. His inclusion, however, suggests not only the growing iconography of the nation's first president, but also betrays the mixture of churchly and national symbols in the public mind. The Constitution, as the fundamental expression of republicanism's "written word," shared in this special aura of God-inspired truth, effusive praise for which could be heard in every July 4th oration, and in many a Sunday sermon.[31]

Various denominational groupings among the churches imitated proudly the organizational structures connoted in the Constitution. The Protestant Episcopal Church developed the House of Bishops and the House of Clerical and Lay Deputies in response to the popularity of the upper and lower houses of Congress.[32] State conventions were developed and took on the authority suggested by the federal system. The Presbyterians were in Philadelphia the same summer as the Founding Fathers, drafting their own constitution, and what emerged was a system of "assemblies" ranging from the "less unto the greater" that were basically similar.[33] The democratizing of most American denominations was perpetuated through the imitation of constitutional structures. One late nineteenth-century academic observed:

> The ecclesiastical side of our constitutional history in this formative period has been generally overlooked. Yet so great movement in the affairs of civil government could hardly have gone on without exerting a powerful influence, by attraction, to borrow a phrase from the grammarians, on our ecclesiastic polity.[34]

The ideals of Hamilton and Madison set forth in *The Federalist,* such as "a correct balance," "equilibrium of power," "the natural limit of a republic," were advantageous maxims for congregations whose roots had been nourished ever since their colonial beginnings with the continuous diet of localism, independence, and anticlericalism. Local congregational autonomy was prevalent throughout all church groups, including Roman Catholic; and, at least to some extent, the model of a republican constitution motivated this claim for local congregational authority. The Constitution, in several ways, had been made in their image.[35]

The republican scheme allowed both nation and churches to distance themselves from European influence whenever it was convenient. What had begun during the American Revolution (blaming a corrupt

England for its political tyranny and its religious decadence) was to blossom into a doctrine of American innocence and moral political virtue by attributing a sense of superiority to the Constitution, unattainable by aristocratic Europe. Americans became almost "obsessed with their virtue," and America's national character was inextricably linked to a political as well as a religious and moral perfectibility.[36] In one way, the need for virtue in a nation came full circle. The earlier argument by Montesquieu and others specified that virtue was needed to sustain a republic. The reverse argument was then put forward by John Adams: the republican ideal was a requirement for a truly virtuous society.[37] In his view the Christian community needed the republican ideal form in order to prosper.

The idealism of the Constitution may have served the American missionary movement with special potency. The boldness and audacity with which missionaries braved the difficulties of their foreign and home mission enterprises reflected not only their strong faith but also the certainty of mind and heart that they represented a superior and triumphant race of people. Their adherence to republican tradition was no small portion of that confidence and bearing.

Both explicit and implicit testimonies to the Constitution fill missionary publications. The Constitution is "the best in the world," said one writer, and "secures to us a larger portion of the natural and unalienable rights of man than any other political charter in existence."[38] This kind of confidence may well have contributed to the excitement and energy of the missionary call. "The Lord is shaking the nation," announced the *Panoplist* journal in 1810, ". . . and unprecedented exertions are making for the spread of Divine knowledge."[39] This "new dispensation of mission," whether on the "Western frontiers" or in the "destitute" regions of Asia, implied the effort to enshrine republican principles in world opinion. Missionary pioneers carried their republican views, if only in subtle ways, wherever they traveled and the Constitution became the political "written word" for the acculturation of the "heathen."

The second major view of the Constitution acknowledged it as a flawed and deficient formula for government. It was understood not so much as a God-inspired instrument for government but as a people-produced document that required some repair and change from time to time. This point of view forces a return to the topic of slavery and the slave trade. Other shortcomings also appeared in federal governance,

as early constitutional amendments give evidence, but the slavery issue
was the most onerous.

The shortcomings of the Constitution were obvious from the very
beginning, even by those who avidly supported its acceptance. Alexander Hamilton, during the 1788 ratification debate in New York, admitted:

> The first thing objected to is that clause which allows a representation
> for three-fifths of the negroes. Much has been said of the impropriety of
> representing men who have no will of their own.

An "accommodation," continued Hamilton, was necessary because
"without this indulgence no union could possibly have been formed."[40]
Hamilton and others could have accepted the accommodation since the
prevailing and seemingly sincere belief was that slavery would sooner
or later wither and die, presumably in a short time. But the impossibility
of a solution was never so clear as when the simple task of writing a
law to end the slave trade on January 1, 1808, mushroomed into a year-
long debate during 1806 and 1807.[41] One Congressman commented:

> I can scarcely recollect an instance in which the members seem so
> generally to agree in the principles of a bill, and yet differ so widely as
> to its details. There seems to be great unanimity respecting the atrocity
> of the crime, but a wide difference of opinion as to the measures neces-
> sary to prevent it.[42]

Another Congressman spoke out in despair, "You have got, gentlemen,
into a great difficulty. You are completely hobbled."[43] The conflict over
a proslavery Constitution had already begun.

A statute prohibiting the importation of slaves was implemented in
time to meet the 1808 date. During the same time, however, one could
survey the recently formed states south of the Northwest Territory
where full constitutional rights were being exercised to expand the system of slavery into their territory. David Rice, a leading antislavery
Presbyterian preacher in Kentucky during that territory's constitutional
convention debates of 1792, had fought hard to defeat the entrance of
slavery, but to no avail.[44] The U.S. Constitution had been drafted to
provide full decision-making privileges to all prospective states, a boon
to those championing the liberty of individual states, but a disaster for
those who, recalling the British antislave trade slogan of "humanity,
justice and policy," were equally concerned over the problem of human
enslavement in the country.[45] Each state was sovereign, revealing the

profound limits of national government under the prevailing interpretation of the Constitution. The prescribed restriction upon federal power to intrude into state affairs became a two-edged sword for much of the political and social reform activity for the next seventy years. The federal government could not rescue a nation from its moral insolvency. Only the energies and strategies of the people of God could recover the rectitude, and for some the perfectibility, among America's citizenry.[46]

The Christian community's response was to set in motion a program, indeed an awakening of several varieties (revivalist, educational, missionary, reformist), that could make up the deficiency due to the "natural limit" of constitutional government. The Constitution, according to Channing, provided the "letter" of the law but it did not by "some magic power" provide for success. Such a view would mean "an idolatrous trust in our free institutions."[47] Consequently, this emphasis moved the churches into a remarkable program of reform, outreach, and educational endeavors. Christians did not see this activity as a movement from the sacred into the secular activities of nation-building, but rather as a church movement endowing sanctifying ministry to the many causes of social and political justice.[48] Initially the reform included the acceptance of gradualism in the removal of slavery. The effort was intended to change the heart of the slaveholder who, in turn, would alter the character of his economic and political views, and then claim his constitutional right to outlaw the peculiar institution.[49]

The church also felt the need to seek the conversion of the slave community, along with the Indians and others, and then to provide education for their eventual freedom. Added to this was the call of every successive generation of citizens to reproduce itself as a righteous society. The evangelical vision was more individualistic and labor-intensive, including colleges, seminaries, religious academies, missionary and benevolent societies, publishing agencies, colporteurs, and local church benevolence support.

The Constitution needed immediate support, given the rapid expansion westward. Lyman Beecher urgently called for evangelical action in his *Plea for the West*.

> But if this nation is, in the providence of God, destined to lead the way in the moral and political emancipation of the world, it is time she understood her high calling, and were harnessed for the work. For mighty causes, like floods from distant mountains, are rushing with accumulating power, to their consummation of good or evil, and soon our character and destiny will be stereotyped forever.[50]

The nation's soul was, in a sense, held in the balance, waiting the response of the churches. This alone, thought Beecher, would fulfill the historical destiny of the nation, as constructed under the Constitution.[51]

The method whereby virtue would be sustained or restored to a nation became supremely important. The Constitution limited the affairs of government to narrow areas. Federal or state officials could not force virtue and righteousness upon anyone. The only acceptable and effectual method was persuasion, which came through the pulpit, the lecture hall, or the religious tract. The Constitution mandated that the churches provide the energy to sanctify the citizenry for the task of responsible involvement.

The larger affairs of European political ideas also needed to be interpreted through the focus of the Christian perspective. The "excesses" of the French Revolution could not be allowed to destabilize and topple the fragile equilibrium of America's constitutional republicanism. It was bad enough to receive the opprobrium of many Europeans who accused the American government of having no "conscience" since it contained no established church. The United States was an "infidel" just as France was during the latter's revolution, some Europeans observed. Americans answered that every denomination of the Christian faith was responsible for the spiritual well-being of the people and the nation.[52] Christian efforts had to be poured into humanitarian strategies in order to Christianize and stabilize America. Perhaps this eventually would cleanse the republic, some Americans reasoned, from the embarrassment of the slave problem.[53]

Part of the debate among Federalists and Republicans at the turn of the century focused on who was going to lead this kind of progress toward American ennoblement and righteousness. The Federalist political elites feared that the Jeffersonian Republicans would tilt too much toward the "anarchy" of the French. The New England Congregationalists, also Federalist in many ways, sought to bring order and design to the moral awakening of America. The two elites complemented each other, with a vision of the Constitution that would allow a kind of moral oversight by a virtuous leadership. The Republicans, also driven by a vision of bringing virtue to America, sought to recover that righteousness from the bottom up, by infusing virtue into the common people, by glorifying personal respect for each one's individual liberty, and thus bringing success for the Constitution as surely as by any elitist oversight.[54] Thus, both Federalist and Republican views implied the need for constant vigilance in order to sustain an imperfect Constitution and to prevent the inanition of the new republic.

One must be cautious in seeing too close a linkage between the Constitution and the Benevolent Empire. Although firmly supporting a republican design of government, most churches professed to be non-political in the fifty years following the American revolution. They resisted involvement in the corrupting arena of politics.[55] Nevertheless, the linkage is there, since the benevolent sensibilities of the period were designed in some measure to foster the success of the Constitution. The coupling, then, may be particularly beneficial in addressing a continuing theme among historians regarding the origins of the humanitarian phenomena.

Ever since Eric Williams expressed his views in *Capitalism and Slavery* (1944), a debate over the origins of humanitarian reform has persisted. Williams argued for an economic interpretation. More recently some historians such as Roger Anstey have argued for a more religious or altruistic view. Both interpretations have merit. The religious interpretation directs attention toward significant leadership of individual clergymen, writers, and thinkers, as well as the influence of churches and denominations. The economic interpretation tends to place the reformist sensibilities of church and individual within a broader context of the industrial revolution, the growth of technology, and the age of capitalism and its emphasis on political economy.

Thomas Haskell has extended the debate in his recent article, "Capitalism and the Origins of the Humanitarian Sensibility."[56] Haskell's principal thesis, drawing clearly from Marxist postulates, is that capitalism precipitated the origins of early nineteenth-century humanitarianism "through changes the market wrought in perception or cognitive style," that is, through "the expansion of the market, the intensification of market discipline."[57] Thus, he joins the economic substructure with the humanitarian activity of the superstructure by "the emergence of a market-oriented form of life."[58] In doing this he rejects the "social control" thesis of David Brion Davis and others as the dominant linkage since this tended to narrow the purpose of the many humanitarian activities to a "class interest" of the ascending entrepreneurial sector of American society.[59]

Although Haskell wishes to pursue a different line of argument than the one I wish to follow, he does present several significant points that seem helpful and that advance the connection between the Constitution and the Benevolent Empire. He skillfully revises the argument

of Davis and others that the antislavery reformers were "generally unaware of the interested character of their ideology."[60] Instead of "self-
deception," Haskell argues that the reformers were consciously "selec-
tive" of the kinds of reform that were possible in their era. Following
this logic, we can give the reformers substantial credit for their actions
and their doctrinaire rhetoric, particularly acknowledging their abilities
to search out the more arcane and tendentious reasons for their actions
from their own hearts and minds. The reformers were intentionally
mindful of their motives and especially how they might implement their
reforms within a republic framed with a written Constitution. Their design for reform matched the civic freedom allowed citizens within a republic.

Central to the explication of his thesis is Haskell's parable of the
"case of the starving stranger." He submits the query: Why do not we
(affluent, humanitarian Westerners) "buy an airline ticket, fly to Bom-
bay or wherever, seek out at least one of these starving strangers, and
save his life, or at the very least extend it"? His answer, that we "always
set limits" to our "moral responsibility," leads Haskell to trace the
"techniques" or "recipes" we use for moral improvement back to the
"market transactions" within the capitalist order.[61]

His reasoning, though labyrinthine at points, contributes particular insight in his use of the "recipe" idea to explain the "rise of humanitarianism." A recipe is a "causal connection" between the "right thing
to do" and the practical implementation needed to accomplish that reform.[62] While acknowledging the incisive disclosures in Haskell's thesis, it seems more straightforward to utilize the same formula of a recipe in a far simpler equation that connects the growth in equalitarian
representation in state and federal government with the rise of humanitarian, reformist activity. The potential success of reordering American
society, given the constitutional mandate for personal and civic liberties of the people, rested on the "recipes" of reforming societies, educational institutions, and missionary agencies. The freedom with which
religious or altruistic persons could organize these societies seems to
correlate, to a measurable degree, with the wave of revivalism and
humanitarianism that washed through the era. Reformism, therefore, is
linked to the newly created recipes engendered by a newly created Constitution.

There is little doubt that the most bitter compromise in the writing
of the Constitution was the impasse over slavery. It was, on one hand,
the symbol of the accommodation that allowed national unity, and, on

the other hand, an early symbol of failure to reach the vision of a political millennium. The humanitarian sensibilities of the Benevolent Empire were responses to these symbols during a period when the shaping of a still inchoate nation seemed promising and creatively malleable. The roots of these sensibilities lay deep in the religious soil of clergy and laity. Some well-known interpretations have been offered to explain the churches' passion for reform in this era. The Benevolent Empire originated, declares one historian, out of the "anxiety" among leaders of New England's Standing Order to retain their leadership.[63] Another historian has suggested that the Benevolent Empire represented the multiple efforts of various religious denominations to "justify their mission" by "legitimating" themselves to the citizenry.[64] Both of these interpretations, however, can be subsumed under a still broader analysis. The new political inauguration of republicanism in 1787 shocked the church leadership into new forms of collaboration with a citizenry who were resolved to reshape a nation. The church and people shared in a search for a new kind of alliance, more informal and voluntaristic than in earlier years. The Constitution had signaled the eventual disestablishment of two major church denominations and consequently had narrowed the definition of church leadership in public life. The Benevolent Empire was the effort to restructure lines of communication and allegiance with a potentially alienated and highly mobile society. Churches needed to consolidate their ministries by recruiting and reclaiming a free people whose constitutional right was to join voluntarily those associations and organizations of their own choosing.[65] The Benevolent Empire was the joint participation in grass-roots efforts of people and church to rebuild their society, in their view, for the better. The Constitution facilitated new categories, and the energies of a people experimenting with these new categories represented a society that recognized the high stakes at risk in their national life. It is to the credit of that remarkably diverse assortment of reforming and religious groups making up the Benevolent Empire that those new categories advanced, in the main, many humanitarian and beneficial contributions to American life. Perhaps the Founding Fathers had some of those humanitarian concerns in mind when they debated the nation's political future during that summer of 1787.

NOTES

1. Forrest McDonald, *Novus Ordo Seclorum: The Intellectual Origins of the Constitution* (Lawrence, Kans.: Univ. Press of Kansas, 1985), 71, 125.

2. The Virginia Declaration of Rights, written by George Mason in 1776, added the phrase, "when they enter into a state of society," to Article I in order to differentiate the African from the "all men" who were "by nature equally free and independent, and have certain inherent rights." William M. Wiecek, *The Sources of Antislavery Constitutionalism in America, 1760–1848* (Ithaca, N.Y.: Cornell Univ. Press, 1977), 51-52.

3. Thomas Clarkson, *An Essay on the Slavery and Commerce of the Human Species, Particularly the African, Translated from a Latin Dissertation, which was honoured with the First Prize in the University of Cambridge, For the Year 1785*, 3d ed. (repr.; Philadelphia: Joseph Crukshank, 1787), ix; Roger Anstey, *The Atlantic Slave Trade and British Abolition, 1760–1810* (London: Macmillan, 1975), 244; Wiecek, *Sources*, 28-29.

4. Wiecek, *Sources*, 38-40; Clarkson, *An Essay*, vi.

5. Wiecek, *Sources*, 45.

6. The occasion was the "Quock Walker" case, which brought a decision related to Article I of the 1780 Massachusetts Declaration of Rights, declaring "All men are born free and equal, and have certain natural, essential and unalienable rights." Wiecek, *Sources*, 43-45.

7. Vermont, however, used a constitutional provision to abolish slavery.

8. Max Farrand, *The Fathers of the Constitution: A Chronicle of the Establishment of the Union* (New Haven, Conn.: Yale Univ. Press, 1921), 121.

9. Ibid., 75-77; Robert Allen Rutland, *The Ordeal of the Antifederalists and the Ratification Struggle of 1787–1788* (Norman, Okla.: Univ. of Oklahoma Press, 1966), 92.

10. Farrand, *Fathers*, 63-70.

11. Howard Temperley, "Anti-Slavery as a Form of Cultural Imperialism," in *Anti-Slavery, Religion, and Reform: Essays in Memory of Roger Anstey*, ed. Christine Bolt and Seymour Drescher (Chatham, Great Britain: Dowson-Archon, 1980), 338; David Brion Davis, *Slavery and Human Progress* (New York: Oxford Univ. Press, 1984), 119, 139, 160.

12. George Bancroft, *History of the Formation of the Constitution of the United States of America*, 2 vols. (New York: D. Appleton & Co., 1885), 2:76-77.

13. Jacques Pierre Brissot de Warville, *A Critical Examination of the Marquis de Chatelleux's Travels in North America, in a Letter addressed to the Marquis Principally intended as a Refutation of his opinions concerning the Quakers, the Negroes, the People, and Mankind* (Philadelphia: Joseph James, 1788), 52.

14. The two periods of debate that focused on the slave problem were 11-13 July and 21-26 Aug. Farrand, *Fathers*, 129-30.

15. The incident regarding Benjamin Franklin's call to prayer on 28 July may be instructive. The suggestion by a not-too-religious man like Franklin to a convention deeply mired in acrimonious stalemate has become a part of America's much-quoted popular history. But far more characteristic among American legislators was the response to Franklin's request. The proposal was not even put to a vote and was set aside as politely as possible given Franklin's patriarchal status. Another illustration may also have some bearing. On 20 Aug. George Mason made a strong plea for the inclusion of sumptuary laws within the new Constitution. According to Madison's account, he was ignored, and the topic was not mentioned again. If we can define "sumptuary law" as broadly as Dwight McDonald suggests to embrace laws involving "police power, such as those regulating, or prohibiting gambling, alcoholic beverages, prostitution, and the like," then again the

framers of the Constitution were sidestepping moral issues that could be understood as items of personal, religious preference or as traditional eighteenth-century religious and social norms. McDonald, *Novus Ordo Seclorum*, 15-16; Jonathan Elliot, ed., *Debates on the Adoption of the Federal Constitution*, 5 vols. (New York: Burt Franklin, 1888), 3:1369.

16. Elliot, *Debates*, 5:457.

17. Farrand, *Fathers*, 130; Jackson Turner Main, *The Antifederalists, Critics of the Constitution, 1781–1788* (Chapel Hill, N.C.: Univ. of North Carolina Press, 1961), 21; Clinton Rossiter, *1787: The Grand Convention* (New York: Macmillan, 1966), 25.

18. James Madison, *The Papers of James Madison*, ed. Henry O. Gilpin, 3 vols. (Washington, D.C.: Langree and O'Sullivan, 1840), 2:1077.

19. Bancroft, *History of the Formation*, 2:221-22.

20. John Adams, *A Defence of the Constitution of the Government of the United States of America* (Philadelphia: Hull and Sellers, Crukshank and Young and McCullock, 1787), iii.

21. See Roger Anstey, "The Pattern of British Abolitionism in the Eighteenth and Nineteenth Centuries," in Bolt and Drescher, eds., *Anti-Slavery, Religion, and Reform*, 20; Davis, *Slavery and Human Progress*, 156.

22. Elliot, *Debates*, 2:41.

23. Ibid., 2:203.

24. Ibid., 2:203-4; Rutland, *The Ordeal of the Antifederalists*, 118.

25. Elliot, *Debates*, 1:373.

26. Ibid., 2:115.

27. Wiecek, *Sources*, 16.

28. Henry D. Thoreau, *Reform Papers*, ed. Wendell Glick (Princeton, N.J.: Princeton Univ. Press, 1973), 103. Neither Jefferson nor Adams were delegates in Philadelphia in the summer of 1787 as Thoreau declares.

29. David Robinson, ed., *William Ellery Channing: Selected Writings* (New York: Paulist Press, 1985), 211.

30. Philadelphia: Temple Univ. Press, 1982, 154.

31. Nathan Hatch in *The Sacred Cause of Liberty: Republican Thought and the Millennium in Revolutionary New England* (New Haven, Conn.: Yale Univ. Press, 1977) has documented some of these sermons and orations in helpful detail.

32. Their constitution was remodeled at the first Triennial Convention of the Protestant Episcopal Church on 28 July 1789, so as to provide for the two houses, one for the bishops, the other for the other clergy and lay representatives. Edward Frank Humphrey, *Nationalism and Religion in America, 1774–1789* (Boston: Chipman Law, 1924), 230; Protestant Episcopal Church in the U.S.A. General Convention, 1799, *Journal of the Proceedings of the Bishops, Clergy, and Laity, on the Protestant Episcopal Church in the United States of America in a Convention held in the City of Philadelphia From Tuesday, June the Eleventh, to Wednesday, June the Nineteenth, 1799* (Philadelphia: John Ormrod, 1799), 5-6.

33. Presbytery of Charleston, *Pastoral Letter of the Presbytery of Charleston, to the Church of the Presbyterian Denomination* (Charleston, S.C.: Benjamin P. Timothy, 1799), 13-14. The four-tiered assembly system of the church included the "Church session" (or "Parochial"), the "Presbyteries," the "Provincial Synods," and finally the "National" or "General Assembly." Humphrey, *Nationalism and Religion in America*, 260-62.

34. William P. Trent, "The Period of Constitution-Making in the American Churches," in *Essays on the Constitutional History in the Formative Period, 1775–1789*, ed. J. Franklin Jameson (Boston: Houghton, Mifflin and Co., 1889), 190.

35. See Numbers 14 and 15 in *The Federalist.*

36. Donald H. Meyer, *The Democratic Enlightenment* (New York: G. P. Putnam's Sons, 1976), 165-67.

37. Ibid., 166.

38. David Sharp, *Obligation of Christians to the Heathen: A Sermon preached before The General Convention of the Baptist Denomination in the United States, in the Baptist Meeting-House in Sansom-St., Philadelphia, April 29, 1829* (Boston: Lincoln and Edmands, n.d.), 8.

39. "Address of the Commissioners for Foreign Missions," *The Panoplist and Missionary Magazine United,* vol. 3, no. 4 (Sept. 1810): 183; Martin E. Marty, *Righteous Empire: The Protestant Experience in America* (New York: Dial Press, 1970), 9, 112.

40. Elliot, *Debates,* 2:205.

41. The House debate centered on such issues as: Should the U.S. government sell confiscated slaves? If the U.S. government freed the slaves, how could southern states protect themselves? How could southern citizens be encouraged to inform on the "crime" of the illegal slave trade when they refused to recognize it as a crime? *Annals of the Congress of the United States,* 9th Cong., 2d sess., 174-264.

42. Ibid., 232.

43. Ibid., 183.

44. Essig, *Bonds of Wickedness,* 86-88; Davis, *Slavery and Human Progress,* 158.

45. Stanley L. Engerman and David Eltis, "Economic Aspects of the Abolition Debate," in Bolt and Drescher, eds., *Anti-Slavery, Religion, and Reform,* 291.

46. Sidney E. Mead, *The Lively Experiment: The Shaping of Christianity in America* (New York: Harper & Row, 1963), 91-92; Henry F. May, *The Enlightenment in America* (New York: Oxford Univ. Press, 1976), 282.

47. Robinson, ed., *William Ellery Channing,* 214-16.

48. David Brion Davis, "An Appreciation of Roger Anstey," in Bolt and Drescher, eds., *Anti-Slavery, Religion, and Reform,* 12.

49. Essig, *Bonds of Wickedness,* 133-34; Davis, *Slavery and Human Progress,* 161.

50. Conrad Cherry, *God's New Israel: Religious Interpretations of American Destiny* (Englewood Cliffs, N.J.: Prentice-Hall, 1971), 120; Constance Rourke, *Trumpets of Jubilee* (New York: Harcourt, Brace and World, 1963), 41.

51. Donald H. Meyer, *The Democratic Enlightenment* (New York: G. P. Putnam's Sons, 1976), 168.

52. Ibid., 180; John Howard Hinton, *The Test of Experience: or The Voluntary Principle in the United States* (London: Albert Cockshaw, 1851), 102; Edward Robert Norman, *The Conscience of the State in North America* (Cambridge: Cambridge Univ. Press, 1968), 75, 80.

53. Essig, *Bonds of Wickedness,* 115.

54. Meyer, *Democratic Enlightenment,* 183.

55. Lois W. Banner, "Religious Benevolence as Social Control: A Critique of an Interpretation," *Journal of American History* 60 (June 1973): 28.

56. *American Historical Review,* Part 1 (April 1985): 339-61; Part 2 (June 1985): 547-66.

57. Ibid., 342.

58. Ibid., 548.

59. Ibid., 341, 343.

60. Ibid., 346.

61. Ibid., 354-57, 555.

62. Haskell's full explanation is far more complex, offering four "preconditions" needed for a successful "recipe."

63. William G. McLoughlin, *Revival, Awakenings, and Reform: An Essay on Religion and Social Change in America, 1607–1977* (Chicago: Univ. of Chicago Press, 1978), 104, 110.

64. Marty, *Righteous Empire,* 90; Banner, "Religious Benevolence," 29.

65. Sidney Earl Mead, *Nathaniel William Taylor, 1786–1858: A Connecticut Liberal* (Archon Books, 1967), 44-45, 50-53.

Anglo-Canadian Perspectives
on the United States Constitution

Paul Marshall

In this chapter I will outline one set of Canadian interpretations of the United States Constitution, that is, "Tory" or "conservative" views, which have been dominant throughout most of Canadian history.[1] There are three reasons why Americans can learn from such views. First, Canada is a country comprised of colonists who abjured the Revolution and, thus, it developed by not being part of the United States. Canadian national self-understanding has been that, while we did not know what we were or wished to be, at least we were *not* Americans, we were *not* republicans, we did *not* rebel, and we did *not* constitute a new polity. Such memorial and political antitheory was the stuff of Toryism, and could shed light on what it means not to be an American, and also on what it means to be an American.

Second, as George Grant, the person to whom I shall devote most attention, constantly reiterates, the United States is the only western society that has no history truly its own from before the age of progress.[2] America has no Toryism, no organic conservatism, no deep respect for hierarchy, order, and tradition. Its "conservatism" is a nineteenth-century liberalism that is not only tinged with but immersed in faith in progress. Hence a neighborly Toryism could provide a perspective not readily found at home.

Third, certain of my comments about Canada have been in the past tense, because Canada's identity as being substantially different from the Great Republic to the south has now been superceded. Its most famous nationalist book was *Lament for a Nation,* published in 1965.[3] This was not a call to defend Canada's identity but was a genuine lament for the loss of Canada, or the loss of anything for which it was worth maintaining an independent state. Canada is being absorbed by

---

AUTHOR'S NOTE: I would like to thank Don Smiley and Janet Ajzenstat for advice on this essay.

the American economy, by American "culture," and by American religion. Its political institutions have, by the 1982 Constitutional Act and "Charter of Rights and Freedoms," been reshaped to an American constitutional image. Because of this development, we can consider the perspective of a country that has often been opposed to the U.S. but has now become like it and has been absorbed by it. It is a view not yet from the belly of the beast, but from the gullet.

Most American references to the Constitution, and especially those at anniversary time, refer to the constitutional documents formulated from 1787–89, and to subsequent amendments to them. It is to some particular written statements, intended as fundamental law, which we refer. However, because of the nature of Toryism, I would like to consider a wider meaning of *constitution*. I will maintain that the constitution of any country properly should be understood as those complexes of attitudes, opinions, theories, and laws that lie at its foundation and that develop, shape, and interact with its fundamental law over time.[4] Hence, in addition to written documents we must, as most legal theorists agree, include the interpretations, glosses, and usages that have been developed over time and are by consent understood to have become part of the Constitution.

In suggesting this I am not defending a particularly activist court or condemning a strict constructivism; I am pointing out an empirical fact about the American and other constitutions. As John Adams maintained, "A constitution is a standard, a pillar, and a bond when it is understood, approved and beloved. But without this intelligence and attachment, it might as well be a kite or a balloon, flying in the air."[5] To which we might add that, if it is a kite, then it is not properly a constitution. Such kites include, for example, the many "constitutions" developed and promulgated in Europe after the First World War. Many of these were modeled on the U.S. Constitution but, despite this happy precedent, most did not survive, and some produced bloody ends. In anything other than the most formal way they were never the foundations of countries.

It is also true that any cogent interpretation of the Constitution becomes, to a large degree, part of the Constitution itself. Let me reemphasize that I am not seeking to laud the modern pastime of finding emanations of halos in the Constitution. For example, in *The American Commonwealth*[6] James Bryce described "some of those features of American government to which its character is chiefly due" that "rest neither upon the Constitution nor upon any statute, but upon usage alone." As instances he gives: "The presidential electors have by usage and by usage only lost the right the Constitution gave them of exercising their discretion in the choice of a chief magistrate. The President is not elected to more than two continuous terms, though the Constitution in no way restricts re-eligibility. The President uses his veto more freely than he did at first, and for a wider range of purposes."[7] Bryce noted that in the United Kingdom such items would be regarded as part of the Constitution; he discusses them in chapter 34, "Development of the Constitution."

Of course some items—for example, Hugo Black's attempt to incorporate Jefferson's correspondence on church and state into the Constitution—are controversial. To the degree that they remain controversial, they are not part of the Constitution. But to the degree that they *are* accepted, they become part of it. Any constitution is rooted in the hearts, minds, and opinions of the people.

Perhaps this stretching of the meaning of *constitution* may seem too vague or not suitable for a bicentenary. However, apart from the arguments suggested above, there is another factor that we should consider. For, whatever its other merits or defects, the notion of constitution just described has at least the merit that it is a *Tory* view. It is how Tories have perceived and judged the United States Constitution, it is what they understood to be the substance of the American polity. They would regard a desire to focus merely on written and formal rules and procedures as itself part of the vice of American liberalism, which attempts to hide its essential nature. Canadian Tory views of the United States often do not trouble much to distinguish these different elements and any insistence on such a distinction would entail a refusal to hear and heed such Toryism.

Bryce opened his study of the United States by remarking on the American predilection for asking surprised European travelers "What do you think of our institutions?"[8] He noted that the habit was not shared by the English, the French, the Germans, or the Italians, and he felt that "the institutions of the United States are deemed by inhabitants . . . to be a matter of . . . general interest." Unfortunately much of the world has not reciprocated this admiration and interest. Certainly Canada has not. Hence, any survey of Canadian views of the U.S. Constitution must first note that there is not too much to survey. Second, we should also note that those views, such as they are, are often distinguished solely by their ignorance. One surveyor of Canadian views in the period leading up to Canadian confederation in 1867 was moved to

remark: "One of the major problems confronting the historian of
Canadian ideas about the American political system is the intellectual
shoddiness of those ideas . . . even Canadians who were sympatheti-
cally inclined toward the United States were unable to reason effectively about American politics beyond a certain point."[9]

Because of, or perhaps in spite of, this general lack of thought and
knowledge, the third general characteristic of Canadian views of the
U.S. Constitution is their overwhelmingly negative assessment, reflecting the fact that Canada was formed as an alternative to the United
States and even, in the words of R. MacGregor Dawson, as a "counter-
America." In general the U.S. was regarded as "too big, too unmanage-
able and too violent."[10] Even in the twentieth century Canada's newspapers "used phases of social and political life in the United States
either as horrible examples to be avoided or as useful patterns to be followed . . . the horrible examples appeared to Canadian editors to pre-
dominate. Notable, also, was the fairly general assumption that
Canadian political institutions are distinct from and much superior to,
those of Canada's neighbor."[11]

The range of criticism included both laws and institutions, and also
the political culture that sustained and was sustained by them. The criticisms of institutions were various and often contradictory, particularly
in assessments of the office of the presidency. As S. F. Wise puts it, "In
the 1850's, it is not unusual to find the same source accusing the President of abusing his vast powers in one context, and in the next breath
deploring the feebleness of the executive in another context."[12]
However, one consistent theme, embracing the presidency but not
limited to it, was the basic criticism that U.S. institutions did not provide for responsible nonpartisan leadership. In 1850 George Brown
wrote that, because of his control over patronage, "the President of the
United States is a despot during his official term, in comparison with
the Queen of England—his power is enormous, and as a political partisan he uses it unblushingly for party purposes."[13]

For Canadians the advantage of monarchs or governors was that
they were above party, could rule for all, and could be a moral force un-
tainted by partisan interest. But in a republic all political offices and
policies were tied to party. One negative result was a politicized civil
service in which the senior staff had to change with each change of
government. This politicization was in turn held to be a result of the
American infatuation with democracy, and a concomitant lack of

authority. Four years before Canadian confederation D'Arcy McGee summed up this theme:

> Where the fault lies *ab origine* in the American constitutions, . . . it is not hard to say. Their authors . . . were so busy looking after their new found liberty that they forgot that they too, could not long govern without authority. Recussants [*sic*] against authority they found it impossible to claim a due portion in the new constitutions for authority. They could not assert the divine origin of government, the natural right of man to be governed, the virtue of civil obedience, and all the other ethical truths, which must every one of them, enter into any human system that ever expects to merit the blessings of Divine Providence.[14]

This infatuation with democracy and self-assertion was in turn thought to lead to impiety. In 1905 Sir Wilfrid Laurier, Canadian Prime Minister and Liberal, during debates in the House of Commons on Canadian schools, said,

> We live by the side of a nation . . . in whose schools for fear that Christian dogmas in which all do not believe might be taught, Christian morals are not taught . . . when I observe in this country of ours, a total absence of lynchings and an almost total absence of divorces and murders, I thank heaven that we are living in a country where the young children of the land are taught Christian morals and Christian dogmas.[15]

In order to trace these general themes a little more closely it is necessary to give a brief historical sketch of some of these Canadian attitudes. At the time of the Revolution, Canada was the recipient of immigrant loyalists. The immigrants were not clear about what they rejected or what they desired. As George Grant states,

> It was an inchoate desire to build, in these cold and forbidding regions, a society with a greater sense of order and restraint than freedom-loving republicans would allow. It was no better defined than a kind of suspicion that we in Canada could be less lawless and have a greater sense of propriety than the United States.[16]

Such people believed that colonies founded on the British constitution had nothing to learn from the upstart Yankees. American independence was thought to show defects in the old colonial American institutions—in particular a weakness of the executive and, more precisely, the weakness of an excess of democracy. The inhabitants took pains to adjust the institutions of British North America to ensure that such faults were not repeated. The Constitutional Act of 1791 was one result. To people such as William Smith, former New Yorker and now

Chief Justice of Lower Canada, this full grant of British institutions had another hope attached to it, specifically that they might yet win back many Americans to the Empire: "As the attempt to govern a continental area under republican forms floundered, and all experienced men knew it must, . . . fragments and the whole of the lost colonies might gravitate back to the standard of ordered liberty and united empire yet flying in the north."[17]

The passage of the U.S. Constitution did not check these imperial hopes. John Graves Simcoe, the Lieutenant Governor of Upper Canada, "advertised like any land agent through the northern states for American settlers. If they would come to clear the lands of Upper Canada, Simcoe was certain British institutions would make them British, as indeed they did."[18] Attitudes such as these certainly do not show much awareness or analysis of American constitutional developments. But they do illustrate a widespread ethos: that American developments were neither very good nor very important.

The attitudes formed during the period of the American founding solidified in the early decades of the nineteenth century. This is perhaps most starkly exemplified in the example of John Strachan, a clergyman who was "teacher, mentor and minister to a whole generation of Tory politicians in Upper Canada" in the earlier decades of the nineteenth century. Strachan's mind has been compared to a megalithic monument: "strong, crude and simple."[19] For Strachan "the two great experiments in America and France to constitute governments productive of virtues and happiness only . . . have completely failed . . . that foolish perfectability with which they had been deluded can never be realized."[20] Or, as a fellow clergyman put it, "Fear thou the Lord and King; and meddle not with them that are given to change."[21]

These statements may be a little extreme but, as the chief commentator on Canadian views of the U.S. in this period writes, "ideological hostility to the United States was already a pervasive part of the cultural *ambiance* of Upper Canada."[22]

The *Kingston Gazette* of 1811 put it this way:

> The characteristic evil of their democratic system is its tendency to foster an uncontrollable spirit of party. Their frequent popular elections of all branches of their government furnish fuel and fan the flame. The rage of their parties has become intolerable. . . . This fervor of party zeal must disturb the harmony and intercourse of social life, and pollute the streams of justice. It must render their tribunals, and especially the popular branch of them, their juries, prejudiced, partial and prone to

favor their co-partizans and condemn those of the opposite party. . . .
These are the practical and perhaps inevitable results of the principle of
democracy, operating upon the passions of human nature.[23]

A more moderate view was expressed by William Warren Baldwin
on the hustings.

In the United States, the want of an hereditary sovereign . . . awoke in
the breast of the American citizen a spirit of personal ambition . . .
[which] will one day or other open the door to a terrific anarchy amongst
that people—even now the spirit of party is so virulent among them.[24]

After the wars this marked antipathy slowly subsided, but it was
renewed with vigor on the occasion of rebellions in Canada in 1837,
which looked partly to the U.S. for inspiration. Despite the near hys-
teria of some of these reactions, there was even, on occasion, a mild
touch of analysis, perhaps influenced by Tocqueville. In 1838, R. B.
Sullivan, in a report on the rebels prepared for the new lieutenant governor, noted the working of the American Constitution.

In the anxiety of the people to leave no power to do evil in the hands of
Government, almost all power has been denied to it. It is true that no individual can be a tyrant, but the tyranny of a majority is less responsible,
and more unrelenting and universal in its application: everything is referred to party, and from the highest to the lowest every functionary of
the Government is dependent upon the will of the majority for his con-
tinuance in office.[25]

Then, as Sullivan's commentator notes, there follows a castigation
of American political anarchy, executive weakness, judicial corruption,
mob law, and "the agitation of a continual election" that does not differ
significantly from those made thirty years before.

The annexation movement of the mid-century brought a further
outpouring of criticism. Particularly vexatious was the view that the
United States was based upon "the blasphemous Whig assumption, that
the people are the source of political power."[26] Indeed, "for the Church
of England, the United States remained what it had always been, a godless republic that had willfully denied the divine origins of government."[27] Even for those rare few who might have found something to
admire in the U.S., there still remained the overwhelming fact of
slavery. As Bishop Mountain stated, slavery was a "monstrous anomaly
. . . the political contradiction unsurpassed, rather unequalled, in the
world." The United States "vaunts itself aloud to the world, as the only

really free country on earth [but has] practically disallowed the consan-
guinity of the family of man."[28]

The first period of extended Canadian study of the U.S. Constitution came when British North America was being formed into one
country, necessitating an overhaul of its own constitution. The example
of the U.S. became the subject of widespread, and occasionally informed, discussion. But even if outright hostility had abated, deep suspicion still remained. George Grant notes the "continual suspicion of
the foundations of the American republic, and their desire to build a
political society with a clearer and firmer doctrine of the comon good
than that at the heart of the liberal democracy to the south."[29] The *Mon-
treal Herald,* a Liberal newspaper, thought it had "stood almost alone
among our contemporaries in having even a decent word to say of
American institutions or American statemen."[30]

As Peter Waite notes, there were basically three prejudices against
the United States. First, "a deep distrust of the North with its continental ambitions and its formidable army." Second, "a strong suspicion that
federation was the cause of the Civil War." Third, "a nearly universal
dislike of American political practice"; "they believed that American
practice had produced . . . the chronic subservience of American politicians to a corrupt and depraved electorate."[31]

The American practice of electing judges was the major example
of partisanship and democracy run wild. The *Globe* (May 19, 1865) ful-
minated fastidiously:

> That the dignified and learned wearer of the ermine, whose proudest dis-
> tinction is his independence from popular clamor and prejudice . . .
> should become a roaring political partisan, and secure or maintain his
> position by force of the unwashed multitudes who boast of universal
> suffrage, is something so abhorent to our traditions and convictions . . .
> that we cannot for a moment think of it.[32]

Themes similar to these, though more diplomatically stated, were
expressed by government figures themselves, so Lord Elgin to Earl
Grey:

> The fact is, that the American system is our old Colonial system with, in
> certain cases, the principle of popular election substituted for that of
> nomination by the Crown. Mr. Filmore stands to his Congress very
> much in the same relation in which I stood to my Assembly in Jamaica.
> There is the same absence of effective responsibility in the conduct of
> legislation, the same want of concurrent action between the parts of the

political machine. . . . For instance, our Reciprocity measure was pressed by us at Washington last session. . . . There was no Government to deal with. The interests of the Union, as a whole and distinct from local and sectional interests, had no organ in the representative bodies.[33]

Some even found much to praise, as Elgin stated: "It is the fashion now to enlarge on the defects of the Constitution of the United States, but I am not one of those who look upon it as a failure. I think and believe that it is one of the most skillful works which human intelligence ever created."[34]

The defects of the presidency were a theme of the future first prime minister of Canada, John A. MacDonald. In 1865 he maintained: "By the election of the President by a majority and for a short period, he is never the sovereign and chief of the nation. He is never looked up to by the whole people as the head and front of the nation. He is at best but the successful leader of a party." He also argued that the president was

in a great measure a despot, a one-man power, with the command of the naval and military forces—with an immense amount of patronage as head of the Executive, and with the veto power as a branch of the legislature, perfectly uncontrolled by responsible advisers, his cabinet being departmental officers merely, whom he is not obliged by the Constitution to consult with, unless he chooses to do so.[35]

Cartier's views were similar, though a little more jaundiced: "In our Federation the monarchical principle would form the leading feature, while on the other side of the lines, judging by the past history and present condition of the country, the ruling power was the will of the mob, the rule of the populace."[36]

In addition to criticism of the role of the president there was also concern about relations between the president and Congress, and between the houses of Congress. As two Toronto newspapers put it, for the president

there were no parliamentary majorities to soothe, no pertinacious reformer to propose awkward questions, no constant reader of blue books to expose inconsistencies. Accordingly questions as such have seldom been debated in the American Senate. On the contrary, there has been much declamation, personal tournaments of power, finished orations, and undoubtedly the exhibition of much mental vigor; but although the party opposed to the President were fully represented, there was no Parliamentary warfare, for nothing was to be gained by it.[37]

The two houses of the American legislatures often come to a dead-lock—one chamber vetoing what the other passes; but then, the division of opinion does not affect the executive . . . [but] unless some one has a direct interest in opposing, almost any measure may be passed. . . . Bills are killed in the senate every year by the score which have been log-rolled through the lower house.[38]

The theme of the lack of genuine national authority in America also reappears, particularly with reference to the Civil War. In general, Canadian politicians thought the war was due to "excessively large state power and insufficient authority in the American national government" and so they called for a stronger central authority in government back home.[39]

The period since Confederation has produced more rounds of the same criticisms, such as the *Globe*'s 1924 jingoism: "The contrast be-tween the two systems" (of the United States and Canada) "is a theme for every student in politics. Is there any doubt as to which is the more modern, more democratic, more rational? Constitutionally the United States is still in the Stone Age."[40] In 1921 *Saturday Night* also recap-tured the ancient hysterical tone quite nicely:

Democracy, as expressed in the American nation, has reached a point where its people are living under laws more oppressive than can be found in any other country on the face of the earth save Russia . . . and what has been the consequence? A wild reaction of extravagance, law-lessness and discontent. To balance these evils we have the still more deplorable spectacle of legal oppression which extends into every home, nay, into every cupboard of the United States. . . . In sheer desire to pre-serve good feeling in this weary world, let us cease to gaze on the foun-tain of so many infectious ills. (May 7, 1921)

Comment was made that the "evils of a system which requires the great majority of public servants to retire with a change of party, can be seen throughout the political history of the United States."[41] But the most general criticism was still of the presidency and of the lack of con-nection between the executive and the legislature. In 1909, Prime Min-ister Sir Wilfrid Laurier maintained that the president "is absolutely su-preme, and if he does anything wrong in the eyes of the nation, there is no force whereby he can be set right." He acknowledged that the Amer-ican system of checks and balance was meant to secure this end but, while he described it as a "bold and noble conception," he still thought it "not as practicable as our own. . . . Ministerial responsibility is far more effective, more prompt, and far less liable to friction than . . . [is]

the American system." As Wise notes, it was "especially easy for Canadians to criticize this particular aspect of the American political system; nothing seemed more unnatural to them than the severance of executive from legislative power. For one thing, it appeared to them to absolve the executive officers from any responsibility to the people, despite the popular election of the President." Sir Hector Langevin observed: "The Ministers there are not responsible to the people. They are responsible to the President of the United States . . . as long as that President holds office and does not violate the constitution of the country."[42] Laurier summed up these views in finding the Canadian and British constitutions "more elastic, more practicable, more amenable to the public weal, and therefore more democratic than the Constitution of the American Republic."[43]

The principal themes of Tory criticism of the U.S. Constitution can be summarized as follows: the weakness of the American presidency due to its elected and nonmonarchical nature; the excessive strength of the presidency due to the lack of responsibility to the legislature; the lack of strong central authority; the lack of coordination of the branches of government; the overwhelming partisanship and general buffoonery that suffused the system due to the wild excesses of democracy and individualism; and the elective nature of virtually all political offices. Beyond these criticisms was a general fear of the American ethos. As a summary of this latter, I can do no better than borrow the words of David Putter's conclusion of a book-length survey of Canadian views of the U.S.:

> Perhaps, fundamentally, what Canadians sensed was that their culture and their system still largely accepted the principle of authority, while American society and the American system did not accept this principle in any comparable degree. . . . Canadians believed that the state, through some authority, should provide moral direction for the society it governed. Moral direction meant discipline, order, responsibility, obedience, even inhibition. America, too, has believed in discipline, order, responsibility, and the rest, but it has believed in them as self-imposed, through the acceptance of a Protestant ethic, not imposed by public authority.[44]

The previous sketch has focused on the views of political leaders and on popular opinion. There were few systematically *argued* Tory appraisals of the U.S. Constitution. An exception to this trend is a very recent one, the work of George Parkin Grant.

Grant came to prominence in Canada when his fourth book, *La-*

ment for a Nation, was published in 1965.[45] Sometimes this book has been portrayed as a defense of Canadian nationalism but it is more strictly a lament for what its subtitle proclaims, *The Defeat of Canadian Nationalism.* Grant lamented that Canada, as something importantly different from the United States, had ended. His lament has been variously described as an innate pessimism or as nostalgia for his vanished age and privilege. He concedes to the latter charge while pointing out that this says nothing of whether or not that vanishing is good. His early political views were liberal, while his first book, *Philosophy in the Mass Age* shows the influence of Hegel.[46] More recent modern influences have been Charles Cochrane, Jacques Ellul, Leo Strauss, Friedrich Nietzsche, and Simone Weil. In the words of Abraham Rotstein, a relatively secular, Jewish economist, "Grant's is a moving plea, evocative, passionate and deeply human. It sounds those hidden chords in all of us that could turn atheists religious and socialists conservative, and have them discover that against the common condition, their own divisions are insignificant."[47] Any short summary of Grant's commentary on the United States will do it and him an injustice, and any expression of his ideas in words other than his will lose much of their power. Nevertheless, I will attempt a summary, using mainly his words.

Grant emphasizes the spiritual uprootedness of the United States:

> The platitude cannot be too often stated that the U.S. is the only society which has no history (truly its own) from before the age of progress. All of us who came made some break in that coming . . . the majestic continent . . . could not be ours in the old way because the making of it ours did not go back before the beginning of conscious memory.

That conquering relation to place has left its mark within us. When we go into the Rockies we may have the sense that gods are there. But if so, they cannot manifest themselves to us as ours. They are the gods of another race, and we cannot know them because of what we are, and what we did. There can be nothing immemorial for us except the environment as object. Even our cities have been encampments on the road to economic mastery.[48]

Because of this uprootedness and commitment to mastery, the

> dominance of the United States is identified with the unequivocal victory of the progressive spirit in the West. The older empires had some residual traditions from before the age of progress. The United States is the only society that has none. The American supremacy is

identified with the belief that questions of human good are to be solved by technology.[49]

Because the overriding public goal is economic mastery, any real diversity is driven to the interstices of life.

As for pluralism, differences in the technological state are able to exist only in private activities: how we eat; how we mate; how we practice ceremonies. Some like pizza, some like steaks; some like girls, some like boys; some like synagogue, some like mass. But we all do it in churches, motels, restaurants indistinguishable from the Atlantic to the Pacific.[50]

American religion has reinforced these trends. At its core is the loneliness of Protestantism, particularly Puritan Calvinism. "The fearful solitariness in the Calvinists' account of the meeting between God and his creatures encouraged that individualism which was at home with a politics essentially defined in terms of individual right. Indeed one can say that the extraordinary compact between God and man in Calvinism strangely prepares people for contractual human relations."[51]

Grant relates the above to American institutions and institutionalized belief. He is particularly disturbed by the "separation" from history and the centrality of freedom that produce the *hubris* that "we" can "ordain and establish" a political order. The root of this political order, according to Grant, lies in the wills of those who found and those who consent.

The social contract represents the consent necessary in any regime proper to human beings whose essence is their autonomous freedom. Because the highest purpose of human life is to will autonomously, the best political regime must be such as could be willed rationally by all its members. In this sense, consent becomes the very substance of the best regimes.[52]

The leading makers of the American Constitution conceived themselves as influenced by political philosophy, which they took in its modern form. . . . The legal and political forms of the U.S. are more purely founded on constitutional contractualism than those of the country where that modernism was first thought comprehensively.[53] This contractualism issues in liberalism—not in the American sense of "progressivism" but as "a set of beliefs which proceed from the central assumption that man's essence is his freedom and therefore that what chiefly concerns man in this life is to shape the world as we want it."[54]

Grant tries to illustrate the nature and consequences of this liberalism particularly by reference to two recent U.S. writings—John Rawls's *A Theory of Justice,* and Justice Blackmun's decision in *Roe vs. Wade.* What Grant notes particularly about Rawls is that he affirms that we can truly understand justice only when it is known as rooted in contract.[55] Rawls understands his own task as one of expressing the truths of contractarianism in forms that pass the strictures of analytic philosophy. "Rawls is in the central tradition of modern liberalism in that his ideal political beings are adult calculators, who freely decide that social cooperation is worthwhile because it is to their individual advantage. The good society is composed of free individuals who agree to live together only on the condition that the rules of cooperation, necessary to that living together, serve the overall purposes of each member of that society."

> That agreement or contract, and the calculating implicit in it, is the only model of political relations adequate to autonomous adults. In the social contract, we agree to government and its limitations upon us because it is to our advantage, in the sense that it protects us from the greatest evil. That contract is the source of our rights because we have consented to be social only upon certain conditions, and our rights are the expressions of those limiting conditions.

"Justice is those convenient arrangements agreed to by sensible men who recognize the state of nature."[56]

The sharp end of such a liberal position is shown in the arguments of *Roe vs. Wade.* Grant does not concern himself directly with the question of abortion but with the mode of argument of the majority decision. Here he sees the essence of contractarianism and the eradication of any notion of justice that could challenge a "right."

> Mr. Justice Blackmun begins his majority decision from the principle that the allocation of rights from within the constitution cannot be decided in terms of any knowledge of what is good. Under the constitution rights are prior to any account of good . . . we must be properly agnostic about any claim to knowledge of moral good. . . . The members of the legislature may have been persuaded by conceptions of goodness in passing the law in question. However, this is not germane to a judge's responsibility, which is to adjudicate between the rights of the mother and those of the legislature. He adjudicates that the particular law infringes the prior right of the other to control her own body in the first six months of pregnancy. He states that fetuses up to six months are not persons, and as non-persons can have no status in the litigation.

The decision then speaks modern liberalism in its pure contractual form: right prior to good; a foundational contract protecting individual rights; the neutrality of the state concerning moral "values"; social pluralism supported by and supporting this neutrality.[57]

But Blackmun cannot wring all of this out of the Constitution, no matter how liberally interpreted, for the Constitution gives no strict guidance as to what constitutes a rights-bearing human being. "Because a distinction between members of the same species has been made, the decision unavoidably opens up the whole question of what our species is. . . . What is it, if anything, about human beings that makes the rights of equal justice their due?"[58] The only feasible answer, given the structure of the argument, seems to be that a rights-bearer is one who can make and enforce a contract. Hence, the end product is a liberal justice that "will exclude . . . those who are too weak to enforce contracts . . . the imprisoned, the mentally unstable, the unborn, the aged, the defeated and sometimes even the morally unconforming."[59]

If what Grant says is true, then why has the United States apparently been so unmodern for many years? One reason is the homogeneity of its political beliefs. As there have been no major theoretical political disagreements in the U.S., then theory could be ignored and practical questions could dominate.

> The principles of our political and legal institutions did not need to be justified in thought, because they were justified in life. They were lived out by practical people for whom they provided the obvious parameters of any decent society.[60]

During the excitement over Sputnik, it was suggested that the Americans were deeply depressed by the Russian success. I thought this was a wrong interpretation. Rather there was a great sigh of relief from the American elites, for now there was an immediate practical objective of competition to be achieved, a new frontier to be conquered—outer space. It provided further excuse not to think about what will make life meaningful when the practical problems are settled.[61]

One beneficial effect of this practicality was the insulation of American life from the "full weight of that public nihilism which in Europe flowered with industrial society."[62] The influence of European philosophy was confined to "intellectuals" outside of the mainstream. The actual content of justice was derived through "common sense" from the tenets of the common religions. But now, with the decline of the strength of these religious traditions, the full implications of justice as contract will be revealed. To American conservatives who deny his charges, Grant says this:

> There is some truth in the claim of American conservatives. Their society does preserve constitutional government and respect for the legal rights of individuals in a way that the eastern tyrannies do not. The perpetuation of these depends on the continuing tradition of Lockian liberalism among influential classes. Bourgeois Protestantism, with its Catholic and Jewish imitations, has survived in the United States and given some sense of the eternal to many people. Nevertheless, these traditions—no longer the heart of American civilization—become more residual every year. Sceptical liberalism becomes increasingly the dominant ideology of those who shape society; and this ideology is the extreme form of progressive modernity.[63]

Hence the U.S. has become "the heart of modernity . . . the spearhead of progress."[64] There are still "old and settled legal institutions which bring forth loyalty from many of the best practical people" but, to quote Richard Neuhaus's summary, "we do not have . . . the tradition of thought which can revitalize for our time the truths from which those institutions emerged."[65]

The sharpness of Grant's criticism of the United States would be even more apparent if we were to consider his contention that "the chief political animation of the United States is that it is an empire."[66] Nevertheless, Grant is no simple anti-American. He is opposed to snobbery:

> To the Europeans we appear as spawned by themselves: the children of some low class servants who once dared to leave the household and who now surprisingly appear as powerful and dominating neighbours masquerading as gentry, whose threat can only be minimised by teaching them a little culture. They express contempt of us as a society barren of anything but the drive to technology; yet their contempt is too obviously permeated with envy to be taken as pure.[67]

He praises modern practicality, which is the American genius and which frequently has the goal and consequence of alleviating human suffering. He is aware that to the poor and starving, "progress" can appear much more of a blessing than it does to many in the West. He is also full of admiration for many American institutions.

> Any sane individual must be glad that we face the unique event of technology within a long legal and political tradition founded on the concep-

tion of justice as requiring liberty and equality. When we compare what is happening to multitudes in Asia . . .[68]

I must also stress Grant's love of liberty. "Liberalism in its generic form is surely something that all decent men accept as good—conservatives included. Insofar as the word 'liberalism' is used to describe the belief that political liberty is a central human good, it is difficult for me to consider as sane those who would deny that they are liberals."[69] I hope that these caveats will help enable an American audience to hear what Grant and, with him, though in a less articulate way, the Canadian Tory tradition has to say about the way the American polity is constituted.

An important aspect of this criticism is that it cannot in any systematic way be assimilated to the American polarities of liberal and conservative.

> The Americans who call themselves "Conservatives" have the right to the title only in a particular sense. In fact, they are old-fashioned liberals. . . . They stand for the freedom of the individual to use his property as he wishes, and for a limited government which must keep out of the market-place. Their concentration on freedom from governmental interference has more to do with nineteenth-century liberalism than with traditional conservatism, which asserts the right of the community to restrain freedom in the name of the common good.[70]

This is true not only for the left/right schema but also for the usual American categories of modes of judicial interpretation. Grant's extended footnote on this matter is worth reproducing in almost its entirety.

> Blackmun's appeal to Holmes illustrates the uncertainties in current American usage of the words "liberal" and "conservative." His decision about abortion has been put in the "liberal" column, when it is in fact based on a strict construction of contractualism which is generally put in the "conservative" column. It is well to remember that Blackmun is a Nixon appointee, and tends in his interpretation of the constitution towards "strict constructionism," and away from that interpretation according to the changing consensus of a progressing people, which characterised the Warren Court. . . . This involved that the constitution be conceived as a foundational contract which established certain rights unaffected by the passage of time. [The] difference concerning judicial interpretation does not alter the fact that both sides to it appeal to a contractual view of the state, related to the acceptance of the consequences of moral pluralism in society. A foundational contract which is viewed

as timeless may seem less oblivious of eternity than an historically
developing contract; but in both views justice is considered contractual.[71]

Such a relativization of categories could, I hope, move Americans
to widen their vocabulary and expand their conceptual structure in
thinking about politics, emphasizing thought outside of the Constitution itself. To an outsider it is remarkable how much American discussion takes place only within the parameters of presumed constitutional
principles. This is true not just in the understandable tendency of legal
figures to argue over what constitutional levers may be available, but
also in more general questions of political theory, especially the nature,
purpose, and limits of the state. Even for those who believe that the U.S.
Constitution is a marvelous and laudable thing it is amazing to encounter the virtual consensus in America that something unconstitutional is wrong. It is almost impossible to find the view that "yes, the
Constitution does say that, but so much the worse for the Constitution."
The fervent arguments about constitutionality draw much of their
strength from the fact that one cannot suggest anything unconstitutional
and hope to have not only any legal but also any moral or political leg
to stand on. This also seems to be one reason for the far-fetched interpretations and pseudoprecedent found in American constitutional law:
if you want to propose something, you have to find it in the Constitution.

In Christian circles the problem is sometimes even worse. Left and
right vie over who holds the true Constitution, as though this were the
same as the question of who holds the truth. The "conservative" stress
on nineteenth-century liberalism as the constitutional and Christian
way seems almost to divinize the document.[72] The religious right
stresses some conservative elements, especially the emphasis on moral
concensus, but even it is associated with a notion of individualism and
rights.

Ironically, as far as Canadian Christians are concerned, we see not
only the new secular liberalism but also the older Christian individualism as evidences of a corruption and betrayal of the faith. In the face of
an assertion of Christian America, present or past, Canadians have
pointed to the U.S. as the lamentable example of what happens to countries that forsake their Christian heritage, as did the U.S. in its founding. Precisely those points that many Americans regard as the marks of

its Christianly formed character are those points that Canadians have regarded as manifestations of a fundamental paganism.

Other possible implications aside, I will draw one main conclusion. The U.S. Constitution, especially in its founding, is a remarkable achievement. Precisely because of that we must avoid being mesmerized by it and we must resist having our thoughts confined within its bounds, or within the bounds of modern discussions of rights, institutions, and functions. These also need to be discerned and judged. Even genuine constitutional thought is no guarantee of Christian thought.

NOTES

1. Hereafter "Canadian" will refer only to English Canada.

2. George Grant, *Technology and Empire* (Toronto: Anansi, 1969), 17.

3. George Grant, *Lament for a Nation* (Toronto: McLelland and Stewart, 1965).

4. Quoted in George Grant, *Time as History* (Toronto: Canadian Broadcasting Corporation, 1969, 1971), 26-27.

5. Quoted in Hannah Arendt, *On Revolution* (New York: Viking, 1965), 145. Many constitutions, such as those of several Latin American countries, are not intended to be law at all, but are rather statements of national ideals and aspirations.

6. James Bryce, *The American Commonwealt`.*, 2 vols. (New York: Macmillan, 1911).

7. Ibid., 1:394-95. Some items Bryce mentioned have changed once again but this does not invalidate his argument.

8. Ibid., 1:1.

9. S. F. Wise and R. C. Brown, eds., *Canada Views the United States: Nineteenth Century Political Attitudes* (Seattle: Univ. of Washington Press, 1967).

10. Ian Lumsden, *Close the 49th Parallel etc.* (Toronto: Univ. of Toronto Press, 1970), 308.

11. H. F. Angus, ed., *Canada and Her Great Neighbour* (Toronto: Ryerson, 1938), 276. "Tory nationalists consider the great works of our history to be those concerned with the maintenance in Canada of a society distinct and separate from that of the United States." Gerald L. Caplan and J. Laxer, "Perspectives on Un-American Traditions in Canada," in Lumsden, *Close the 49th Parallel etc.,* 307.

12. Wise and Brown, *Canada Views the U.S.,* 76.

13. *Globe,* 31 Oct. 1850, quoted in ibid.

14. Wise and Brown, *Canada Views the U.S.,* 120.

15. *House of Commons Debates,* 27 Feb. 1905, 1458-59; Wise and Brown, *Canada Views the U.S.,* 118.

16. Grant, *Lament,* 69-70. See also David Bell, "The Loyalist Tradition in Canada," *Journal of Canadian Studies,* vol. 5, no. 2 (1970): 22-33; H. A. Morton, "The American Revolution: A View from the North," *Journal of Canadian Studies,* vol. 7, no. 2 (1972): 43-53.

17. W. L. Morton, *The Canadian Identity* (Toronto: Univ. of Toronto Press, 1961), 25-26.

18. Ibid.

19. S. F. Wise, "Sermon Literature and Canadian Intellectual History," in J. M. Bumsted, ed., *Canadian History Before Confederation* (Georgetown, Ont.: Irwin-Dorsey, 1979), 259.

20. Ibid., 260.

21. Ibid., 258.

22. Wise and Brown, *Canada Views the U.S.,* 19.

23. Ibid., 18.

24. Ibid., 21.

25. Ibid., 41. See also Gerald M. Craig, ed., *The Durham Report* (Oxford: Clarendon Press, 1975); J. Ajzenstat, "Modern Mixed Government: A Liberal Defence of Inequality," *Canadian Journal of Political Science,* vol. 18, no. 1 (March 1985): 119-43.

26. Wise and Brown, *Canada Views the U.S.,* 49.

27. Ibid., 48.

28. Ibid., 51.

29. Grant, *Technology*, 68.

30. 24 Nov. 1866 in Peter Waite, *The Life and Times of Confederation, 1864–1867* (Toronto: Univ. of Toronto Press, 1962), 30.

31. Ibid., 34.

32. Ibid., 13.

33. W. P. M. Kennedy, ed., *Documents of the Canadian Constitution 1759–1915* (Toronto: Oxford Univ. Press, 1918), 586-87 (letter dated 1 Nov. 1850).

34. Ibid., 605 (17 Dec. 1850).

35. Wise and Brown, *Canada Views the U.S.*, 100.

36. Kennedy, *Documents*, 625.

37. *Toronto Leader*, 22 Jan. 1861, in Wise and Brown, *Canada Views the U.S.*, 88-89.

38. *Globe*, 19 Oct. 1852, in Wise and Brown, *Canada Views the U.S.*, 79.

39. Dawson, *op. cit.*, p. 11. Canadians, however, remained happily vague about constitutional niceties: the British North America Act of 1867 called for "A Constitution Similar in Principle to that of the United Kingdom." The citizenship oath is still not to a form of law but to a person—the monarch.

40. Angus, *Canada and Her Great Neighbour*, 274-75.

41. Bourinet (1899), quoted in Wise, "Sermon Literature," 104.

42. Wise and Brown, *Canada Views the U.S.*, 101.

43. Ibid., 114.

44. Ibid., 128-29.

45. See also J. W. Daly, "Toward a Philosophic Basis for Canadian Conservatism," *Journal of Canadian Studies*, vol. 5, no. 4 (1970): 50-58; T. Cook, "The Canadian Conservative Tradition," *Journal of Canadian Studies*, vol. 7, no. 4 (1973): 31-39.

46. The best book on Grant is Joan O'Donovan, *The Twilight of Justice* (Toronto: Univ. of Toronto Press, 1984). A good introduction is the collection in L. Schmidt, ed., *George Grant in Process* (Toronto: Anansi, 1978). Grant's *Technology and Justice* was published by Anansi in late 1986.

47. Quotation on back cover of *Technology and Empire*. Grant is more skeptical of his worth and says it took him from the age of twenty to the age of thirty just to cope with sex—"and it took my thirties and into my forties to cope with earning a living for my family. Now it's taken the rest of my life to try and formulate the questions . . . and you silly buggers want answers." *Globe and Mail*, 13 Feb. 1980.

48. Grant, *Technology*, 17. This theme is perhaps most radically stated in Tom Paine's assertion, "We have it in our power to begin the world over again."

49. Ibid., 71.

50. Ibid., 26.

51. George Grant, *English Speaking Justice* (Sackville: Mount Allison, 1974), 62-63. On this point, see David Little, *Religion, Order and Law* (New York: Harper & Row, 1969). In this respect it is worth noting that no state has been able to join the Union without first proposing a Constitution.

52. Grant, *English*, 29. On the relation of contract and will, see my *Human Rights Theories in Christian Pespective* (Toronto: Institute for Christian Studies, 1982); Patrick Riley, *Will and Political Legitimacy* (Cambridge, Mass.: Harvard Univ. Press, 1982).

53. Grant, *English*, 59.

54. Grant, *Technology*, 114.

55. Ibid.

56. Ibid., 17, 16, 19. Cf. Lord Durham to Lord Glenelg, 9 Aug. 1838: "Differing as the Americans do, from all other nations . . . in a habit which belongs to all ranks, of calculation as to the future." Kennedy, *Documents*, 459.

57. Grant, *Technology*, 74-75. Cf. Grant's reference to Edward S. Corwins's statement, in "The 'Higher Law' Background of American Constitutional Law," *Harvard Law Review*, 42 (1928): 152: "The attribution of supremacy to the Constitution on the ground solely of its rootage in popular will represents . . . a comparatively late outgrowth of American constitutional theory. Earlier the supremacy accorded to constitutions was ascribed less to their putative source than to their supposed content, to their embodiment of essential and unchanging justice."

58. Grant, *English*, 75-77.

59. Ibid., 89.

60. Ibid., 71.

61. George Grant, *Philosophy in the Mass Age* (Toronto: Copp, Clark, 1959), 87-88.

62. Grant, *Technology*, 37.

63. Grant, *Lament*, 63.

64. Ibid., 54.

65. R. J. Neuhaus, "Review" of *English Speaking Justice* (1985 ed.), in *Chronicles of Culture*, Aug. 1985, 26-27. See also Grant, "The Battle Between Teaching and Research," *Globe and Mail*, 18 April 1980.

66. Grant, *Time as History*, 8; see also *Technology*, 64, and Introduction to J. Laxer and R. Laxer, *The Liberal Idea of Canada* (Toronto: James Lorimer, 1977), 9.

67. Grant, *Technology*, 11.

68. Grant, *English*, 87.

69. Ibid., 4.

70. Grant, *Lament*, 64.

71. Grant, *English*, 110-11. Nor should Grant's criticism be construed in the form of the debate between "interpretivism" and "noninterpretivism." The rights view he criticizes can be found in both, and other, schools. Cf. J. H. Ely, *Democracy and Discontent: A Theory of Judicial Review* (Cambridge, Mass.: Harvard Univ. Press, 1980); T. C. Grey, "Do We Have An Unwritten Constitution?" *Stanford Law Review* 27 (1975), 703.

72. As, e.g., Senator Helms's claim that the Founding Fathers were particularly inspired by God and so the Constitution has virtual revelatory status.

Separation of Church and State in the American and German Constitutions

Richard V. Pierard

S eparation of church and state is an idea that has arrived on the scene only lately in human history, but increasingly people have realized that it is the surest foundation for religious liberty. Officially recognized churches or establishments of religion constrict the freedom of a polity's entire population, and dissenters are by definition second-class citizens. Moreover, ties between the public authority and a church or other religious body have a deleterious effect upon the spiritual organ as well. In my judgment, one of the greatest disasters in the history of the Christian church was the conversion of the Roman ruler Constantine and the subsequent recognition of Christianity as the official faith of the empire. Not only was the Christian gospel harnessed to a political system and gradually emptied of its spiritual dynamic, but Christians felt a need to sanctify the public order. Before long, the concept of a sacral society and the holy nation under God became fixed in the minds of Christian theologians and political philosophers, and it has been, so to say, "a long time a-dying." If anything, in the 1980s it is enjoying a resurgence.

Nevertheless, we live in the age in which the alternative to a sacral polity and established religion, a free church in a free state, has gained wide acceptance. The idea emerged in the thinking of the Anabaptists, those sixteenth-century pioneers of religious freedom and nonviolent action, whose farsightedness has come to be appreciated in our own times, and given clear expression a century later by the early English Baptists, the Quakers, and that remarkable Calvinist in New England, Roger Williams, whose likeness is enshrined with the other heroes of the Reformed faith in the celebrated Reformation monument in

AUTHOR'S NOTE: The author acknowledges with gratitude a grant from the Research Committee of Indiana State University which aided him in preparing this essay. He would also like to express appreciation to the library personnel at the Kirchliche Hochschule, West Berlin, Evangelischer Bund, Bensheim, West Germany, and Indiana State University for their assistance.

88

LIBERTY AND LAW

Geneva. The constitutional expression of the idea is the doctrine of the separation of church and state, where the secular state maintains peace and order in accordance with an autonomous law of nature or reason, and where religious truth and moral truth are not regarded as necessarily the same.

Civil or public morality, in such a situation, is determined independently of particular religious beliefs or authorities. Full freedom of conscience exists, whether to believe or disbelieve, and no coercion of any kind is brought upon the individual to conform to the religious views of the society's leaders or the majority of the populace.[1] As Williams put it, the state is responsible for enforcing the second table of the Decalogue concerning basic social relations among human beings in the "moral and civil" sphere of life, but not the first table regarding the relations between human beings and God. In the latter, the religious realm, conscience must have free reign, while the civil and moral sphere is governed by the "natural law," a moral standard applicable to all people regardless of their religious affiliation. Thus, to enact into law certain biblical prescriptions just because they are believed to be "God's word" is not desirable, since this "bloody tenent," to use Williams's immortal phrase, would result in religious strife and persecution. This is particularly true in a pluralistic society, because it would require the state to favor one particular religious rationale for morality over others.[2]

Only in the later eighteenth century did statesmen, under the impact of Enlightenment rationalism, begin to give serious attention to these principles. In the United States both the Virginia Bill of Rights in 1776 and the First Amendment to the Federal Constitution in 1791 guaranteed the free exercise of religion to all citizens, and the latter document also denied recognition to an establishment of religion. The French constitutions of 1791 and 1793 affirmed the freedom of religious belief, and the National Convention in February 1795 adopted a strong measure spelling out the details of a formal separation between the state and the church. The idea of religious liberty gained increasing acceptance in the following century as the various state constitutions in the United States incorporated provisions regarding it. Moreover, the constitution of 1847 adopted by the Swiss canton of Basel contained a modest guarantee of religious freedom, the Frankfurt National Assembly of 1848–49 included a clause in its document rejecting a state church, and Mexico amended its constitution in 1873 to declare church and state independent of one another and to forbid the congress from establishing or prohibiting any religion.[3]

By the modern era three different forms of legal relationships between the ecclesiastical and political authorities had become evident.[4] In the first form, the regime recognized a single church. In England, Scandinavia, and some Swiss cantons one church had official status. The state had a role in appointments to high ecclesiastical offices, and the Parliament passed laws applying to church matters, while dissenting communions were guaranteed full freedom to organize, worship, and evangelize. In some countries, such as Italy and Spain, the Roman Catholic Church was granted exclusive recognition through a concordat (a treaty with the Holy See), while non-Catholic bodies were given a restricted measure of religious liberty.

The second type was accommodation. Here a cooperative relationship between church and state existed, which in some places amounted virtually to an establishment. This was the situation in Germany, Austria, and a few Swiss cantons, where the church was allowed internal freedom but the state assisted it in various ways, such as collecting church taxes, authorizing religious instruction in the public schools, maintaining theological faculties in the universities, and giving clerics the status of civil servants. Dissenting groups were accorded full religious liberty but given no state help.

The third model was separation. In the United States this took the form of a constitutional barrier between the two, whereby the state did nothing to aid church bodies materially. Religious training in the public schools or subsidies for parochial schools were forbidden. At the same time the state permitted the churches almost unrestricted rights to carry out their religious functions and only interfered when clergy or churches violated laws applicable to the entire population, such as fraud, bigamy, health regulations, and building codes.

Unlike the United States where the term *separation of church and state* was not used in statute law, France went much further and on December 9, 1905, adopted a measure formally severing all ties between the two. As worked out in subsequent legislation over the next three years, the Roman Catholic Church was deprived of its standing in public law, its role in education was curtailed, and its properties were put under state (i.e., lay) supervision. Some of the restrictions were eventually relaxed, but similar actions took place in Geneva (1909), Basel (1911), and Mexico (1917).

The most extreme form of separation occurred in Soviet Russia, where decrees in early 1918 totally separated the church from the state, abolished religious education, restricted religious gatherings, and secularized church properties. These principles were carried over into the Soviet constitution of 1936. In 1939 the German National Socialist regime adopted virtually the same ideas in the Warthegau, a region seized from Poland that was intended to serve as the model for the new Nazi order. All churches there were deprived of their status as private associations and put under strict state supervision, and only adults were allowed to attend services.

The concept of the established or officially recognized "state" church is rapidly dying out and, in Protestant and Catholic countries alike, the relationship is becoming essentially one of accommodation. However, the other two are alive and well, as a comparative analysis of the United States and German situations will reveal.

A heated debate has been going on in the United States for some decades over what *separation of church and state* means, and during the Reagan years this debate took on what, to some, seemed like ominous political overtones. This resulted from the manner in which the president together with Chief Justice William Rehnquist, Attorney-General Edwin Meese, Secretary of Education William Bennett, and lesser lights in the administration aligned themselves with a broad coalition of right-wing politicians, conservative evangelicals, Roman Catholics, and neoconservative Jews to promote an accommodationist conception of church-state relations. They directed their energies toward counteracting the drift toward strict separation that had accompanied the growth of religious pluralism in the twentieth century, especially as revealed in Supreme Court decisions since the early 1940s. Court watchers recognized that the rulings were at times confusing and inconsistent as well as highly unpopular. Of all the actions by the highest tribunal, probably only those in the realm of civil rights did more to stir public passions than the religious ones. The body of literature on the issue is enormous, and the positions taken by scholars and polemicists are strong ones.[5]

Does the Constitution really guarantee separation? The founding document only makes one reference to religion, in the last clause of Article Six, which reads: "No religious test shall ever be required as a qualification to any office or public trust under the United States." The Bill of Rights, adopted in the first session of the new congress, also addresses the matter in one place. The First Amendment states:

Congress shall make no law respecting an establishment of religion, or prohibiting the free exercise thereof; or abridging the freedom of speech, or the press; or the right of the people peaceably to assemble and to petition the Government for a redress of grievances.

The term *separation* does not enter into the picture until a decade after the ratification of the Bill of Rights. The Baptists in Connecticut were most unhappy about the Congregationalist establishment there, and they began protesting regularly to the state assembly. At the same time, a three-man committee representing the Danbury Baptist Association sent an address to President Thomas Jefferson complaining about the situation, and he replied with the famous lines:

Believing with you that religion is a matter which lies solely between man and his God, that he owes account to none other for his faith or his worship, that the legitimate powers of government reach actions only, and not opinions, I contemplate with sovereign reverence that act of the whole American people which declared that their legislature should "make no law respecting an establishment of religion, or prohibiting the free exercise thereof," thus building a wall of separation between Church and State.[6]

This interpretation was largely overlooked until the Supreme Court in the *Everson* (1947) and *McCollum* (1948) cases affirmed that the First Amendment was intended to erect a "wall of separation between church and state."

What was the intent of the Founding Fathers? The evidence is clear that James Madison, an active participant in the Constitutional Convention of 1787 and drafter of the amendments that made up the Bill of Rights, believed the religious realm had been made off-limits to the state, and squarely behind him stood Jefferson (at the time serving in Paris), whose views he shared and represented. Madison was satisfied that the Constitution, which did not mention God and forbade religious tests, sufficiently protected liberty because the existence of a multiplicity of sects would forestall the creation of an establishment, but he was also responsive to those who felt a more specific guarantee of rights was needed.[7]

Madison's deep commitment to religious freedom was evidenced by several factors: his role in persuading the Virginia Convention in June 1776 to include a phrase in its Declaration of Rights acknowledging that "all men are equally entitled to the full and free exercise of religion, according to the dictates of conscience";[8] his use of the phrase "separation between Religion and Government";[9] his opposition to presidential thanksgiving proclamations and to chaplains for Congress and the military being paid out of public funds; and, especially in the *Memorial and Remonstrance Against Religious Assessments,* which is one of the most eloquent defenses of liberty ever made. Madison prepared this statement in 1784 to combat a bill before the Virginia legislature to authorize a tax to support religious teachers (i.e., ministers). He declared that

> We hold it for a fundamental and undeniable truth, "that Religion or the duty we owe to our Creator and the manner of discharging it, can be directed only by reason and conviction, not by force or violence." The Religion then of every man must be left to the conviction and conscience of every man; and it is the right of every man to exercise it as these may dictate. This right is in its nature an unalienable right. It is unalienable; because the opinions of men, depending only on the evidence contemplated by their own minds, cannot follow the dictates of other men. . . . We maintain therefore that in matters of Religion, no man's right is abridged by the institution of Civil Society, and that religion is wholly exempt from its cognizance.

He then went on to develop fourteen additional arguments for liberty of conscience that denied the right of the state assembly or any other governmental organ to meddle in religious beliefs and practices and that the Christian religion needed civil support. Moreover, such assistance would be harmful to religion itself because it bred strife and persecution and hindered the diffusion of Christianity.[10]

In December 1785 Madison succeeded in defeating the assessment measure, and straightway he called up Jefferson's Bill for Establishing Religious Freedom, which had been languishing in limbo since 1779. After a few modifications were made in a conference committee, the Virginia Assembly passed the bill on January 16, 1786. This formalized the disestablishment that had already taken place in Virginia, where laws had been repealed that required dissenters to support the established church (1776) and members of the Episcopal Church to contribute to the support of their ministry (1779). It is the expression of Jefferson's and Madison's views on religious liberty and reflects the thinking that went into the writing and adoption of the First Amendment.

The Virginia Statute affirmed that God made man's mind free and thus religion should be propagated by reason and not coercion. However, legislators and rulers have established and maintained false religions, and it is sinful and tyrannical to force people to support religious teachers, whether they accept or reject them. One's civil rights were not based on one's religious opinions, and to impose religious tests for public office only leads to corruption. Opinions were not under the jurisdiction of civil government, "truth is great and will prevail if left to herself," and "she is the proper and sufficient antagonist to error" when allowed to use "her natural weapons, free argument and debate." The act then stated that no one was required to attend or support any religious worship or place of ministry or suffer discrimination because of religious beliefs, and all are free to profess their opinions in matters of religion. The principles of the measure were, in Jefferson's words, based on "the natural rights of mankind." Writing later in his autobiography (1821), Jefferson observed that the assembly "meant to comprehend, within the mantle of its protection, the Jew and the Gentile, the Christian and Mahometan, the Hindoo, and Infidel of every denomination."[11]

In a familiar passage in his *Notes on Virginia* (1782), Jefferson referred to the "error" that the operations of the mind as well as the acts of the body are subject to the coercion of the laws. Instead, he asserted, rulers have no power of rights of conscience and they may only be concerned with such acts that are injurious to others:

> But it does me no injury for my neighbor to say there are twenty gods, or no God. It neither picks my pocket nor breaks my leg.
>
> Difference of opinion is advantageous in religion. The several sects perform the office of a *censor morum* over each other. Is uniformity attainable? Millions of innocent men, women, and children, since the introduction of Christianity, have been burnt, tortured, fined, imprisoned; yet we have not advanced one inch toward uniformity. What has been the effect of coercion? To make one half the world fools, and the other half hypocrites.[12]

Thus, Jefferson's affirmation of the "wall of separation" flowed naturally from his understanding of the Constitution and Bill of Rights. His response to the Danbury Baptists was not an offhand comment; rather, he had used the occasion to express something that concerned him deeply. In fact, he sent the draft of the letter to Attorney-General Levi Lincoln for a critical reading and told him that the Baptist address provided the opportunity for

> a condemnation of the alliance between Church and State, under the authority of the Constitution. It furnishes an occasion, too, which I have

long wished to find, of saying why I do not proclaim fastings and thanksgivings, as my predecessors did.[13]

Six years later Jefferson wrote to a Presbyterian clergyman, the Reverend Robert Miller of Washington, regarding the demand that he as president should recommend a day of fasting and prayer:

> I consider the government of the United States as interdicted by the Constitution from intermeddling with religious institutions, their doctrines, discipline, or exercises. This results not only from the provision that no law shall be made respecting the establishment or free exercise of religion, but from that also which reserves to the States the powers not delegated to the United States. Certainly, no power to prescribe any religious exercise, or to assume authority in religious discipline, has been delegated to the General Government. . . . I do not believe it is for the interest of religion to invite the civil magistrate to direct its exercises, its discipline, or its doctrines.

Jefferson added that only civil powers had been given to the president and he had no authority to direct the religious exercises of his constituents.[14]

Madison affirmed a similar viewpoint in a letter to Robert Walsh on March 2, 1819. He praised the American experiment in religious freedom and pointed to the great expansion of Christian activity that resulted from it. He noted the experience of Virginia, which showed that the civil government could stand without the prop of a religious establishment and that the church prospered without legal support for its clergy.

> The Civil Government, though bereft of everything like an associated hierarchy, possesses the requisite stability, and peforms its functions with complete success; whilst the number, the industry, and the morality of the Priesthood, and the devotion of the people, have been manifestly increased by the total separation of the church from the State.[15]

Although the doctrine of total separation was brought to the fore in the above-mentioned rulings in 1947 and 1948, attention had been drawn to it much earlier. In the most important religious liberty decision in the nineteenth century, *Reynolds vs. United States* (1878), the Mormon polygamy case, the Supreme Court held that the Free Exercise clause could not be evoked as a defense of the practice in question or other "acts inimical to the peace, good order, and morals of society." The professed doctrines of religious belief could not be superior to the criminal laws of the land. Surveying the historical background and intent of the First Amendment, Chief Justice Morrison R. Waite, writer of the opinion, cited the Virginia Statute for Establishing Religious Freedom as the place where one may find "the true distinction between what properly belongs to the Church and what to the State." Then he quoted Jefferson's letter to the Danbury Baptists and concluded: "Coming as it does from an acknowledged leader of the advocates of the measure, it may be accepted almost as an authoritative declaration of the scope and effect of the amendment."[16]

An important aspect of the separation question is whether the First Amendment guarantees applied to the states. At first glance the matter seems to be of no consequence since all the states included affirmations of religious freedom in their constitutions.[17] Some of these were essentially restatements of provisions in the Constitution and Bill of Rights, while others spelled out in great detail the liberties their citizens possessed. Moreover, the language of the respective constitutions shows that their writers borrowed heavily from one another. An example of religious provisions in a state bill of rights is that included in the Indiana constitution:

> Sec. 2. All men shall be secured in their natural right to worship Almighty God according to the dictates of their own consciences.
> Sec. 3. No law shall in any case, whatever, control the free exercise and enjoyment of religious opinions, or interfere with the right of conscience.
> Sec. 4. No preference shall be given, by law, to any creed, religious society or mode of worship, and no man shall be compelled to attend, erect, or support any place of worship or to maintain any ministry against his consent.
> Sec. 5. No religious test shall be required as a qualification for any office of trust or profit.
> Sec. 6. No money shall be drawn from the treasury for the benefit of any religious or theological institution.
> Sec. 7. No person shall be rendered incompetent as a witness in consequence of his opinion in matters of religion.[18]

Another is Article 1, Section 3 of the Maine constitution, which declared:

> All men have a natural and unalienable right to worship Almighty God according to the dictates of their own consciences, and no one shall be hurt, molested or restrained in his person, liberty, or estate for worshipping God in the manner and season most agreeable to the dictates of his conscience, nor for his religious professions or sentiments, provided he does not disturb the public peace, nor obstruct others in their religious

worship;—and all persons demeaning themselves peaceably, as good members of the State, shall be equally under the protection of the laws, and no subordination nor preference of any one sect or denomination to another shall ever be established by law, nor shall any religious test be required as a qualification for any office or trust under the State; and all religious societies in this State, whether incorporate or unincorporate, shall at all times have the exclusive right of electing their public teachers and contracting with them for their support and maintenance.[19]

In *Barron vs. Baltimore,* a case in 1833 that dealt with a Fifth Amendment question (not with religion *per se*), the Supreme Court ruled that the Bill of Rights did not apply to the states but constituted only a limitation on the exercise of power by the federal government. This of course had implications for the religious realm, even though the states had included religious liberty guarantees in their constitutions. Thus, in 1791 four of the original thirteen states still had religious establishments (the last to abolish theirs was Massachusetts in 1833), many had religious tests for public office, Sunday closing laws existed in nearly all of them, Catholics suffered discrimination in some states and communities, and intrachurch conflicts were frequently litigated in state courts. These things were possible in spite of the *de jure* separation, because in nineteenth-century America a *de facto* establishment of Protestantism existed.

After the Civil War Congress passed the Fourteenth Amendment to overrule *Barron vs. Baltimore* and make the Bill of Rights applicable to the states. The key provision was Section 1, which affirmed:

No State shall make or enforce any law which shall abridge the privileges or immunities of citizens of the United States: nor shall any State deprive any person of life, liberty, or property without due process of law; nor deny to any person within its jurisdiction the equal protection of the laws.

It was clear in the deliberations over the amendment that its congressional drafters intended to make the liberties in the Bill of Rights binding upon state governments as well as the federal one. In the so-called Slaughter House Cases of 1873 the Supreme Court held that the "privileges and immunities" mentioned here were only those inhering in national citizenship, such as the right to vote for congressmen and presidential electors, and not those in the first eight amendments. But beginning in the 1920s with some freedom of speech cases, the court expanded the term *liberty* in the Due Process clause of the Fourteenth

Amendment, and through this means made the Bill of Rights applicable to the states.[20]

Religious freedom became a prominent issue in the Jehovah's Witnesses cases in the early 1940s, beginning with the landmark ruling of the high court in *Cantwell vs. Connecticut* (1940):

> The fundamental concept of liberty embodied in the Amendment embraces the liberties guaranteed by the First Amendment. The First Amendment declares that Congress shall make no law respecting an establishment of religion or prohibiting the free exercise thereof. The Fourteenth Amendment has rendered the legislatures of the states as incompetent as Congress to enact such laws.[21]

The tribunal expanded upon this in *Minersville School District vs. Gobitis* (1940), where it affirmed:

> Centuries of strife over the erection of particular dogmas as exclusive or all-comprehending faiths led to the inclusion of a guarantee for religious freedom in the Bill of Rights. The First Amendment, and the Fourteenth through its absorption of the First, sought to guard against repetition of those bitter religious struggles by prohibiting the establishment of a state religion and by securing to every sect the free exercise of its faith.[22]

The reason church-state separation has become such a controversial matter in the United States today is that these principal actions of the Supreme Court struck at the roots of the establishment of Protestantism at the state level and even of Christianity itself. They opened the door to eliminating religious instruction, prayers, and Bible readings in the public schools, state religious tests for officeholders, public support for church-related schools, the display of religious symbols in public places, and morals legislation that was religiously based, such as bans on abortions and the sale of contraceptives. Pluralism has carried the day and the judicial bodies have decreed that governmental organs must be religiously *neutral*.

The current debate is over how strict and total the separation between state and religion shall become, and in this respect the struggle is far from over. Yet, it is clear that in spite of the constitutional restraints on the public support of religious institutions, the population of the United States is by far the most apparently religious of any industrialized nation in the world. Separation of church and state, apparently, has worked here.

In the Protestant areas of Germany a close tie existed between the

churches and the political order that had all the appearance of a state
church situation, and in fact it was commonly referred to as the "union
of throne and altar." The two organs mutually supported one another
but it was not a state-controlled church in the sense, say, of Russian Or-
thodoxy. Each kingdom, principality, and free city possessed a territorial church *(Landeskirche)* that encompassed the entire population,
and the ruler generally was the *summus episcopus,* the supreme governor of the church. The church was ultimately responsible to God, but
the prince was the highest authority in ecclesiastical affairs. This was a
vestige of the Reformation era *cujus regio ejus religio* principle, but by
the nineteenth century nearly all states had mixed Protestant-Catholic
and Lutheran-Reformed populations together with a scattering of free
churches or "sects" as they were often pejoratively labeled.

In the Second Reich (1871–1918) there were thirty-two separate
Landeskirchen, a number that shrank to twenty-eight in 1919 through
the consolidation of some small Thuringian churches. Three types existed—Lutheran, Reformed, and United, the last of which was exemplified by the Old Prussian Union Church, an organizational merger
of the two Protestant communions effected in 1817 by Frederick William III, ruler of the largest state, which contained half of all the Protestants in Germany.

The *Landeskirchen* received state help in collecting church taxes,
usually through a surcharge on an individual's regular tax fee, as well
as direct subsidies to support schools and to pay church officials. Most
churches were governed by a synodical-presbyterial system paralleled
by consistorial organs that were occupied by clerical bureaucrats who
received their authority from the territorial monarch. In some places the
state ministry of education and public worship *(Kultusministerium)* exercised supervisory authority as well. By the end of the century rulers
seldom directly interfered in church affairs, but the structure still was
rather authoritarian. The clergy loyally supported the militaristic,
nationalistic, and imperialistic actions of the state that eventually led to
war in 1914, while laypeople were schooled in the virtues of obedience
to authority, patriotism, and cheerful acceptance of one's lot in life.

The emphasis in the nineteenth century was on the creation of a
national Protestant church *(Volkskirche),* especially in Prussia. This was
rooted in the connection between pietism and the German national
awakening of the Napoleonic years, which encouraged the flowering
of patriotism under the protective cover of religion. As the century pro-
gressed, God in Lutheran parlance became less the tender, loving Re-

deemer and more the one who led his people to victory—the "Lord of Peoples and Kingdoms," "Great God of Battles," "Almighty Judge and Avenger."

The highest place in the divine structure of creation was occupied by the *Volk* and its concrete political form, the nation. The struggle for the *Volkstum* (peopledom) became a struggle for God's order, indeed, for God himself. Service for *Volk* and fatherland consequently was God's service, and devotion to the community was the highest moral demand placed upon an individual. The revelation of God was worked out in German history, which meant that political unity, monarchical power, and freedom within a structure of authority were the fulfillment of the divine dictates. The Reformation stress on the justifying power of faith had been supplanted by the proclamation of the nationality and its God, and national mission became the new gospel.[23] At the same time, the possibility of loosening or even ending the church-state tie was seriously discussed. As early as 1799 theologian Friedrich Schleiermacher had argued for this, and King Frederick William IV convened a general synod in 1846 to consider greater freedom of action for his church, while provisions in the Prussian constitutions of 1848 and 1850 granted a modicum of autonomy. The Frankfurt National Assembly (1848–49) proclaimed full freedom of conscience and the end of state preference for any church. The Prussian, North German Confederation (1867), and Reich (1871) constitutions dropped most confessional requirements for the exercise of political and civil rights, as was the case in the smaller states as well.

Liberal and Progressive politicians alike criticized the linkage of throne and altar, while the Social Democratic Party's Erfurt Program (1891) advocated making religion a private matter, curtailing public expenditures for religious purposes, converting church bodies into private corporations, and discontinuing religious instruction in the public schools. Catholics also called for greater freedom of movement, but they firmly rejected a secularistic separation like that which occurred in France. Many Protestants assessed the American experience in positive terms and maintained that a similar arrangement would be desirable for Germany. Theologians and churchmen, such as Wilhelm Kahl, Adolf Stoecker, Martin Rade, and Friedrich Naumann, recognized the benefits that a "*Volkskirche* free of state control" could bring. To be sure, in 1914 the discussion was shelved for the duration as the spiritual leaders rallied behind the war effort, but the ground had been prepared for the far-reaching changes in church-state relationships that were soon to come.[24]

As the end of World War I approached and the political power of Socialists, Catholics, and secularized liberals increasingly threatened the survival of the conservative, monarchical order, many churchmen believed the whole idea of the "Christian state" was in jeopardy and with it the privileged status of the church and its confessional schools. Since, for example, the Old Prussian Union Church in 1918 drew 34 percent of its income from property holdings, capital investments, and pension funds, 39 percent from church taxes, and 27 percent from direct state contributions, its leaders were convinced that disestablishment would be an incalculable disaster.[25] Also, the continuation of confessional religious training in the public schools was endangered, as many teachers were hostile to clergymen supervising ("inspecting") such instruction. In fact, churchmen regarded progressive educators and "materialist" Socialists as the mortal enemies of all they stood for. With the dawning of the age of democratic and radical politics, it was apparent to many that the Protestant churches no longer were important in public life and thus they faced an ominous future.

Events in the fall of 1918—the military debacle, sudden parliamentarization of Germany from above, forced abdication of Kaiser William II, creation of the German Republic, and conclusion of the armistice that in reality was a surrender—confirmed the Protestant clerics' worst fears. On November 12, only three days after Socialist Friedrich Ebert had taken up the reins of power in the new republic, his government announced that the free exercise of religion would be guaranteed, and no one would be compelled to engage in religious exercises. The next day the more radical Socialist regime in Prussia declared that the schools there were to be liberated from the tutelage of the church and the separation of church and state would take place.

At the same time Adolf Hoffmann, a notoriously anticlerical, left-wing Socialist, was appointed as co-minister in the *Kultusministerium*.[26] His first actions were to relax the procedures for withdrawal from church membership and to decree that immediate steps would be taken to separate church and state and to cut off the flow of subsidies by April 1, 1919. Moreover, he forbade religious exercises and instruction and clerical supervision in the public schools. The Protestant leaders were extremely alarmed at the turn of events and cooperated with their Catholic counterparts to resist these actions. The result was that Hoffmann was forced out of office within two months and the state organs became accommodating to clerics' wishes. Although these events were unsettling for the churchmen, they discovered that the new regime was not prepared to implement a radical program of separation.[27]

Meanwhile, at the national level the moderate Socialists in the Provisional Government gained control of the situation, thwarted the intentions of radicals to set up a class dictatorship through revolutionary councils, and called for elections for a national assembly to write a constitution for the new Germany. Elections took place in January 1919 and the body convened in the provincial city of Weimar the following month. By then the churches had closed ranks to defend their interests, and much of the extreme separationist steam was gone from the revolution.

In the elections the churches threw their support behind the parties of the right, a behavior pattern that would persist throughout the history of the short-lived Weimar Republic. Unprepared as they were to adapt spiritually to the new political order, clerical bureaucrats and pastors clung firmly to the ideals of the past and fervently longed for the restoration of monarchical government, social stability, and national pride.[28] Although the right-wing parties did not fare particularly well, a number of key church people (sixteen pastors and lay leaders) were elected to the National Assembly.[29] They included Friedrich Naumann, a pastor turned politician, Professor Wilhelm Kahl, a church law expert, and clerics Reinhard Mumm and Gottfried Traub.

By participating actively in the Weimar Assembly's Constitution Committee, they played significant roles in the drafting of the church and school provisions of the document. Meanwhile, the churches engaged in a nationwide public relations campaign and petition drive as well as in direct lobbying efforts to influence assembly deputies. Other than the issue of secular schools, where their demands were not heeded, the *Landeskirchen* ended up retaining most of what they had before the change. As two recent commentators on the topic noted, "In their external form church-state relations changed amazingly little as a result of Weimar deliberations," and "many important points desired by the church were incorporated into the principles of the constitution."[30]

The section in the part of the constitution entitled "Fundamental Rights and Duties of Germans," which dealt with "Religion and Religious Bodies" (Arts. 135-41) comprised two printed pages. Articles 142-50 treated "Education and Schools" and covered three pages.[31] The document assured full liberty of belief and conscience and the right to engage in worship (Art. 135). Civil and political rights and duties were not dependent on one's religious beliefs, and no one was required to reveal his membership in a religious body (except for statistical purposes), participate in a religious ceremony, or take an oath in a religious form (Art. 136).

Article 137, the most widely discussed one, began with the affirmation: "There is no state church." It then spelled out the rights of religious bodies. They were allowed freedom of association, the right to run their internal affairs as they saw fit (within the limits of law), and the right to make clerical or other appointments without any involvement of the civil authorities. Existing religious societies that were incorporated *(Körperschaften des öffentlichen Rechtes)* remained so, and others were to be granted the same privilege if by their constitution and membership they offered the guarantee of permanence. Such bodies were entitled to levy taxes on their members on the basis of the civil tax rolls. Associations that were formed to foster a worldview *(Weltanschauung)* had the same status as the religious ones.

Those ongoing state contributions to religious bodies that were based on a statutory, contractual, or special legal basis were to be commuted, that is, the state governments involved would arrange some sort of legal settlement and thereby terminate the subsidy. Their right to own property for religious, instructional, and social service purposes also was secured (Art. 138). Sundays and public holidays remained legally protected as days of rest from labor and of spiritual edification (Art. 139). Members of the armed forces were to be given the necessary free time to fulfill their religious obligations (Art. 140). Religious bodies were allowed to provide worship and pastoral care in the military installations, hospitals, prisons, and other public institutions, but on a strictly voluntary basis (Art. 141).

The public schools were put on a secular basis under state supervision (Art. 144), but the parents' wishes were to be taken into consideration, especially with regard to religious instruction, which would be a regular subject in all schools except those classified as "purely secular" ones. Instruction was given in accordance with the religious doctrines of the various denominations, but the state would supervise it. Teachers had the discretion whether or not to give religious instruction and perform religious ceremonies, and parents were to decide whether their child would take part in these (Arts. 146, 149). If there was no public elementary school in a community that reflected the religious faith or worldview of a minority of parents, the licensing of a private school for this purpose would be allowed (Art. 147). The theological faculties at the universities were to be maintained (Art. 150).

The Weimar Constitution was a skillful blend of religious establishment and liberty. The individual was guaranteed freedom of worship and extensive rights that were in no way dependent on belief. Jewish congregations, free churches, and secular worldview societies were given equal standing with the existing *Landeskirchen,* and churches were accorded property rights and were freed from most state controls. At the same time, the churches as public corporations could utilize the taxing mechanism to raise funds but were curtailed by some measure of state oversight. In this way everyone on the parish rolls supported the church, regardless of whether they were involved in the life of the congregation at all, and wealth steadily flowed into church coffers. Legislation to effect the commutation of state contributions never was adopted, so the subsidies continued. Churches provided chaplains for public institutions and the state enforced Christian holidays. Religious instruction remained a regular subject in public schools, and the theological training of clergy took place at universities as before.

Although conservative churchmen constantly railed upon the Weimar Republic as a "religionless state" because it ostensibly severed the tie with the church and recognized all creeds as equal before the law, in reality the regime had bent over backward to conciliate the church. Nevertheless, even this moderate accommodationist stance failed to produce a strong German church. The level of popular involvement in terms of attendance at worship services continued to decline, and many persons formally withdrew from the church in order to avoid paying the tax to support something that no longer had any meaning to them. However, the most important index of the church's failure was its anemic response to the development of National Socialism and Hitler's accession to power.[32]

The German church emerged from the inferno of World War II a sadder but not necessarily wiser body. To be sure, the development of the Confessing Church, the drafting of the Barmen Declaration of 1934, the resistance of people like Dietrich Bonhoeffer and Martin Niemöller, and the unsung heroes of the church struggle all indicated that not every pastor or parishioner had bowed before the German Baal that was Adolf Hitler. Unfortunately, those who reconstituted the shattered church after 1945 were not able to make a clean break with the past. The idea of the *Volkskirche* and the Christian state still had its old fascination, but now

there was a new situation. Germany was occupied by the victors of
World War II, and two different political systems were evolving in the
western and eastern parts of the divided country. Two models of church-
state relationships emerged: the accommodationist in the western Federal Republic of Germany and the separationist in the eastern German
Democratic Republic.

The West German constitution, the Basic Law *(Grundgesetz),*
adopted May 23, 1949, incorporated as Article 140 the provisions of
Articles 136, 137, 138, 139, and 141 of the German Constitution of
August 11, 1919 as "an integral part," while Article 135 was recast as
Article 4 of the "Basic Rights" section. Weimar Article 140 (right of
soldiers to exercise their religious faith) was deliberately omitted because the Federal Republic had no army at the time. The right of parents
to decide whether their child should receive religious instruction and
the authorization of public schools to give such instruction (in accordance with the tenets of the religious communities) were contained in
Article 7 of the Basic Rights.[33] Thus, the Protestant church in West Germany resumed the constitutional relationship with the state that it had
during the Weimar Republic. The Weimar Constitution was not actually abolished during the Nazi era; it was simply ignored by the regime.
However, the continuing accommodationist relationship has not
fostered church growth, either in numbers or in spiritual depth, and in
recent years there has been considerable debate, both inside and outside of the church circles, as to whether the idea of the *Volkskirche*
should be abandoned altogether and the evangelical (Protestant) church
be allowed to go it alone as a free church.[34]

The German Democratic Republic, on the other hand, at its outset
was somewhat equivocal, but the later revisions of its constitution more
firmly expressed separation.[35] For example, the 1949 document contained language drawn directly from the Weimar Constitution with respect to individual freedom of belief and the rights of religious communities. Although there was "no state church," people had the right to
form religious societies, which were guaranteed the status of public corporations and could even utilize a church tax (Art. 43). The church was
permitted to give religious instruction on school premises (Art. 44). Religious bodies were given the right to hold services and give pastoral
help in hospitals and prisons (Art. 46). Legal procedures had to be followed in order to withdraw from a religious body (Art. 47). Parents had
the right to determine whether their children under fifteen should be
members of a religious body (Art. 48).

In the next few years deep tensions arose between the socialist state in East Germany and the traditionalist church, especially over the church's close link with the West German church and officially fostered atheism. As the possibility of a unification of the two German states faded, the G.D.R. church increasingly had to draw upon its own resources and work out a *modus vivendi* with the regime.[36] The drastically revised 1968 constitution continued to guarantee freedom of conscience and belief, and every citizen had the right to profess a religious creed and to carry out religious activities. However, the lengthy section on churches was scaled down to read:

> The churches and other religious communities conduct their affairs and carry out their activities in conformity with the Constitution and the legal regulations of the German Democratic Republic. Details can be settled by agreement. (Art. 39, Sec. 2)

The same wording is in the 1974 constitution.

In 1968–69 all formal ties between the East and West German church bodies were dissolved. The only state support it would now receive was for charitable institutions, restoration of old church buildings, and the maintenance of theological faculties at six universities. Also, a political organization known as the Christian Democratic Union (formed in 1945) represented Christian concerns and maintained a public presence in governmental bodies and through its own press. In 1978 an understanding was worked out between the head of state and church leaders which allowed the churches more freedom of action, while in turn the latter agreed to function in the role of "the church within socialism." That meant that Christians would minister within the system, not against it or under it. Thus, taking into consideration the very different political systems, the G.D.R. in effect adopted a separationist stance roughly analogous to that of the United States while the Federal Republic continued an accommodationist one. The difference between the G.D.R. and the U.S.A. is that the latter's position is one of benevolent neutrality toward religion, whereas in accordance with the official ideology the Marxist-Leninist regime in East Germany views religion with suspicion.

Although the wealth and power of the East German church is far less than its West German counterpart and some are discouraged because the old ties no longer bind, it is clear to people who have spent time in the country that some sort of spiritual awakening is taking place. To be sure, churches are not growing rapidly, because there is no intrin-

sic benefit to church membership, but those who do choose to make
commitments to Christ and his community are sincere and dedicated
people. The evidence leads to the conclusion that a church which is not
linked to the state but rather witnesses to it and to the society at large
in word and deed about the love of Christ will be one that is spiritually
strong.

NOTES

1. David Little, "Theological Dimensions of Church-State Relations," in *Conceived in Conscience*, ed. Richard I. Rutyna and John W. Kuehl (Norfolk, Va.: Donning, 1983), 91-92.

2. David Little, "Roger Williams and the Separation of Church and State," in *Religion and the State: Essays in Honor of Leo Pfeffer*, ed. James E. Wood, Jr. (Waco, Tex.: Baylor Univ. Press, 1985), 13-14, 16.

3. A useful collection of documents on the topic is Zaccaria Giacometti, ed., *Quellen zur Geschichte der Trennung von Staat und Kirche* (Tübingen: J. C. B. Mohr, 1926). Although the book was reprinted in 1961, it unfortunately was not updated. In addition, it does not contain any material on German and Dutch developments.

4. This schema is utilized by Ulrich Scheuner in his article "Kirche and Staat" in *Die Religion in Geschichte und Gegenwart*, 3d ed. (1959), 3:1332-34.

5. The most eloquent exponent of separation is Leo Pfeffer, whose major works include *Church, State, and Freedom* (Boston: Beacon Press, 1953; rev. ed., 1967); *Church and State in the United States*, with Anson Phelps Stokes (New York: Harper & Row, 1964); *God, Caesar, and the Constitution* (Boston: Beacon Press, 1975); and *Religion, State and the Burger Court* (Buffalo: Prometheus, 1985). A number of the contemporary advocates of separation contributed essays to the Pfeffer *Festschrift* mentioned in note 2, and their works are cited on pages 569-72. The latest proseparation books include Thomas J. Curry, *The First Freedoms: Church and State in America to the Passage of the First Amendment* (New York: Oxford Univ. Press), and Leonard W. Levy, *The Establishment Clause: Religion and the First Amendment* (New York: Macmillan, 1986). On the other side of the issue are Chester J. Antieau et al., *Freedom from Federal Establishment: Formation and Early History of the First Amendment Religion Clauses* (Milwaukee: Bruce, 1964); Walter Berns, *The First Amendment and the Future of American Democracy* (New York: Basic Books, 1976); Michael J. Malbin, *Religion and Politics: The Intentions of the Authors of the First Amendment* (Washington, D.C.: American Enterprise Institute, 1978); Robert L. Cord, *Separation of Church and State: Historical Fact and Current Fiction* (New York: Lambeth Press, 1982); George Goldberg, *Reconsecrating America* (Grand Rapids: Wm. B. Eerdmans, 1984); and Richard John Neuhaus, *The Naked Public Square* (Grand Rapids: Wm. B. Eerdmans, 1984). A useful although outdated document collection is Joseph L. Blau, ed., *Cornerstones of Religious Freedom in America* (New York: Harper & Row, 1964), while indispensable for understanding the development of religious liberty is Anson Phelps Stokes, *Church and State in the United States*, 3 vols. (New York: Harper & Brothers, 1950).

6. *The Writings of Thomas Jefferson*, ed. H. A. Washington (New York: Riker, Thorne, 1853–54), 8:8. An examination of a photographic reproduction of the manuscript of the letter (in Stokes, *Church and State in the U.S.*, vol. 1, plate 24) reveals that the published Jefferson papers incorrectly rendered the word *legitimate* as *legislative*.

7. *The Writings of James Madison*, ed. Gaillard Hunt (New York: Putnam, 1900–1910), 5:176, 271-72.

8. *The Papers of James Madison*, ed. William T. Hutchinson and William M. E. Rachal (Chicago: Univ. of Chicago Press, 1962), 1:174-75.

9. Elizabeth Fleet, ed., "Madison's Detached Memoranda," *William and Mary Quarterly*, 3d ser., 3 (Oct. 1946): 555. On Madison's religious views see the thoughtful essay by Ralph L. Ketcham in *James Madison on Religious Liberty*, ed. Robert S. Alley (Buffalo, N.Y.: Prometheus, 1985), 175-96.

10. *Writings of Madison*, 2:184-91.

108   LIBERTY AND LAW

11. Blau, *Cornerstones of Religious Freedom*, 77-78; *Writings of Thomas Jefferson*, 1:45. A moving account of the background and struggle to secure passage of the bill is William Lee Miller, *The First Liberty: Religion and the American Republic* (New York: Alfred A. Knopf, 1986), 1-75.

12. *Writings of Jefferson*, 8:400-401.

13. Ibid., 5:236-37.

14. Ibid., 9:428-30.

15. *Letters and Other Writings of James Madison* (New York: R. Worthington, 1884), 3:125.

16. 98 U.S. 163-64 (1878).

17. The texts of the religious provisions included in all the various state constitutions up to 1913 are found in Giacometti, *Quellen zur Geschichte der Trennung von Staat und Kirche*, 678-733.

18. Ibid., 702-3.

19. Ibid., 707-8.

20. This development is discussed in Pfeffer, *Church, State and Freedom*, 142-49.

21. 310 U.S. 303 (1940).

22. 310 U.S. 593 (1940).

23. Klaus Scholder, "Neuere deutsche Geschichte und protestantischer Theologie," *Evangelische Theologie* 23 (Oct. 1963): 525-30; Daniel R. Borg, "*Volkskirche*, 'Christian State,' and the Weimar Republic," *Church History* 35 (June 1966): 186-206.

24. Wilhelm Kahl, *Aphorismen zur Trennung von Staat und Kirche* (Berlin: Gustav Schade, 1908); Karl Rothenbücher, *Die Trennung von Staat und Kirche* (Munich: Beck, 1908); Leopold Zscharnack, *Trennung von Staat und Kirche* (Berlin: Evangelischer Bund, 1919), 16-32; Ulrich Krüger, *Das Prinzip der Trennung von Staat und Kirche in Deutschland* (Berlin: VEB Deutscher Zentralverlag, 1958), 4-12; Claus Motschmann, *Evangelischer Kirche und preussischer Staat in den Anfängen der Weimarer Republik* (Lübeck: Matthiesen, 1969), 11, 33-37.

25. Daniel R. Borg, *The Old-Prussian Church and the Weimar Republic: A Study in Political Adjustment, 1917–1927* (Hanover, N.H.: Univ. Press of New England, 1984), 46-47.

26. In 1892 he had published a slashing attack on the church entitled *The Ten Commandments and the Owner Class*, which by 1922 had sold 190,000 copies, making it one of the most popular Socialist books of the time. Wolfgang Stribrny, "Evangelische Kirche und Staat in der Weimarer Republik," in *Zeitgeist im Wandel: Zeitgeist der Weimarer Republik*, ed. Hans Joachim Schoeps (Stuttgart: Ernst Klett, 1968), 163.

27. See the discussion in Borg, *Old-Prussian Church*, 58-66; Motschmann, *Evangelische Kirche*, 27-33; and Jochen Jacke, *Kirche zwischen Monarchie und Republik: Der preussische Protestantismus nach dem Zusammenbruch von 1918* (Hamburg: Christians, 1976), 44-47. The stance of the church during this troubled time is analyzed in Gottfried Mehnert, *Evangelische Kirche und Politik 1917–1919: Die politischen Strömungen des deutschen Protestantismus von der Julikrise 1917 bis zum Herbst 1919* (Düsseldorf: Droste, 1959).

28. A substantial body of literature validates this generalization, and most observers feel it was a prime factor in the alienation of the Protestant church from the urban working classes. The latest and most substantial treatment is Kurt Nowak, *Evangelische Kirche und Weimarer Republik: Zum politischen Weg des deutschen Protestantismus zwischen 1918 und 1932* (Göttingen: Vandenhoeck & Ruprecht, 1981). See also Karl-Wilhelm Dahm, *Pfarrer und Politik: Soziale Position und politische Mentalität des deutschen evangelischen Pfarrerstandes zwischen 1918 und 1933* (Cologne: Westdeutscher Verlag, 1965); J. R. C. Wright, *'Above Parties': The Political Attitudes of the German Protestant*

Church Leadership 1918–1933 (Oxford: Oxford Univ. Press, 1974); and Georg Hoffmann, "Das Nachwirken deutscher staatskirchlicher Tradition im evangelischen Kirchenbewusstsein nach 1918," in *Ecclesia und Res Publica,* ed. Georg Kretschmar and Bernhard Lohse (Göttingen: Vandenhoeck & Ruprecht, 1961), 125-41.

29. Mehnert, *Evangelische Kirche,* 180-82, 236-39.

30. Borg, *Old-Prussian Church,* 96; Nowak, *Evangelische Kirche,* 74. The tortuous negotiations over church-state matters in the Weimar Assembly are detailed in Borg, 83-97, and Jacke, *Kirche zwischen Monarchie und Republik,* 119-49.

31. Constitution of the German Reich (Weimar Constitution), 11 Aug. 1919. The German text is in *Die deutschen Verfassungen des 19. und 20. Jahrhunderts,* ed. Horst Hildebrand, 12th ed. (Paderborn: Ferdinand Schöningh, 1983), and the English in Heinrich Oppenheimer, *The Constitution of the German Republic* (London: Stevens and Sons, 1923).

32. For a discussion of this problem see Richard V. Pierard, "Why Did German Protestants Welcome Hitler?" *Fides et Historia* 10 (Spring 1978): 8-29.

33. German text, *Die deutschen Verfassungen des 19. und 20. Jahrhunderts;* ET, *The Bonn Constitution* (New York: Press and Information Office of the Federal Republic of Germany, n.d.).

34. For an indication of the directions in which the debate is going see Wilhelm Kewenig, "Das Grundgesetz und die staatliche Förderung der Religionsgemeinschaften," *Essener Gespräche zum Thema Staat und Kirche* 6 (1972): 9-53; Peter Rath, ed., *Trennung von Staat und Kirche? Dokumente und Argumente* (Hamburg: Rowohlt, 1974); Georg Denzler, ed., *Kirche und Staat auf Distanz: Historische und aktuelle Perspektiven* (Munich: Kösel-Verlag, 1977; and Paul Mikat, ed., *Kirche und Staat in der neueren Entwicklung* (Darmstadt: Wissenschaftliche Buchgesellschaft, 1980).

35. The texts of the 1949 and 1974 constitutions are in *Die Deutschen Verfassungen des 19. und 20. Jahrhunderts,* and the 1968 one in *The Constitution of the German Democratic Republic* (Berlin: Staatsverlag der DDR, 1968).

36. Works that provide some useful information about the activities of the church in East Germany include *Auf dem Wege zur gemeinsamen humanistischen Verantwortung: Eine Sammlung kirchenpolitischer Dokumente 1945 bis 1966* (Berlin: Union Verlag, 1967); *Christen und Kirchen: Eine Information aus der Deutschen Demokratischen Republik* (Berlin: Panorama DDR, 1983); and Albrecht Schönherr, *Zum Weg der evangelischen Kirchen in der DDR* (Berlin: Union Verlag, 1986).

The American and South African Constitutions: A Comparative Study

Johan D. van der Vyver

A nalogies are in the eyes of the beholder. Much depends on the basis of comparison the analyst has selected. A comparative investigation, however, is not entirely a matter of subjective predilection. The things to be compared should at least belong to a distinct category of analogous objects, and the yardstick of a comparative study ought to reflect the particular characteristics of the phenomena under consideration.

A superficial examination of the South African and American constitutions would reveal many conspicuous discrepancies:

- The South African Constitution emerged from a British-type (Westminster) system of government, while the American constitutional dispensation was established in reaction to, and with deliberate censure of, the traditional English notion of government.

- The South African Constitution is essentially a formalistic instrument that simply regulates the establishment, composition, and functions of the major agencies of government, whereas its American counterpart in addition to such structural provisions also embodies an elaborate Bill of Rights that brings the entire spectrum of substantive and procedural law within the confines of constitutional domain.

- The South African and the American constitutions both created a republican form of government, but the South African republic is constituted as a union with a particularly potent centralized administration, while the United States is made up of federal units with a multitude of decentralized power structures; the Republic of South Africa, echoing its British constitutional heritage, disavowed all pretenses of a separation of powers, while the central and regional governmental institutions of the United States to a large extent uphold the Montesquieuan model of political power constraint; the South African political system reflects the country's balance of power securely vested in the hands of a privileged white elite, while the American Constitution is firmly committed to the demands of a representative and egalitarian democracy.

•The South African Constitution is meticulously (though badly) worded in legal language reminiscent of British positivism, whereas the American Constitution is noted for its loose and sweeping phraseology and its propensity of law-creating interpretations in response to changing circumstances and adjustments in public opinion.

With these general aspects of the South African and American constitutions in mind, one could for purposes of comparison go into many more particular details, seeking, for instance, to uncover similarities and differences between the multiparty, tricameral composition of the South African Parliament as against the bicameral structure of the American legislatures, or the distinct legislative procedures, administrative arrangements, and court systems of the two jurisdictions concerned. Although many of these issues will arise in the context of this survey, they are not to be the focus of my analysis. I propose to confine my comparative outline to more general issues, using as the basis of comparison what I regard as the fundamental characteristics of the Republic of South Africa Constitution Act 110 of 1983. I thus intend to approach the subject with a definite South African bent. I do so on the assumption that the reader is familiar with the American constitutional system.

I premise my evaluation of the South African Constitution on the conviction that constitutions are not destined so much to grant political power as to *curtail* the exercise of state authority. Political systems should then be judged according to the objective of maintaining a fair balance between effective government and precautions against the abuse of power. To arrive at a reasonable assessment I would commend the pragmatic approach of a pessimist: simply imagine what might lawfully occur if your greatest political adversary or the most unscrupulous person or party imaginable were to be in command and entrusted with the powers authorized by the constitution in question.

With these directives in mind, I shall in this chapter (a) briefly outline the basic principles underlying the South African Constitution; (b) analyze some of the western democratic measures for the curtailment of political power and, in each instance, evaluate the performance of South Africa and the United States with regard to those measures; and (c) compare the general characteristics of the South African and American constitutional systems.

The Republic of South Africa Constitution Act 110 of 1983 was enacted with two objectives in mind: (1) To terminate in South Africa the (British orientated) Westminster system of government of parliamentary supremacy and to enact a system in which the powers of the executive would be supreme; and (2) to extend to Coloureds[1] and Indians political rights that had been monopolized by the White minority. The main elements of this constitutional arrangement can be summarized as follows:

1. Racialism. The Constitution is racially based in the sense that the participation of Whites, Coloureds, and Indians in the concerned procedures and institutions is conditional upon their racial classification in terms of the Population Registration Act 30 of 1950. Similarly, Africans, by virtue of their color, are excluded from the benefits of citizenship.

2. Dualism. The Constitution reflects an attempt to accommodate, on a racially defined basis, the dual premise of (a) self-determination of the participating population groups in matters supposedly affecting their respective interests only; and (b) joint responsibility of the participating population groups in matters of common interest.

The Constitution thus makes provision for three distinct and racially segregated Ministers' Councils—one for each participating population group—to administer matters of state concerning the "own affairs" of that population group.[2] A multiracial Cabinet is provided to administer departments of state for "general affairs" that affect the common interests of all the participating population groups.[3]

Parliament, the supreme legislative organ of the Republic, is similarly composed of three racially segregated Houses: the 178-member all-White House of Assembly, the 85-member Coloured House of Representatives, and the 45-member Indian House of Delegates. Legislation pertaining to "own affairs" is enacted by the House serving the population group whose "own affairs" are at stake. "General affairs" legislation must be approved, in separate sessions, by all three Houses of Parliament, and if the Houses should fail to agree, the state president may refer the bill for final settlement to the President's Council, which is a substitute legislative body comprised of twenty White members designated by the House of Assembly, ten Coloured members designated by the House of Representatives, five Indian members designated by the House of Delegates, and twenty-five state president nominees (ten of whom must come from the opposition parties in the three Houses of Parliament).[4]

In empirical reality, "own affairs" and "general affairs" do not

exist. Everyone within any particular jurisdiction is involved in and affected by all matters administered and regulated by state authority. Thus
these concepts cannot be defined with the measure of precision required
for effective law enforcement. In order to overcome this difficulty, the
legislature entrusted the state president with the power to label arbi-
trarily any matter as either "own affairs" or "general affairs." Provided
he has complied with an elementary prior procedure,[5] the state president's decision in this regard can under no circumstances whatsoever
be challenged in a court of law.[6]

3. An Executive Dictatorship. The 1983 Constitution created an
extremely powerful executive branch, prominently featuring the State
President. His power to designate matters as "own affairs" or "general
affairs," coupled with his entitlement to decide or overcome deadlock
situations, vested in him the power to manipulate legislation and the administration of affairs of state. Important in this regard is the fact that
the President's Council, the substitute legislature, is paced with state
president appointees. His powers are reminiscent of an executive dictatorship.

4. Pseudoconsociationalism. Proponents of the 1983 Constitution
claimed that the new arrangement would include the basic elements of
a consociational form of government. That is not at all the case. A consociational democracy is one in which segments of the population in a
divided society are proportionally represented in the legislative and executive organs of state authority, the emphasis is on consensus rather
than conflict, and each segment has the power of veto in important matters.[7] In matters designated by the state president as "general affairs,"
mechanisms are set in motion to achieve consensus; but consensus ap-
plies only insofar as all the participating segments agree. If they disagree, procedures can be set in motion to overrule the dissidents. It is
important to note that in the President's Council the representatives of
the (White) House of Assembly, together with the state president nominees, constitute a clear majority. The balance of power is thus safely
concentrated in the hands of the White component of government.

5. The Absence of Legitimacy. The 1983 Constitution was instituted without the necessary legitimacy. On November 2, 1983, the
White electorate of South Africa was given the opportunity to vote on
the issue of enacting the Constitution. An overwhelming majority of
65.9 percent voted Yes. It was decided at the time not to hold similar
referendums of Coloureds and Indians, but to give members of these
communities the opportunity to express their wishes in the forthcom-

ing elections. The only way in which Coloured and Indians could therefore express disagreement with the Constitution was to abstain from
voting in the elections. In August 1984 the elections were held for the
House of Representatives and the House of Delegates, garnering approximately 30 percent of the Coloured vote and 20 percent of the Indian vote. The turnout in the urban areas was substantially lower than
these averages—in some instances as low as 2 and 3 percent. Furthermore, a large percentage of the eligible electorate in those communities, in protest against the Constitution, declined to register as voters.

Taking into consideration the usual circumstances that contribute
to political apathy or to preventing voters from participating in elections, but bearing in mind that absenteeism constituted the only means
for Coloureds and Indians to record their rejection of the new constitutional dispensation, it is fair to conclude that the 1983 Constitution
lacked credibility. Because the new dispensation lacked legitimacy, the
inauguration of the Constitution on September 3, 1984, was attended
with unrest and violence from which South Africa has not yet re-
covered.

With the possession of political power comes the tendency to play
the tyrant. This truism has been eloquently paraphrased in many telling
aphorisms: "Power tends to corrupt, and absolute power corrupts absolutely," said Lord Acton;[8] or, in the words of Emil Brunner, "To possess
power is a constant temptation to abuse power."[9]

The corruptive tendency of political power has necessitated many
constitutional devices for the retrenchment of state authority. The
search for such devices has become a common recurring theme in
political science. Over the years many feasible strategies for counteracting the suppressive nature of political power have emerged:

1. Representative government in a democratic society is perhaps
the oldest method of power constraint known to western civilization. It
has its roots in early Greek culture and operates on the assumption that
a government that does not comply with the popular demands of the
people may be deprived of its governmental authority in periodic elections. It might be noted that whereas the political system of the United
States does conform to the *essentialia* of a representative democracy,
the South African structures of government can be described more ac-
curately as a racially based aristocracy. That is, in South Africa the right
to vote and to be represented in the legislative branch of government is
confined to a racially defined minority of Whites, Coloureds, and Indi-

ans, and the balance of power is concentrated in the hands of the White population group.

2. Separation of powers is perhaps the most neglected power constraint measure in western democracies. John Locke (1652–1704)[10] designed the first modern doctrine of *trias politica,* but Baron de Montesquieu (1689–1755) must be credited for refining these doctrines in certain passages of his *L'Esprit des Loix* (1948).[11] As currently interpreted, the notion of separation of powers embraces four basic principles: state authority is formally broken into the separate powers of legislation, administration, and adjudication; persons are not permitted to serve in more than one branch of government; the functions of government are delegated to separate institutions so that each institution is entrusted with only one category of responsibility and is not permitted to perform the functions of another subdivision of state authority; and the principle of checks and balances restrains the two other branches of government in the exercise of their powers.

Except for formally classifying the repositories of state authority into the legislative, executive, and judicial branches of government and upholding an independent judiciary, South Africa does not even remotely adhere to the doctrine of the separation of powers. For example, the state president is an integral part of the legislative organ of state authority[12] and also heads the executive;[13] members of the cabinet are required to be, or within a period of twelve months to become, Members of Parliament;[14] Parliament has been given the powers of a court of law for the purpose of conducting trial proceedings in cases of contempt of Parliament;[15] legislative functions are often delegated to members of the executive;[16] magistrates' courts and administrative tribunals constitute part of the executive branch of government, and so on.

The governmental structures of the United States, perhaps more so than those of any other western democracy, comply to a large extent with the contemporary principles of the separation of powers. The elaborate American system of checks and balances, however, has resulted in several violations of the ideal of a separation of functions. The presidental veto of congressional legislation, for instance, is essentially a legislative function being carried out by the head of the executive branch; the power of the Senate to impeach the president and members of the judiciary adds up to a judicial function being performed by a legislative organ; and the courts' power of substantive review, in conjunction with the sweeping language of the national and state constitutions, vests elaborate legislative powers in the judiciary branch.

3. Decentralization of state authority and the concomitant autonomy of local authorities probably emerged as a response of European communities to medieval federalism. Theoretical expositions of the concept of autonomous regional control are particularly evident in the writings of German-Lutheran political scientists of the nineteenth century. Georg Friedrich Puchta (1798–1846) professed that urban communities—which he called "corporations" and defined as "microcosmic states"—were entitled to a "degree of self-reliance in the administration of their internal affairs."[17] Georg Beseler (1809–1888) spoke of the *ius particulare* of a region, province, or town[18]—as opposed to the *ius commune* of the state—and maintained that such local rules of law derive from "the will capable of legal expression (autonomy) of a corporation which finds expression, in the same way as legislation, in a particular Act that constitutes a rule of law."[19] Beseler defined autonomy as "the power belonging to certain corporations to enact in their own discretion their own law (decrees, statutes, options) within the district governed by them or in any event in relation to their own affairs"[20] and proclaimed "that a corporation is entitled autonomously and according to their own discretion to regulate their internal affairs."[21]

The political entity currently constituting the Republic of South Africa was established in 1910 as a union and not a federation; the bulk of political powers were vested in the central and not the regional authorities. Over the years the South African Parliament has tended to centralize further the powers of legislation and administration by depriving the provinces of their jurisdiction in important matters[22] and over several regions within their borders.[23] In most instances, Parliament's actions were unconstitutional.[24] In 1986 provincial councils were altogether abolished.[25]

It is interesting to note, though, that the later dismantling of provincial jurisdictions coincided with the creation of a new type of regional autonomy with a racial foundation. The establishment of Bantustans, homelands or national states with various degrees of autonomy for the African population groups,[26] seems to indicate that South Africa is moving toward a federal political structure, but one founded on racial distinction. The United States in 1787 selected for itself a federal composition. Here, too, there has been a tendency to diminish the regional autonomy of the states. In America federalism as a means of

power constraint did not live up to expectations; the states rather than
the central administration and legislature have tended to abuse their
powers.

4. The doctrine of sphere sovereignty is the contribution of contemporary Calvinism toward the development of power constraint
strategies. The notion of sovereign spheres emerged from controversies
specifically regarding state-church relations but subsequently acquired
a much wider area of application. Eventually, it included the idea that
the state should confine its activities to a particular set of functions determined by its own typical leading function (the establishment and
maintenance of a public legal order within a particular territory)[27] and
ought not to interfere in the sovereign spheres of other (apolitical) social entities, such as a religious denomination, the family circle, a business enterprise, an educational institution, a cultural organization, a
sports club, and the like. Sphere sovereignty, in a word, cuts political
power down to size by requiring the state to mind its own business.

The idea was first mooted by the early legal philosopher John Al-
thusius (1557–1638), who maintained that every social entity is
governed by its own typical laws that are conditioned by the special
characteristics of the social entity concerned.[28] Puchta similarly proclaimed the church to be "self-reliant" as a "social institution alongside
the state"[29] and distinguished from the state "on account of the difference in nature thereof."[30] Groen van Prinsterer (1801–1876), pioneer
of Calvinistic political science in the Netherlands, coined the phrase
"sovereignty within its own sphere";[31] Abraham Kuyper (1837–1920)
popularized the idea in Dutch Calvinistic circles,[32] and Herman
Dooyeweerd (1894–1975) expanded the doctrine into an elaborate
sociological principle with substantial intellectual and practical appeal.[33]

Totalitarianism results when a government oversteps the confines
of its own sovereign sphere and encroaches upon the territories of
apolitical social institutions. A government that entertains a racially
based sports policy,[34] uses legal coercion to uphold the particular cultural heritage or racial identity of its subjects,[35] controls on nonaca-
demic grounds student admission to institutions of tertiary education,[36]
regulates on nonreligious grounds the attendance of church services,[37]
and lays down other than biotical-orientated requirements for valid
marriages[38] has clearly crossed the line of sphere sovereignty to em-
bark upon the road to totalitarianism. All such instances of excessive
juridical control, in the case of South Africa, were prompted by the ra-

cial problem; and, paradoxically, the current regime in Pretoria has seemingly abandoned its initial resolve to manipulate human relations through coercive social engineering. Most of these instances of totalitarianism have, in recent years, disappeared from the South African Statute book.[39]

Whereas South Africa overstepped the bounds of sphere sovereignty with a meddlesome legislature, the United States in particular state-church relations erred in the opposite direction. The "wall of separation between church and state" of which Thomas Jefferson (1743–1826) spoke[40] and which the U.S. Supreme Court, in the words of Justice Black, believed should be "kept high and impregnable"[41] resulted in, among other things, the courts' failure to perform their primary function as instruments to settle interindividual disputes. Whenever an interdenominational quarrel or a conflict of interests between a church and its members cannot be resolved without an inquiry into doctrinal issues, civil courts decline to exercise jurisdiction in the matter.[42] In *Serbian Orthodox Diocese vs. Milivojevich*[43] it was said in this regard, "religious controversies are not the proper subject of civil inquiry, and . . . a civil court must accept the ecclesiastical decision of church tribunals as it finds them."

It should be noted that the principle of sphere sovereignty requires the judicial branch of state authority to respect the jurisdiction and decisions of domestic tribunals of all nonpolitical social entities and never to interfere in purely internal disputes of such institutions, but whenever such disputes are of an interindividual adversary nature, state courts are charged with the responsibility of ensuring that the demands of natural justice (e.g., the rule of *audi alteram partem*) have been complied with. A court of law should thus never intervene to upset the decision of a church council regarding, for instance, ecclesiastical liturgy, but should feel free to review on the basis of the norms of natural justice decisions of a domestic church tribunal concerning, for instance, the contract of service of its pastor. In such cases the court of law should never substitute its own opinion for that of the domestic tribunal but should simply consider the matter in view of the most basic requirements of a fair trial. Property disputes following a religious schism would no longer be domestic in nature and would fall within the jurisdiction of state courts.

It is a fact of empirical reality that all social entities within a particular territorial region interact in numerous ways and cannot be isolated from one another. A church, for instance, also acts within the juridical sphere of the state when it buys, sells, or owns property, or through its organs vicariously commits a tort; and, similarly, the members of a government might also worship and pray. Furthermore, the same individual who as a member of a particular church is subject to the laws of that denomination would, as a citizen, also be subject to the national legal system of his particular country. The conflicts that might arise from this state of affairs are numerous and difficult to resolve. The truth is, though, that they never can be settled by unrealistically closing one's eyes to the interrelated nature of social life, or what Dooyeweerd called, in his own unique term, the encaptic intertwinement of societal institutions.[44] Sphere sovereignty requires that the state should not assume the function of a church; it does not imply that the state should decline to resolve a conflict simply because an ecclesiastical institution is a party in the dispute.

5. The rule of law is a notion introduced into political science by the English constitutional lawyer A. V. Dicey (1835–1922) and means in essence the "supremacy of law."[45] It constitutes another constraint worthy of discussion in the context of the present survey. The concept includes several principles,[46] and many more have been added by subsequent interpolations of Dicey's exposition of these principles.[47] The one particularly pertinent to the question of political power is that the rights and duties of the subordinates to state authority as well as the competencies and responsibilities of these powers ought to be circumscribed and executed by clearly defined rules of law. The opposite of the rule of law in this sense is arbitrary powers of the repositories of state authority.

In principle the legal system of the United States complies with this idea in that governmental powers, including those of the legislative and executive branches, must be exercised subject to the substantive and procedural provisions of the federal and state constitutions. The only criticism in this regard might be that those constitutions lack the measure of precision required by the Dicenian conception of the rule of law. We shall examine this aspect of the American Constitution later.

In South Africa, on the other hand, it is not uncommon for the legislature to confer arbitrary powers on members of the executive government. The ultimate in legally sanctioned licentiousness is found in the phenomenon of "detention for interrogation" in South Africa's security legislation. This variety of detention without trial, as regulated by Section 29 of the Internal Security Act 74 of 1982, permits indefinite solitary confinement of persons who are suspected by the police of having committed, or having intended to commit, terrorism, or who are thought to possess information relating to terrorism or subversion. The section expressly deprives courts of law of the jurisdiction "to pronounce upon the validity of any action taken in terms of this section, or to order the release of any person detained in terms of the provisions of this section."[48] In this way the legislature has given the security police almost unlimited powers to extract information from a detainee; and consequently the security police over the years[49] have established a dismal record of physical and mental intimidation and insolent brutality.[50] More than fifty people have thus far died while in detention under South Africa's security legislation: some in consequence of being manhandled (with *de facto* immunity) by the police (e.g., Steve Biko, who died in September 1977), some having been driven to suicide (e.g., Neil Aggett, who died in February 1982), and many others under extremely suspicious circumstances.

Nothing in the South African Constitution can prevent this kind of legislation. Prior to the 1983 Constitution the South African Parliament, in fact, regarded itself as above the law,[51] a view shared by many constitutional lawyers[52] and by the Cape Provincial Division of the Supreme Court.[53] Under the 1983 Constitution the Supreme Court's right of procedural review has clearly been established, but parliamentary legislation still cannot be tested in view of its substantive provisions.[54]

6. The institution of ombudsman is a particularly useful device for overseeing the exercise of executive powers. This Swedish invention requires a number of politically independent officials with the authority to scrutinize administrative conduct, including those acts of the executive that belong to the "darker reaches of government," in order to establish that the interests of the subordinates of state authority are duly considered, respected, and protected. The office of ombudsman has become a regular institution in American executive structures. At the last count six states have instituted an ombudsman, while six others have appointed such officials to monitor penal institutions. Woodrow Wilson once said, "Everyone knows that corruption thrives in secret places, and avoids public places, and we believe it a fair presumption that secrecy means impropriety."[55] Not only does South Africa not have an ombudsman in the true sense, but the confidentiality regarding governmental conduct is stretched to the extreme.[56] The Advocate General Act 118 of 1975, which purported to establish South Africa's own poor imitation of a public interest guardian, in fact created a framework for the government effectively to obscure all allegations of, in-

quiries into, and findings indicating executive misconduct.[57] Such legislation is so much more alarming since the present government is on record for maladministering public funds for its own party's political gain,[58] lying to Parliament about the misallocation,[59] and for refusing to take joint responsibility for such conduct and for the lie.

7. These preceding factors lead to a discussion of a constitutional bill of rights as a means of restricting governmental powers. The idea of protecting the fundamental freedoms of a defined enclave against administrative and legislative encroachment is clearly based on the doctrine of the natural rights of man. We can define a bill of rights as a statutory act primarily designed to protect the basic rights and fundamental freedoms of the individual by restricting the government's power to curtail those rights and freedoms. The American constitutional system includes statutory directives designed to bar governmental and legislative intervention in a fairly comprehensive list of individual rights and freedoms; and in 1803, in the well-known case of *Marbury vs. Madison,*[60] the United States Supreme Court endorsed the judiciary's authority to test and, if necessary, to invalidate legislative and executive acts inconsistent with the pertinent constitutional provisions.

The Bill of Rights of the U.S. Constitution is perhaps no longer the ideal model of a constitutional freedom charter. The sweeping language of the American Constitution—its failure to specify the exact content of the protected rights and freedoms, and its ill-defined limitations on and exceptions to those entitlements—might be seen as conferring on the judiciary too much law-creating power. It would thus violate the norm of *trias politica* embodied in the maxim *iudicis est ius dicere sed non dare.*[61] The one-sided emphasis upon the people's rights and freedoms without reference to their corresponding duties might support the construction of absolute entitlements; the rudimentary nature of the American inventory of fundamental rights, coupled with the notion of preferred freedoms,[62] might distort the equilibrium of all juridical rights in accordance with the notion of commutative justice as expressed in the norm *sic utere tuo et alienum non laedas* (the problem of reconciling freedom of speech and the individual's right to dignity *[dignitas]* and reputation *[fama]* seems to present difficulties in the United States); the individualistic disposition of the American Bill of Rights, reflected in its almost exclusive reference to rights and freedoms of the individual, admittedly has been conducive to the low-key treatment of group interests; the First Amendment was seemingly drafted to confine its application to public-law (state against citizen) relations ("Congress shall make no law . . .") and to exclude the horizontal operation of its provisions in private-law (citizen against citizen) relations. Nevertheless, congressional and state legislation also regulates the latter type of conflicts, making it impossible in the final analysis to avoid the *Drittwirkung* (tripartite functioning) of the Bill of Rights,[63] and so on.

A bill of rights is primarily destined to limit governmental powers and not to govern person-to-person relations. If the provisions of a freedom charter were extended to operate horizontally and acquire a tripartite application, it might become oppressive of the possession and enjoyment of certain basic civil rights.[64] These points of criticism do not intend to suggest that the American Bill of Rights is not suitable to the needs and circumstances of the United States. My concerns address the special demands of human rights protection within a South African setting; I explore them here with the goal of possibly incorporating into the South African Constitution an American-type bill of rights.

The South African Constitution does not contain an elaborate bill of rights. The provisions granting special protection to the "equal freedom, rights and privileges" of the two official languages, Afrikaans and English (with certain concessions pertaining to indigenous African languages)[65] are indeed comparable to a bill of rights,[66] but that is all. Other clauses in the Constitution[67] safeguard the racial foundation of the South African Constitutional system[68] as well as the far-reaching powers of the state president.[69] Those provisions can by no stretch of the imagination be likened to a bill of rights: a freedom charter does not sanctify constitutional racism or endeavor to perpetuate a particular constitutional system or persons in authority; rather, it protects the rights and freedoms of the subordinates of state authority.

South Africa's constitution-makers present many reasons why the country ought not to have a bill of rights:[70] the so-called humanist emphasis on individual rights over against the authority of the state is in conflict with the Calvinistic tradition of the Afrikaner people; a bill of rights is incompatible with the Westminster (British/South African) concept of parliamentary sovereignty; persistent international criticism, founded on human rights ideals, of South Africa's social, juridical, and political institutions has created in the minds of South Africans a negative view of this ideology; human rights are without substantive juridical content, have not been securely defined, and lack a fixed meaning; the testing right of law courts is conducive to politicizing of the judiciary; South African law, so they say, already adequately pro-

tects the basic rights and freedoms of the individual; constitutional
guarantees are only as effective as law enforcement agencies might
wish them to be; the one-sided emphasis on individual rights without
also specifying the duties of the citizen and the rights of the government *(sic!)* would disturb the legal order within the body politic, and so
on. These arguments range from unconvincing to being utter rubbish![71]
The fact is, though, that the current South African Constitution cannot
offer meaningful protection of basic human rights.

It has been generally accepted that any meaningful implementation of human rights ideals requires satisfaction of two basic juridical
principles: (1) the people's right to self-determination, which includes
the full and free participation of all adult citizens of a particular community in the legislative and administrative processes of that community; and (2) the principle of justice, which requires the equal treatment
of every individual within a particular political community by and
before the law, and which permits a classification of persons for purposes of the law, only where a definite reasonable foundation for the legally sanctioned differentiation can be demonstrated.

A constitution that excludes a section of the population from the
instruments of state authority and is structured upon racial discrimination would make a mockery of a freedom charter. Instead of a genuine
bill of rights, the South African Constitution of 1983 contains in its
preamble a Declaration of Intent.[72] A constitutional *credo* has two essential characteristics: it spells out national objectives that the government of the day promises to pursue, and it is not legally binding.[73]
Though not of the same fabric as an enforceable bill of rights, a constitutional Declaration of Intent could be of great value as a directive for
governmental action and legal reform, provided that certain conditions
are satisfied.

- The objectives enunciated in the Declaration of Intent should reflect the
  resolve of the present government, as well as that of possible future rulers
  of the country.

- The constitutional objectives should not be contradicted by the constitution in which they are contained.

- Those objectives must be reasonably achievable in the not-too-distant
  future.

- Inasmuch as the current constitution does not reach the objectives in
  question, a governmental plan of action to remedy the situation should
  be designed and implemented immediately.

The Declaration of Intent should thus transcend party-political differences. It ought to entail principles based on transsectional consensus.

The South African Declaration of Intent does not as a whole satisfy any of these demands. The aims enunciated therein did not ensue from negotiations between all interest groups within the country but reflect the desires of a small section of the population only; the promise to further and protect the self-determination of the population groups of South Africa was clearly inserted in the Declaration to depict and perpetuate the policy of separate development as defended by only the National Party and some of its political consorts; in view of the current regime's continued policies of racial discrimination, the stipulation to respect and protect the dignity, life, liberty, and property of all persons almost entirely lacks credibility.

Many prominent South Africans, including several academics[74] and members of the judiciary,[75] have advanced over the years convincing reasons why South Africa should select the option of a bill of rights for constraining governmental powers. In 1979 an opposition Member of Parliament introduced a private member's bill "to provide for the recognition and protection of freedom and democratic right,"[76] but his draft, modeled after the Canadian Bill of Rights of 1960,[77] was not pursued to its final conclusion. In 1977 the Republic of Bophuthatswana was established within the borders of the Republic of South Africa with a Bill of Rights (based on the European Convention of Human Rights) in its Constitution.[78] The South African Minister of Justice recently announced that the government has now recognized the urgent need for a bill of rights and that the matter has been referred to the Law Commission.[79]

South Africa, in all likelihood, will not imitate the American system of human rights protection. I would prefer a bill of rights formulated in precise and unambiguous terms, specifying with meticulous accuracy the conditions for and exceptions to the specified protections, and detailing exactly the procedures required for the amendment or repeal of its provisions. As far as enforcement mechanisms are concerned, there are interesting alternatives to the American censure of decisive and immediate unconstitutionality: in the Netherlands, for instance, the Bill of Rights constitutes a guide to be considered and applied by the legislature itself;[80] in France a constitutional court can be called upon to consider the constitutionality of legislation before, but not after, its promulgation;[81] the Canadian Constitution Act of 1982 authorizes the Canadian Parliament to retain legislation, by means of an express declaration, after the legislation in question was found by a court of law to be in conflict with the Canadian Charter of Rights and Freedoms;[82] the constitutional court of the Federal Republic of Germany developed an exciting procedure whereby the legislature is often given a fixed time within which to remedy any human rights shortcomings in existing law,[83] and so on.

8. For the purposes of this survey, we must carefully scrutinize one further method of political constraint: parliamentary sovereignty. It seems ironic to suppose that the power of persons in authority can be restrained effectively by vesting supreme powers in Parliament, but that is the British method. In actuality, the Westminster formula to restrict excesses in governmental power is not only to vest power in the legislature but also to uphold certain conventions with a solid historical foundation, which admittedly are not legally enforceable but ought to be maintained as a matter of honor and respectability.[84]

The British notion of parliamentary sovereignty evolved over several centuries, but clearly culminated in the seventeenth-century conflict between the British legislature and the dynasty of Stuart kings.[85] Parliament emerged from this dispute as a champion of the interests and aspirations of the people, acting as their mediator in the struggle for liberty and fair play. Following the Glorious Revolution of 1688, in which James II was dethroned, the Bill of Rights was enacted in 1689 to outlaw the type of arbitrary executive actions for which the Stuart dynasty had become notorious and to endorse power in the legislature to control the executive branch of state authority.

It is important to note that these successes of Parliament also marked the victory of *the people* over administrative immoderation. In order to protect and promote the people's fundamental rights and freedoms, Parliament had to possess supreme authority. Provided that the principles of representative democracy are present, parliamentary sovereignty in its proper historical context should be seen as the Bill of Rights of the Westminster system of government.

While the British Parliament has, in general, quite admirably discharged its functions as the patron of egalitarian and libertarian principles in relation to the subjects it represents, it has not been so successful in matters affecting the British colonies. In these situations, Parliament had a reputation for indiscriminately enacting a series of "transportation laws" that could be used to enlarge the White labor force in the colonies, for imposing taxes without representation, and, on the whole, for establishing the legal framework facilitating the exploitation of colonial resources to enrich the motherland. The Januslike behavior of the British Parliament in their colonial experience prompted the Founding Fathers of the United States not to entrust the protection of human rights to a sovereign legislature. Within a federalist framework, they opted for alternative political control mechanisms: separation of powers, a system of checks and balances, and a Bill of Rights *regime*.

When the Union of South Africa was established in 1910, the constitutional structure of the new state was modeled on the British system and included the principle of a sovereign legislature.[86] The South African Parliament, however, lacked the legacy of the British liberal tradition and, with political power overwhelmingly concentrated in the hands of a White minority, it fell short of the basic principle of representative democracy.[87] Lacking a truly democratic design, the sovereign South African Parliament was soon disfigured by favoritism, partiality, and sectional bias, emanating from the distinct interests of its privileged White constituency.

While avoiding the morbid details of South Africa's unjust legislation, I should mention, however, that the most detrimental manifestation of distorted legislative power is the institutionalization of racial discrimination. Looking beyond the semantics of textbook law to the vulgar facts of this statutory law, one is greeted with the strange, almost incredible world of legal acquiescence to social misery and human suffering. Parliament not only used its supremacy to suppress persons of color, it also set itself above its own Constitution.[88] Instead of restraining the powers of government, in many instances it entrusted the executive with sweeping legislative powers,[89] arbitrary administrative entitlements,[90] and extensive jurisdiction to adjudicate civil and criminal matters.[91] Furthermore, on many occasions Parliament condoned unlawful conduct of the executive,[92] opened the way for ever-increasing clandestine operations of the bureaucracy,[93] and permitted itself to become a forum for the lies[94] and cheating[95] of the government.

The saga of constitutional impropriety in South Africa under the Westminster system of government would be incomplete without mentioning the constitutional scandal of the 1950s, which centered upon the disfranchisement of the Cape Coloureds. The scandal originated when the Separate Representation of Voters Act 46 of 1951 was taken through its various stages in Parliament without compliance with the special procedures prescribed in the Constitution for such legislation.[96] The

Appellate Division of the Supreme Court consequently declared the Act null and void.[97] Parliament reacted by passing legislation to exclude the review powers of the Supreme Court and converted itself into a constitutional court to test the validity of its own legislation.[98] When this legislation was also declared invalid by the Appellate Division,[99] the government loaded the Senate[100] to create the two-thirds majority required by the Constitution to pass the Act. Thus, in a "constitutional" manner Parliament deprived the Coloureds of their voting rights.[101] A sovereign Parliament deprived of the moral constraints embedded in British constitutional history (and finding expression in a sense of honor and conventional propriety) turned out in practice to radiate the ambivalent caricature of a law-maker that frequently excelled in its own infamous lawlessness.

The South African constitutional system, as a product of the Westminster tradition, differs fundamentally from the American constitutional system in certain key elements. The first concerns the question of political sovereignty: Where or in whom is political supremacy concentrated? In Great Britain, as we already know, sovereignty in the sense of supreme political powers is an attribute of the legislature. Prior to the introduction of the Republic of South Africa Constitution Act 110 of 1983, that was, at least in theory, also the case in South Africa. The 1983 Constitution officially exchanged parliamentary sovereignty for a system of executive supremacy. As we have seen, however, the South African Parliament clearly had already sacrificed much power to the executive. So, in a sense, the 1983 Constitution merely brought the *de jure* situation into conformity with the *de facto* state of affairs. In fact, the new Constitution actually went further, vesting wide-ranging executive and legislative control in one person, the state president, thereby paving the way for an executive dictatorship.

Most American constitutional lawyers maintain that in the United States sovereignty rests with the people and the Constitution is supreme over any particular branch of state authority. That, in my opinion, is mere theory. Considering the courts' wide-ranging powers to invalidate legislation and administrative acts, and taking into account the arbitrary criteria for the execution of those powers inherent in the sweeping language of the federal and states' constitutions, I find inevitable the conclusion that the judiciary in fact possesses the balance of power in the United States.

The second matter to be considered is the question of flexibility of the United States and South African constitutions. The United Kingdom is said to have a flexible constitution; that is, the constitutional law can be amended by means of ordinary legislative procedures. The U.S. Constitution, on the other hand, is relatively inflexible in the sense that it is amendable only after a difficult and cumbersome process. But, again, in practice the opposite is true. The almost unbridled power of the U.S. Supreme Court to reinterpret the general provisions of the American Bill of Rights so as to accommodate the court's evaluation of public opinion and changing circumstances renders the U.S. Constitution extremely flexible, while British traditionalism virtually excludes instantaneous adjustments, even through legislation, of constitutional practices. Since British traditions never carried much weight in South Africa, the South African Constitution, except for a few entrenched clauses, had always been in theory and in practice quite flexible. The 1983 Constitution, however, introduced a new inflexibility into the law of governmental structures.

We have already established that the legislature in 1983 introduced a set of provisions designed to uphold the newly designed constitutional system.[102] The 1983 Constitution also made special provision to safeguard the continuation of the system in case, for instance, any of the three participating population groups (the Whites, the Coloureds, and the Indians) should "walk out on the system." A "failsafe" clause provides that, if any one or two of the Houses of Parliament should be unable to perform its functions, the remaining House(s) would constitute Parliament.[103] However, in order to amend or repeal any of the existing clauses in the Constitution, the legislature had contemplated the consensus of all three Houses of Parliament.[104] It is possible that if the structures of government should start to crumble because of its inherent weaknesses, the "failsafe" provision might prove to be a convenient means of perpetuating the system but would at the same time leave the legislature in need of mechanisms for constitutional reform. Circumstances might, in a word, arise in which Parliament is left without the apparatus to remedy the weak spots that caused a breakdown in the system.

Finally, a comparison of the comprehensiveness of legal provisions for the protection of human rights would be instructive. The primary concern here is with a natural-law versus a positivistic approach to the question of the source of a person's legal rights and competencies: Does a legal subject derive his rights and freedoms from a source other than positive law (e.g., nature, the nature of man, God, reason, etc.), or does he possess only those rights and freedoms allotted to him by the law? In this respect, theory and practice of the two systems again point in two opposite directions.

South African law, which proclaims "a kind of residual freedom, everything being permitted which is not expressly forbidden,"[105] clearly upholds the natural-law approach. In *Stoffberg vs. Elliott*[106] this principle was vividly stated: "In the eyes of the law, every person has certain absolute rights which the law protects. They are not dependent upon a statute or a contract, but they are rights to be respected, and one of those rights is the right to absolute security of the person." In *Nestor & others vs. Minister of Police & others*,[107] for instance, the Supreme Court of South West Africa/Namibia, applying this approach, decided that a prisoner was entitled to all reasonable privileges (i.e., in that case, a cell of reasonable size, hygienic conditions, no solitary confinement, the opportunity to work, and the right to exercise in the open air) and not only those expressly mentioned in the security proclamation under which the plaintiffs were being detained.[108]

Natural-law proponents, however, would concede that the individual's "natural rights and freedoms" can be constrained by law. The legislature cannot do so indiscriminately, but the limitations have never been clearly demarcated. The fact is, though, that the South African legislature has over the years abundantly restrained its subordinates in the exercise of their natural and civil rights, and furthermore has done so on a racially discriminatory basis.

In the first century of United States constitutional history the American courts clearly reflected a philosophy of natural law; a commitment to libertarian ideals was not without practical legal significance. Prior to the enactment in 1868 of the Fourteenth Amendment, the protection of human rights against the legislatures and executive governments of the different states lacked express constitutional backing, but the U.S. Supreme Court, relying heavily on the then current ideas of natural law, notably those pertaining to the unassailability of vested rights,[109] nevertheless subjected the states to many of the same restraints established by the Bill of Rights that applied to the federal executive and legislature. For instance, in *Van Horne's Lessee vs. Dorrance*[110] Justice Patterson described "the right of acquiring and possessing property and having it protected" as "one of the natural, inherent and inalienable rights of man." In *Wilkinson vs. Leland*[111] Justice Story, who was commonly regarded as the champion of vested rights, said: "The fundamental maxims of free government seem to require that the rights of personal liberty and private property should be held sacred"; and in an earlier judgment he referred to vested rights as "consonant with the common sense of mankind and the maxims of eternal justice."[112] In *Savings and Loan Association vs. Topeka*[113] Justice Miller singled out the right to life, liberty, and property as being "rights in every government beyond the control of the State."

Following the enactment of the Fourteenth Amendment, and under the influence of nineteenth-century positivism, there was a marked decline in the tendency of American courts to base the sanctity of human rights upon the liberal decrees of natural law. Toward the end of the century, Judge President Lucas of West Virginia aptly summarized the development in constitutional-law thought when he said:

> A further principle, at one time held in some doubt, but now, we think, finally decided, is that the judiciary cannot annul or pronounce void any act of the legislature upon any other ground than that of repugnancy to the constitution. It was at one time supposed that the judiciary could resort to the principles of natural justice or common right, and pronounce a legislative act void because in conflict with such supposed principles. This view, however, I think we may regard as finally abandoned.[114]

These sentiments are well supported by prominent American advocates of legal positivism.[115] Most commentators nevertheless conceded that certain earlier judgments of the U.S. Supreme Court had been inspired by natural-law ideas,[116] although the commentaries with a positivistic bias tended to disparage the actual influence of those ideas.[117]

In spite of their eventual positivistic orientation, American courts have had no difficulty in applying the current notions of human rights to the constitutions of the United States. This, again, was made possible by the vague and undefined language of the bills of rights embodied in those constitutions.

Thus, what from a strictly legalistic point of view might be seen as weaknesses of the American constitutional system—sweeping provisions, judicial activism, and extensive law-creating adjudication—were put to good use to convert the jurisprudence of the United States into an excellent and commendable model of human rights protection.

NOTES

1. In the South African context the word *Coloured* is most commonly used to denote all South Africans who are not classified as either Whites, African, or Asians. Included in the Coloured community are descendants of the early Hottentots who lived in the Cape at the time of the first White settlement in the territory (in 1652), those of Malayan slaves imported into the Cape Colony in the seventeenth and eighteenth centuries, and persons of mixed White-Black extraction.

2. In each Ministers' Council provision is currently made for departments of health services and welfare; local government, housing, and agriculture; education and culture; and the budget.

3. State President P. W. Botha included in his first Cabinet under the new Constitution one Coloured minister, Dr. Alan Hendrikse, and one Indian minister, Mr. Amichand Rajbansi; both are ministers without portfolio.

4. The President's Council cannot easily amend the bill but must endorse a version of it that has been approved by at least one House.

5. In terms of Sec. 17(2) the state president must consult the Speaker of Parliament and the chairpersons of each House of Parliament, and since the question whether or not a matter is an "own affair" is itself a "general affair" (Sec. 16[1][b]), he must act "in consultation with the Ministers who are members of the Cabinet" (Sec. 19[1][b]). The first of these two formalities is subject to judicial review, but the second is not (Sec. 34[2][a] read with Sec. 18[1]). The state president is in any event not in any way bound by the opinions of the persons consulted.

6. Sec. 18(2).

7. Arend Lijphart, *Democracy in Plural Societies: A Comparative Exploration* (Cambridge, Mass.: Yale Univ. Press, 1977), 25-52, distinguished four basic elements of the consociational model: (1) Governmental functions are to be exercised in a "grand coalition" by the leaders of all the major segments in a plural society; (2) decisions would require the consent of a defined percentage of the participating political segments (it could be a simple majority), coupled with a mutual right of veto as an additional safeguard against the concentration of power and the domination of one segment over the others; (3) representation in the political and civil institutions of the state, and the distribution of state revenues, should be based on the principle of proportionality; and (4) every segment ought to be afforded a high degree of autonomy in its own internal affairs. See also T. Hanf, H. Weiland, and G. Vierdag, *South Africa: The Prospects of Peaceful Change* (1981), 383-86; L. J. Boulle, *South Africa and the Consociational Option: A Constitutional Analysis* (1984), 46-51.

8. J. E. E. Dalton-Acton, *Essays on Freedom and Power,* ed. G. Himmelfarb (Boston, Mass., 1949), 364.

9. Emil Brunner, *Justice and the Social Order,* trans. M. Hottinger (London, 1945), 188.

10. Locke in his *Two Treatises of Civil Government* (1690): 2.12., 143ff. distinguished between the legislative, executive, and the federative functions of government. He included the judiciary under the executive branch of government and confined the federative functions to what today we might call "foreign affairs."

11. Chap. 11.6, entitled "De la Constitution d'Angleterre."

12. Sec. 24(1) of the Republic of South Africa Constitution Act 110 of 1983.

13. Ibid., Sec. 16(1).

14. Ibid., Sec. 20(3).

15. Sec. 4 of the Powers and Privileges of Parliament Act 91 of 1963.

16. E.g., in terms of Sec. 25 of the Black Administration Act 38 of 1927 the state president has been entrusted with comprehensive powers to enact, to amend, or to repeal statutory provisions applying to Africans only; in terms of Sec. 38 of the South West Africa Constitution Act 39 of 1968 the state president has similar legislative powers in respect to Namibia, to be exercised "with a view to the eventual acquisition of independence by the said territory, the administration of Walfish Bay and the regulation of any other matter." In both instances the state president is required to consult beforehand the ministers who are members of the Cabinet (cf. Sec. 19[1][b] of the Republic of South Africa Constitution Act 110 of 1983).

17. *Cursus der Institutionen* (1841) 6e neu vermehrte Auflage . . . besorgt von Dr. A. E. Rudorff (Leipzig 1865), 1.1.14 (pp. 30-31). ("Grad von Selbstständigkeit in der Verwaltung ihren inneren Angelegenheiten.")

18. System des gemeinen deutschen Privatrechts (4e vermehrte und verbesserte Auflage) (Berlin, 1885), 1.1.1.1 (p. 4).

19. Ibid., 1.2.1.17 (p. 49). (". . . in dem zur Rechtserzeugung befugten Willen [der Autonomie] einer Corporation, welche sich ähnlich, wie die Gesetzgebung es thut, in einem bstimmten, die Rechtsregel constituirenden Act offenbar.")

20. Ibid., 1.2.1.1. B 26 (pp. 76-77). (". . . die gewissen Corporationen zustehende Befugnisz, sich innerhalb des von ihnen beherrschten Kreises oder doch für ihre besonderen Angelegenheiten nach freiem Ermessen ihr eigenes Recht [Willkühren, Statute, Beliebungen] zu setzen.")

21. Ibid., 1.2.1.1. B 27 (p. 79). (". . . dasz die Corporation befugt ist, ihre inneren Angelegenheiten nach freiem Ermessen autonomisch zu ordnen.")

22. In terms of the Black Education Act 47 of 1953 the jurisdiction of the provinces with regard to African education was terminated.

23. The so-called independent republics of Transkei, Bophuthatswana, Venda, and Ciskei were carved from the various provincial territories. See the Status of Transkei Act 100 of 1976; the Status of Bophuthatswana Act 89 of 1977; the Status of Venda Act 107 of 1979, and the Status of Ciskei Act 110 of 1981. In terms of the Alteration of Provincial Boundaries Act 36 of 1978, Griqualand East, formerly part of the Cape Province, was incorporated into Natal. The Bophuthatswana Border Extension Act 8 of 1978 enlarged the territories of Bophuthatswana at the expense of the Cape Province and Transvaal. The Borders of Particular States Extension Act 2 of 1980 entrusted the state president with the competence to shift provincial borders so as to consolidate the territories of the "independent" national states.

24. See J. D. van der Vyver, "The Section 114 Controversy—and Governmental Anarchy," *The South African Law Journal* 97 (1980): 363, and "Depriving Westminster of its Moral Constraints: A Survey of Constitutional Development in South Africa," *Harvard Civil Rights Civil Liberties Law Review,* vol. 20, no. 2 (1985): 308-11; and see also the *obiter dictum* of J. van den Heever in *Cowburn vs. Nasopie (Edms) Bpk & andere* 1980 (2) SA 547 (NC), 554; and cf., contra, *Mpangela vs. Botha* (2) 1982 (3) SA 638 (C). Sec. 149 of the South Africa Act, 1909 (9 Edw VII c 9—this is an Act of the British Parliament) guaranteed the territorial integrity of the provinces and was subsequently amended by Sec. 1 of the South Africa Act Amendment Act 45 of 1934 also to guarantee the powers of the provincial councils. The guarantee consisted of a special procedure to be followed if Parliament should wish to change the boundaries of a province or amend or abolish any of the powers of a provincial council. This provision, as amended in 1934, was subsequently embodied in Sec. 114 of the Republic of South Africa Constitution Act 32 of 1961. With the enactment of none of the Acts referred to in notes 22 and 23 was this procedural provision (involving Parliament to be petitioned by the provincial council concerned) complied with. Sec. 7 of the Republic of South Africa Constitution Sec-

ond Amendment Act 101 of 1981 amended with retroactive effect Sec. 114 of the 1961 Constitution so as to *ex post facto* legalize the statutes of an earlier date mentioned in note 23 above and to pave the way for the enactment of those of a later date mentioned in the same footnote. In terms of Sec. 8 of Schedule 2 Part 1 of the Republic of South Africa Constitution Act 110 of 1983 the special protection afforded to the powers and territorial integrity of the provinces was altogether abolished.

25. A multiracial, appointed administrative body (without legislative powers) has been instituted in its stead in each one of the four provinces.

26. The national states developed through three pre-"independence" constitutional stages: In the first stage an administrative regional authority was established in terms of the Black Authorities Act 68 of 1951; in the second stage the national state was afforded responsible government and a legislative assembly (with limited legislative powers) in terms of Chap. 1 of the National States Constitution Act 21 of 1971; and in the final stage the national state acquired self-government in terms of Sec. 26 of the National States Constitution Act 21 of 1971. See F. Venter, *Die Suid-Afrikaanse Bantoestaatsreg* (LL.D. thesis, Potchefstroom, 1978), 483ff. If the national state so requests, it can then become "fully independent." Besides the four "independent" national states (Transkei, Bophuthatswana, Venda, and Ciskei), all the others (Gazankulu, KaNgwane, KwaNdebele, Kwazulu, Lebowa, and Qua-Qua) have reached the third stage of development. KwaNdebele was scheduled to become "independent" in December 1986 but has recently again decided against it. "Independence" brings about the greatest possible measure of regional autonomy but carries with it the disadvantages attending nonrecognition by the international community of states and of the nationals of such Black states being deprived of their South African citizenship.

27. H. Dooyeweerd, *A New Critique of Theoretical Thought* (Philadelphia: Presbyterian and Reformed, 1969), 3:414, defined the leading function of the body politic as "an internal monopolistic organization of the power of the sword over a particular cultural area within territorial boundaries."

28. *Politica Methodiae Digesta* (3e Aufl) Herborn 1614, [cap 1. 19] (p. 7): "Propriae leges sunt cujusque consociationis peculiares, quibus illa regitur. Atque hae in singulis speciebus consociationis aliae atque diversae sunt, prout natura cujusque postulat."

29. *Cursus der Institutionen,* 1.1.14 (p. 31).

30. Ibid., 1.2.25 (p. 65).

31. *Ter Nagedachtenis van Stahl* (Amsterdam, 1862), 30-31.

32. Once having grasped the notion of sphere sovereignty, Kuyper became so obsessed with the idea that he proclaimed all and sundry to be "circles" that vis-à-vis state authority could lay claim to sovereign powers. In *Ons Program* (Amsterdam: J. H. Kruyt, 1879), 30, for instance, he singled out as components of society that "do not derive their impulse from the State," the family, church, local population (of a town or city), trade, industry, science, art, and so on. Not all of these institutions are of course social entities within the meaning of the doctrine of sphere sovereignty. See also *Lectures on Calvinism* (Grand Rapids: Wm. B. Eerdmans, 1953), 90, where he speaks of "the family, the business, science, art and so forth" as being "social spheres, which do not owe their existence to the state, and which do not derive the law of their life from the superiority of the state, but obey a high authority within their bosom." His lack of academic precision in the identification of "social spheres" led J. D. Dengerink to conclude that Kuyper's conception of sphere sovereignty was "no more than a mighty, intuitive stroke." *Critisch-Historisch Onderzoek naar de Sociologische Ontwikkeling der Beginsel der "Souvereiniteit in Eigen Kring"* (Kampen, 1948), 112.

33. See, e.g., *A New Critique of Theoretical Thought,* 3:169-70; *De Strijd om het Souvereiniteitsbegrip in de Moderne Rechts-en Staatsleer* (Amsterdam, 1950), 51;

Verkenningen in de Wijsbegeerte, de Sociologie en de Rechtsgeschiedenis (Amsterdam, 1962), 80. Basic to his notion of sphere sovereignty is the conviction "that a matrimonial community, a State, a Church, etc. have a constant inner nature, determined by their internal structural principle" and "that the inner nature of these types of societal relationships cannot be dependent on variable historical conditions of human society." *A New Critique of Theoretical Thought*, 3:170.

34. Dr. H. F. Verwoerd (1901–1966), prime minister of South Africa in the period 1958–1966, in September 1965 announced the government's sports policy in which racially mixed teams would not be allowed to compete in the Republic against White teams. In 1968 Prime Minister John Vorster (1915–1983) announced that he would refuse entry into the country of a British cricket team if a certain Basil d'Oliviera, a Coloured man who was born and raised in South Africa and subsequently settled in England, were to be included in the side. The British team thereupon canceled its tour to South Africa. The sports policy was therefore amended to allow foreign teams to include whoever they wish in their own teams. Racial integration in sports within South Africa commenced in 1971 and today there are no longer any legal or policy restrictions on the selection of teams or participation in sports on racial grounds.

35. The government's misplaced sense of responsibility in this regard has in the past been an important impetus of apartheid legislation.

36. The Extension of University Education Act 45 of 1959. The provision in the act that authorized state control of student admissions on racial grounds (Sec. 32) was repealed by the Universities Amendment Act 83 of 1983.

37. Sec. 9(7) of the Black (Urban Areas) Consolidation Act 25 of 1945. This clause was to the best of my knowledge never actually implemented, and has now been abolished. Abolition of Influx Control Act 68 of 1986.

38. The Prohibition of Mixed Marriages Act 55 of 1949. This act was repealed by the Immorality and Prohibition of Mixed Marriages Amendment Act 72 of 1985.

39. See notes 34, 36, and 38 above.

40. A. P. Stokes, *Church and State in the United States* (New York: Harper & Row, 1950), 335.

41. *Everson vs. Board of Education* 330 US 1 (1947), 18.

42. *Watson vs. Jones* 13 Wall 679 (1871); *Kedrof vs. St. Nicholas Cathedral* 344 US 94 (1952); *Presbyterian Church vs. Hull Church* 393 US 440 (1969); *Md. & Va. Churches vs. Sharpsburg Church* 396 US 367 (1970); *Serbian Orthodox Diocese vs. Milivojevic* 426 US 696 (1972).

43. Supra note 42, p. 713.

44. Dooyeweerd defined "encapsis" as "an intertwinement of intrinsically different structures." *Verkenningen in de Wijsbegeerte, de Sociologie en de Rechtsgeschiedenis*, 102-3.

45. A. V. Dicey, *Introduction to the Study of the Law of the Constitution* (1885; 10th ed., London, 1959), 184.

46. Dicey (ibid., 188-203) subdivided the rule of law into three basic norms: (1) transgressions of the law are to be established in accordance with the law in the ordinary legal manner and before the regular courts, and persons in authority are therefore not to be entrusted with arbitrary, prerogative, or discretionary powers; (2) no person is above the law and every subject is therefore entitled to equal treatment before the law; and (3) constitutional rights of the subjects are to be determined in the ordinary course of justice and no special significance is to be attached to constitutional law.

47. For an overview of some of those interpretations, see J. D. van der Vyver, *Seven Lectures on Human Rights* (Cape Town/Wynberg/Johannesburg: Juta & Co., 1976), 108-17.

48. Sec. 29(6).

49. Sec. 29 of the Internal Security Act of 1982 was preceded by a similar provision contained in Sec. 6 of the Terrorism Act 83 of 1967.

50. A fair summary of current methods of interrogation has been listed by John Dugard, *Report on the Rabie Report: An Examination of Security Legislation in South Africa* (Center for Applied Legal Studies, University of the Witwatersrand, Johannesburg, March 1982), 26-32. It includes physical assault, psychological coercion, degrading and humiliating treatment, standing for long periods of time, long and persistent interrogation, deprivation of food and sleep, subjection to noise, and solitary confinement. The Directions Regarding the Detention of Persons in Terms of Sec. 29(1) of the Internal Security Act 1982 (GN 877 of 1982 in *Government Gazette* 8467 of 3 Dec. 1982) have proved to be hopelessly inadequate to restrain misconduct of the police when interrogating a detainee.

51. See, e.g., note 24 above.

52. E.g., H. J. May, *The South African Constitution*, 3d ed. (1985), 385; E. Kahn, "Republic Outside the Commonwealth" 1961 *Annual Survey of South African Law*, 10-11 and 1962 *Annual Survey of South African Law*, 12-14; C. W. H. Schmidt, "Section 114 of the Constitution and Sovereignty of Parliament," *The South African Law Journal* 79 (1962): 319-21; R. E. Goldblatt, "Constitutional Law" in W. A. Joubert, ed., *The Law of South Africa* V (1978) para. 6 n.2; L. J. Boulle, "The Second Republic: Its Constitutional Lineage," *Comparative and International Law Journal of South Africa* 13 (1980): 3, n.26.

53. *Mpangela vs. Botha* (2) (supra, note 24).

54. See J. D. van der Vyver, "Judicial Review under the New Constitution," *The South African Law Journal* 103 (1986): 238-39.

55. *The New Freedom: A Call for the Emancipation of the Generous Energies of a People* (1913), 112.

56. Freedom of the news media to publish reports on official administrative conduct has been unduly restricted in the case of, e.g., the Defence Force (see, e.g., Sec. 118 of the Defence Act 44 of 1957), police activity (Sec. 27B of the Police Act 7 of 1958, and see also Sec. 45[8] of the South African Transport Services Act 65 of 1981 in relation to the South African Railway Police), the administration of prisons (Sec. 44[1][f] of the Prisons Act 8 of 1959), and mental health institutions (Sec. 66A[b] of the Mental Health Act 88 of 1977). The Protection of Information Act 84 of 1982 substantially expanded the range of classified information in public administration by basing culpability for disclosure of information on undefined generalities, such as "prejudicial to the security or interests of the Republic," and also by conferring on the executive unlimited authority to specify localities that would qualify as a "prohibited place" for purposes of coerced confidentiality, and to identify foreign institutions as being "a hostile organization" to which communications of certain information would be an offense. Sec. 66 of the Internal Security Act 74 of 1982 also entrusted the executive with arbitrary powers to defeat the ends of justice under the guise of "state security" withholding evidence in court proceedings.

57. The advocate general can be called upon to investigate allegations of the maladministration of state funds only. An investigation by the advocate general would render the matter *sub judice,* and it is within the discretion of the state president to publish or not to publish his findings and report.

58. The "information scandal" of the 1970s—South Africa's own Watergate—centered upon the clandestine spending of large sums of tax money by quite improper means to promote South Africa's international image, and included the financing of an English language newspaper, *The Citizen,* to propagate National Party policies.

59. Dr. Connie Mulder, the minister of information, denied in Parliament that public funds were being used for the financing of a newspaper. *House of Assembly Debates,*

10 May 1978, col. 6612; and see also the *Supplementary Report of the Commission of Inquiry into Alleged Irregularities in the Former Department of Information* (RP 63/1979), para. 3, 52-55.

60. I Cranch 137.

61. My own reservations in this regard are more fully substantiated in "Rigidity and Flexibility in Constitutions: The Judiciary, the Rule of Law and Constitutional Amendment" in A. Benyon, ed., *Constitutional Change in South Africa* (Pietermaritzburg: Univ. of Natal, 1978), 52, 59-63.

62. This doctrine originated in a footnote remark of J. Stone in *United States vs. Carolene Products Co.* 304 US 114 (1938) and claims that the presumption of legality of legislation can more readily be rebutted when such legislation restricts First Amendment freedoms (freedom of speech, the press, religion, and assembly) than would be the case when economically qualified rights are at stake.

63. E.g., in *Martin vs. City of Struthers* 319 US 141 (1943) the right to privacy of the individual was sacrificed for the sake of the "religious freedom" of Jehovah's Witnesses to knock on doors and ring doorbells for the purpose of handing out handbills and literature; in *New York Times Co. vs. Sullivan* 376 US 254 (1964) the right of public officials to their reputation had to give way to freedom of the press by confining the capacity of such officials to claim compensation for libel to cases where it could be shown that a false statement was published with knowledge that it was false or with reckless disregard for its inaccuracy; in *Regents of the University of California vs. Bakke* 438 US 265 (1978) the court, with a view to the equal protection provision of the Fourteenth Amendment, scrutinized and overruled the student admission policy of a university, and so on.

64. The examples in note 63 illustrate the undermining in person-to-person relations of, respectively, the right to privacy, the personal right to reputation, and contractual freedom.

65. Sec. 89. In terms of Sec. 99(2) the constitutional provisions regulating the language rights can be amended or repealed only by a two-thirds majority in each one of the three Houses of Parliament (the White House of Assembly, the Coloured House of Representatives, and the Indian House of Delegates).

66. It is interesting to note that this single bill of rights provision affords entrenched protection to group interests and not to individual rights.

67. Those provisions require for their amendment or repeal a simple majority in each and every House of Parliament (see note 65 above) (Sec. 99[3]).

68. As reflected in the composition of an electoral college responsible for the designation, and if need be the impeachment, of the state president (Sec. 7[1][b]); the composition of the Cabinet (Sec. 20), Councils of Ministers (Sec. 21); Parliament (Sec. 37[1]), the House of Assembly (Secs. 41[1] and 53), the House of Representatives (Secs. 42[1] and 53), the House of Delegates (Secs. 43[1] and 53) and the President's Council (Secs. 70[1] and 71[1], [3][b], and [3][c]); the distinction between "own affairs" and "general affairs" (Secs. 14, 15, 19, and 31[1]); the franchise (Secs. 52 and 53), and so on.

69. E.g., his competence to designate "own affairs" (Sec. 16[1]); to prevent amendments to an "own affairs" bill by the House entrusted with its enactment (Sec. 31[2]); in the event of a dispute among the Houses of Parliament concerning a "general affairs" bill to refer the bill for final settlement to the President's Council (Secs. 32[1], [2], and [3] and 78[5]); to withhold his assent to legislation on the grounds of a procedural oversight in the course of its enactment (Sec. 33); to dissolve Parliament (Sec. 39[2]), and so on.

70. *Second Report of the Constitutional Committee of the President's Council on the Adaptation of Constitutional Structures in South Africa* (PC 4 of 1981), 70-77; and see also the rather silly speech of the minister of justice, Mr. Kobie Coetzee, "Hoekom nie 'n Verklaring van Menseregte nie?" *Journal for Juridical Science* 9 (1984): 5. Other South

African human-rights skeptics include three public-law academics of Potchefstroom University: F. Venter, *Die Staatsreg van Afsonderlike Ontwikkeling* (Potchefstroom: PU vir CHO, 1981), 316ff. and "Menseregteperspektief in Perspektief," *Woord en Daad,* June 1984, 13; J. A. Robinson, "Menseregte, Militêre Diensplig en Geloofsbeswaardes," *Woord en Daad,* Dec. 1983, 12 and "Menseregte, Militêre Diensplig en Geloofsbeswaardes," *Tydskrif vir Hedendaagse Romeins-Hollandse Reg* 47 (1984): 210; and S. C. Jacobs, "Grundrechte und Verfassungsreform in Südafrika," in Georg Ress, ed., *Verfassungsreform in Südafrika und Verfassungsgebung für Namibia/Südwestafrika* (Heidelberg: C. F. Muller, 1986), 107.

71. For a detailed analysis thereof, see J. D. van der Vyver, "The Bill-of-Rights Issue," *Journal for Juridical Science* 10 (1985): 1.

72. The Declaration of Intent specifies the following objectives:

- "To uphold Christian values and civilized norms, with recognition and protection of freedom of faith and worship,
- To safeguard the integrity and freedom of our country,
- To uphold the independence of the judiciary and the equality of all under the law,
- To secure the maintenance of law and order,
- To further the contentment and the spiritual and material welfare of all,
- To respect and to protect the human dignity, life, liberty and property of all in our midst,
- To respect, to further and to protect the self-determination of population groups and peoples,
- To further private initiative and effective competition."

73. Being part of the preamble to a statute, the Declaration of Intent is not altogether juridically irrelevant, but its legal significance is confined to rules of interpretation: In the case of ambiguity or obscurity in the Constitution Act itself (not in any other legislation), the preamble can be utilized for purposes of establishing the intention of the legislature. See, e.g., *Law Union and Rock Insurance Co. Ltd vs. Carmichael's Executor* 1917 AD 593, p. 597; L. J. Boulle, *South Africa and the Constitutional Option* (Cape Town/Wetton/Johannesburg: Juta & Co., 1984), 208.

74. E.g., B. Beinart, "The Rule of Law," *Acta Juridica* 99 (1962): 137; D. B. Molteno, "The Rules Behind the Rule of Law," *Acta Juridica* (1965–66): 147-48 and "Change the Methods of Change," in P. Randall, ed., *Law, Justice and Society. Report of the Spro-Cas Legal Commission* (Johannesburg, 1972), 96-97; J. Dugard, *Human Rights and the South African Legal Order* (Princeton, N.J.: Princeton Univ. Press, 1978), 401-2; I. M. Rautenbach, "Die Juridiese Werking van Menseregte-Aktes en die Nuwe Grondwetlike Bedeling," in S. C. Jacobs, ed., *'n Nuwe Grondwetlike Bedeling vir Suid-Afrika: Enkele Regsaspekte* (Durban: Butterworths, 1981), 151. My own appeals for a South African bill of rights are reflected in, inter alia, *Die Beskerming van Menseregte in Suid-Afrika* (Cape Town/Wetton/Johannesburg: Juta & Co., 1975), 184-85, *Seven Lectures on Human Rights,* 76-77, 102, and "The Bill-of-Rights Issue," 1ff.

75. E.g., V. G. Hiemstra, "Constitutions of Liberty," *The South African Law Journal* 88 (1971): 47; M. M. Corbett, "Human Rights. The Road Ahead," *Acta Juridica* (1979): 1, also published in *The South African Law Journal* 96 (1979): 192; R. N. Leon, "A Bill of Rights for South Africa," *South African Journal on Human Rights* 2 (1986): 60.

76. B 33 of 1979.

77. 8 & 9 Eliz II c 44.

78. Chap. 2 of the Republic of Bophuthatswana Constitution Act 18 of 1977. On the strength of its provisions, the courts have declared unconstitutional certain security

legislation that had been taken over from South Africa (*S vs. Marwana* 1982 [3] SA 717 [A]) as well as an act restricting bail privileges (*Smith vs. Attorney-General, Bophuthatswana* 1984 [1] SA 196 [Bp]). The Appeal Court of Bophuthatswana declined, however, to find that the death penalty was incompatible with the provisions proscribing cruel and inhuman punishments (*S vs. Chabalala* 1986 [3] SA 623 [Bp AD]).

79. See *The Sunday Star*, 21 Sept. 1986.

80. Sec. 120 of the 1983 Constitution of the Netherlands provides that judges are not competent to test statutes and treaties for their constitutionality. It is the duty of the legislature itself to consider proposed legislation with a view to the basic rights outlined in Chap. 1 of the Constitution. See D. Pieters, *Sociale Grondrechten op Prestaties in de Grondwetten van de Landen van de Europese Gemeenschap* (Antwerp: Kluwer, 1985), 428.

81. Ibid., 280.

82. Enacted as Schedule B to the Canada Act 1982 (of the United Kingdom), c 11. See Sec. 33 of the act.

83. The Basic Law for the Federal Republic of Germany was enacted in 1949.

84. The main characteristics of the Westminster system of government are, briefly, no strict separation of powers; Parliament is sovereign in the sense of having comprehensive and overriding legislative powers, its enactments not being subject to judicial review, and the executive being accountable to it; a bicameral legislature representing two distinct interest groups, the lords and the commons; representative democracy in relation to the House of Commons, but membership of the House of Lords stemming mostly from hereditary peerage; a head of state with symbolic functions only; a cabinet consisting of appointees of the leader of the political party that emerged victorious in the most recent parliamentary elections; members of the Cabinet are required to become members of the legislature so as to answer to Parliament for their administrative actions; an independent judiciary, protected from being influenced or intimidated by the legislature and the executive.

85. I have canvassed this theme more fully in my inaugural address "Parliamentary Sovereignty, Fundamental Freedoms and a Bill of Rights," *The South African Law Journal* 99 (1982): 557 and in the Frederick William Atherton Lecture delivered at Harvard University on 10 April 1984, "Depriving Westminster of its Moral Constraints: A Survey of Constitutional Development in South Africa" (supra, note 24).

86. The sovereignty of Parliament reached complete maturity when, by virtue of the Statute of Westminster 1931 (21 & 22 Geo V c 4) and the Status of Union Act 69 of 1934, the union became fully independent. When the union was converted from a monarchy into a republic in 1961, the new Constitution (the Republic of South Africa Constitution Act 32 of 1961) retained its own simulated image of the Westminster system of government. The basic structures of that system were, however, abandoned with the entering into force (on Sept. 3, 1984) of the Republic of South Africa Constitution Act 110 of 1983.

87. The relatively few Africans who under a qualified franchise system had the right to vote were deprived of that vote by the Representation of Natives Act 12 of 1936, and the Cape Coloureds were finally disfranchised by the South Africa Act Amendment Act 9 of 1956. See the text to notes 96-119 hereafter.

88. See, e.g., the events recorded in note 24.

89. See, e.g., note 16 above.

90. See, e.g., the text to notes 48-50 above.

91. The general rule is that magistrates' courts can try civil cases in which the amount in issue does not exceed R1,500 (Sec. 29 of the Magistrates' Courts Act 32 of 1944); a regional court magistrate can in criminal cases impose sentences as high as a fine of R10,000 and imprisonment for a period of ten years (ibid., Sec. 92).

92. For instance, in 1975, when the Citizen Force was charged with military combat in the Angolan Civil War, the South African Defense Force acted in breach of Sec. 95 of the Defense Act 44 of 1957. Instead of a fitting reprimand—let alone retributive action—Parliament retroactively amended the act to *ex post facto* legalize the unlawful conduct of the military authorities. See Sec. 1 of the Defense Amendment Act 1 of 1976.

93. See note 57 above.

94. See note 60 above.

95. E.g., many material misrepresentations attended the granting of so-called independence to the (Black) national states (homelands): The "independence" of Transkei in 1976 was preceded by promises that citizens of the new state would be afforded the privileges of foreigners in South Africa and would consequently no longer be subject to the segregation laws of South Africa; Bophuthatswana accepted "independence" in 1977 under the express condition that the rights of its citizens to remain in urban areas in South Africa (granted in terms of Sec. 10 of the Black [Urban Areas] Consolidation Act 25 of 1945) would not be affected by the change in status of the territory—only subsequently to find that the legislation concerned guaranteed such rights of current citizens only and not of their offspring (Sec. 6[4] of the Status of Bophuthatswana Act 89 of 1977; see also Sec. 6[3] of the Status of Transkei Act 100 of 1976; Sec. 6[3] of the Status of Venda Act 107 of 1979; Sec. 6[3] of the Status of Ciskei Act 110 of 1981).

96. Secs. 35 and 152 of the South Africa Act 1909 (9 Edw VII c 9) protected the political rights of the Coloureds by requiring a two-thirds majority, at the third reading of a bill amending or abolishing those rights, in a joint session of the House of Assembly and the Senate.

97. *Harris & others vs. Minister of the Interior & another* 1952 (2) SA 428 (A).

98. The High Court of Parliament Act 33 of 1952.

99. *Minister of the Interior & another vs. Harris & others* 1952 (4) SA 769 (A).

100. The Senate Act 53 of 1955.

101. The South Africa Amendment Act 9 of 1956, the constitutionality of which was upheld in *Collins vs. Minister of the Interior* 1957 (1) SA 552 (A).

102. See notes 67-69.

103. Sec. 37(2).

104. See J. D. van der Vyver, "Judicial Review under the New Constitution," 254; W. H. B. Dean, "A New Constitution for South Africa," *Jahrbuch des öffentlichen Rechts der Gegenwart* 459 (1985): 506-7.

105. A. S. Mathews, *Law, Order and Liberty in South Africa* (Cape Town/Wynberg/Johannesburg: Juta & Co., 1971), 32.

106. 1923 CPD 148, p. 148.

107. 1984 (4) SA 230 (SWA).

108. Procl AG 9 of 1977 (SWA).

109. J. Chase defined a vested right as "the power to do certain actions; or to possess certain things according to the law of the land." *Calder vs. Bull* 3 Dall 386 (1798), 394.

110. 2 Dall 304 (1795), 309.

111. 2 Pet 627 (1829), 657.

112. *Terrett vs. Taylor* 9 Cranch 43 (1815), 50.

113. 20 Wall 655 (1875), 622.

114. For earlier judicial opinions to the same effect, see, e.g., Collier, *Ex Parte Dorsey* 7 Porter 293 (Ala 1838), 417-18: "In this country, it cannot be endured, that the judges should declare a statute void, because, in their opinions it is incompatible with the abstract principles of civil liberty, unless it also opposes the constitution"; Ruffin, *Raleigh & Gastow Railroad Co vs. Davis* 2 Dev & Bat 451 (N Ca 1837), 459-60: "The natural right and justice of compensation, and the nature of free institutions, were also relied on

as sufficient in themselves to create the supposed restriction on this power [to assail vested rights]. But the sense of right and wrong varies so much in different individuals, and the principles of what is called natural justice are so uncertain, that they cannot be referred to as a sure standard of constitutional power"; Scott, *Walker vs. City of Cincinnati et al.* 21 Ohio St 14 (1871), 41: "Courts cannot, in our judgment, nullify the act of legislation, on the vague ground that they think it opposed to a general 'latent spirit,' supposed to pervade or underlie the constitution, but which neither its terms nor its implications clearly disclose in any of its parts."

115. See, e.g., J. E. Keeler, "Survival of the Theory of Natural Rights in Judicial Decisions," *Yale Law Journal* 5 (1895): 24-25, who characterized the doctrine of natural rights as "jurisprudence in the air"; A. W. Specer, "The Revival of Natural Law," *Central Law Journal* 80 (1915): 346, who maintained that it would be difficult to find "any conspicuous modern representative of a clearly defined doctrine of natural law"; Oliver Wendell Holmes, "Natural Law," *Harvard Law Review* 30 (1918): 41, who wrote: "The jurists who believe in natural law seem to me to be in that naive state of mind that accepts what has been familiar and accepted by them and their neighbors as something that must be accepted by all men everywhere"; Nathan Isaacs, "John Marshall on Contracts: A Study in Early American Juristic Theory," *Virginia Law Review* 7 (1921): 419, who referred to "the sweeping phraseology of the cosmopolitan law-of-nature school, with its rights of man in the abstract"; J. M. Zane, "Paul Vinogradoff: Custom and Right," *Yale Law Journal* 35 (1925–26): 1026, who thought that "the analytical or the historical or the *jus naturale* school" were "old and worthless chaff" and represented "the work of men and not of lawyers."

116. See esp. C. G. Haines, "The Law of Nature in State and Federal Judicial Decisions," *Yale Law Journal* 25 (1916): 625, who asserted "the tendency to use natural law principles as a direct basis to invalidate legislation and also as an implied ground to broaden and render more effective the specific language of written constitutions in the development of judicial review of legislation"; M. O. Hudson, "Advisory Opinions of National and International Courts," *Harvard Law Review* 37 (1924): 970, who claimed that the concept of natural law was "an experiment which played a useful role in the formation period of American law," but added, "we have now consigned them to the museum of juristic relics" (p. 971).

117. R. P. Reeder, "Constitutional and Extra-Constitutional Restraints," *University of Pennsylvania Law Review* 61 (1913): 456-57, referring to natural-law concepts in judicial opinions, maintained that "the premise upon which they are based has been abandoned by thoughtful men for over a century"; according to (Mr. Justice) H. L. Black, *A Constitutional Faith* (New York, 1969), 35, "these natural law devotees were few and far between"; and J. E. Keeler, "Survival of the Theory of Natural Rights in Judicial Decisions," 24, who even went so far as to say that "there is no case in which a law in any state having a constitution at the time of its enactment has by the Court been held invalid except where in conflict with constitutional provisions."

The Constitution and Religious Pluralism Today

Kathryn J. Pulley

When I mention religion I mean the Christian religion; and not only the Christian religion, but the Protestant religion, and not only the Protestant religion, but the Church of England.

Parson Thwackum asserted the above statement in Henry Fielding's *Tom Jones*. Such a narrow perspective, in which one's own religious view is believed to be the only correct view, cannot be regarded too seriously in a society that is religiously pluralistic. While in the history of America some would have agreed with Parson Thwackum, the majority would not have agreed. Religious pluralism was a reality during the formation of our republic and it continues to be a reality today.

In the following chapter I will describe the various forms of pluralism, discuss the role of tolerance, and address the influence of the First Amendment. Finally, I will consider some of the possible implications of continued pluralism, especially from the Christian perspective. I shall approach the topic from a generalist position, with the intent of providing an overview of this large topic within which meaningful discussion can occur.

In the most basic definition, religious pluralism is nonuniformity among religious groups. At the time of the writing of the Constitution the colonies were considered to be pluralistic because of the great religious diversity throughout, although chiefly among Protestant groups. Many colonies had had difficulty tolerating much diversity and in such Puritan strongholds as New Hampshire, Connecticut, and Massachusetts there was still an unwillingness to give up hope for an established religion. The early history of the colonies reflects a great deal of intolerance toward groups that strayed too far from the mainstream. A prime example of this is Rhode Island, where Baptists and Quakers, among others, sought religious freedom because it was not granted to them in Massachusetts.

Religious pluralism emerged not so much because of the high-minded intentions of the early religious leaders but because of the unintended consequences of their particular situation. Despite the early settlers' interest in religious freedom, the idea of religious pluralism had not been planned. It was typical for Protestant groups to perceive themselves as the only true established church until they became a religious minority. Then they would argue strongly for religious freedom for all.

The situation was somewhat enhanced by Enlightenment thinking. This movement, which encouraged rationalism and individualism, encouraged both civil and religious leaders to accept greater religious diversity by the Revolutionary War period. Robert Handy summarizes this period well when he says,

> Tensions among the multiplying religious groups, the unsettling contributions of much Enlightenment thought, and the excitements of the Great Awakening all played a role in the crisis and erosion of religious establishments. But the idea of maintaining a Christian society was deeply embedded in the culture, and was by no means given up.[1]

From the political perspective, the framers of the Constitution were committed primarily to a legal system that would ensure democracy in the new republic; however, as Handy pointed out, the Judeo-Christian heritage was deeply embedded in the culture. The First Amendment, "Congress shall make no law respecting an establishment of religion, or prohibiting the free exercise thereof," resulted from both civil and ecclesiastical concerns for protection of each person's rights to be guided by her/his conscience in regard to religious commitment.

Church leaders were very active and influential during the Revolutionary War period,[2] and most Protestant clergy accepted the Constitution and the First Amendment. This acceptance relied, at least partially, upon the belief that each individual receives her/his identity from her/his relationship to God, and not from any civil or ecclesiastical institution.[3]

As mentioned above, the framers of the Constitution were greatly influenced by Enlightenment thinking. Yet it is doubtful that they would have had much reason to disagree with the presuppositions of the clergy in regard to the individual's identity. On this particular issue Protestant thought and deistic thought easily blended, and provided the beginnings of a new kind of religious pluralism, which was legally and philosophically committed to the individual and to the necessity of tolerance in regard to a diversity of religious beliefs.

The theory of toleration played a key role in early Enlightenment thinking and it continues to be the *sine qua non* from which the practice of religious pluralism is possible. John Locke, for example, was the English philosopher who, in 1688, attempted to counter Christian arguments for suppression by writing a *Letter Concerning Toleration,* in which he argued that toleration could help a society in overcoming religious warfare and aid in the development of a rationale for religious freedom. Ideally, such freedom would encompass more than indifference or apathy toward religion; it would acknowledge the goodness of religious pluralism in and of itself.[4] Lockean thinking greatly influenced the writers of the Constitution, and they produced a document that promulgated tolerance, although, out of necessity, it was a legally binding tolerance.

While tolerance and religious pluralism were considered to be the ideal, only legislated tolerance made possible the ideal. It did not necessarily change attitudes or opinions. Therefore, after the Revolutionary War, the republic entered into a two-dimensional understanding of religious tolerance. On the one side was a grudging acceptance of the necessity of supporting religious diversity. The majority of both the civil and ecclesiastical leaders rejected established religion; therefore, it was only logical to support the tolerant approach to religious life. On the other side, tolerance was viewed not only as necessary, but as the right principle and the highest good for the republic. The tolerance approach was good as long as there was no serious conflict. However, this view's inherent weakness is that tolerance implies that a stronger group bears with a weaker group, or, tolerance puts up with and accepts what is supposedly unworthy and unacceptable.[5] For example, our society does not use the word *tolerate* to describe our feelings about the medical profession. However, it would be very common to use this word to express the majority of the society's sentiments toward prostitution.

The Enlightenment hopes for toleration among warring factions served that particular time and situation well. However, the doctrine of toleration has not sufficiently given today's American society a means of implementing and directing attitudinal changes toward an acceptance of true religious pluralism.

John Cudihhy, in his book *No Offense: Civil Religion and Protestant Taste,* has argued that there is reason for optimism in the United

States, because America has moved beyond tolerance out of necessity to tolerance as a principle:

> The story of religion in America involves two phases: an early cognitive phase, in which each religion on arrival "learns of the existence of the other diverse religions, and accommodates to them in a provisional, grudging, "utilitarism" way . . . and a later, ethical phase, in which this diversity and pluralism is gradually, internally accepted, as somehow not only inevitable, but also right and meaningful, and good: what was merely descriptive of an external situation becomes normative and religiously legitimate.[6]

The writers of the Constitution envisioned what they believed to be the ideal situation when they wrote the First Amendment; however, the ideal had not been tested or proven workable in any nation. There is much truth in Catherine Albanese's statement that the writers of the Constitution "bequeathed its heirs a theoretical pluralism . . . and in contemporary America that theoretical pluralism has become actuality."[7]

If Cudihhy is correct that America has moved into a phase of real acceptance of religious pluralism, then it is important to direct our attention toward contemporary America and focus on what the theoretical pluralism of the late 1700s has become in twentieth-century America. In modern America religious pluralism is both a political and a theological issue, and the scope of its definition goes far beyond how it would have been understood two hundred years ago.

Today, religious pluralism shows at least three distinct faces in this nation. The first, perhaps the most familiar and prevalent, is denominational pluralism. This represents the continuing differences between and within the many Christian groups. Much of what is currently written about pluralism in America focuses on this aspect. A second face of religious pluralism is that which exists between the major world religions. As the United States has become more global, increased exposure to Islam and the Eastern traditions has been inevitable. We are just beginning to address this kind of pluralism. Only a small percentage of the population belongs to religious traditions outside of the Judeo-Christian heritage; however, the percentage is increasing and it seems unavoidable that America will become more multifaith oriented.[8] Serious discussion of this type of pluralism seems to be taking place primarily in seminaries and is commonly referred to as "universal theology." A third face of religious pluralism includes those who react negatively to the subject of religion. Whether these individuals refer to themselves as agnostics, atheists, unchurched, or simply secularists who believe that religion no longer serves a useful function, they too are a serious force with which to deal.

From the political perspective, the First Amendment protects religious diversity in its many and varied manifestations. As Albanese has said, it is largely because of the theoretical pluralism bequeathed to America by the Constitution's writers that such a pluralism is becoming actualized in contemporary times. Indeed, the First Amendment has effectively legitimated religious freedom in America.

The Judeo-Christian roots alone would not have created the acceptance of religious nonuniformity. The history of Christianity verifies this. Many situations have occurred in which Christianity did not serve to bring equality and religious freedom to a culture. Thus far, the peculiar American situation has been the prime example of how well Christianity has thrived when governmental power kept it well in check. The First Amendment was an effort to ensure that government would not favor one religion over another and that it would not prohibit the actions of any group. And all of this was done in the name of protecting the individual and her/his rights as a free person.

Religious freedom has influenced the society in various ways, and perhaps the most obvious has been the pluralism that resulted from the prescribed freedom. In America, religious pluralism has meant not only diversity but also activity and voluntarism. The First Amendment gave freedom to individuals not only to practice their religion but also to be as active as they chose and to do so in a totally voluntary way. The result has been that there has been much participation in religion. However, the First Amendment cannot adequately address the theological issues that have arisen from religious pluralism, and no legal document could be expected to do so.

Denominational pluralism does not present the same kind of theological dilemmas as the other types of pluralism because there is a shared Christian and civil belief system. Often, this kind of pluralism recognizes doctrinal differences, but focuses primarily on its common civil component and its common beliefs and values. When one belongs to a denomination he/she makes a commitment to the society and its values, as well as to the church. Within American society, doctrinal pluralism is one of those values, and it is well accepted.

Ecumenism has grown in recent years because of church leaders' efforts to stress their commonalities and to work together in a more unified manner. Many religious groups who do not participate in the ecumenical movement still practice tolerance toward other groups because of their shared civil beliefs. Although denominational pluralism definitely exists, it does not present the nation or the religious structure with very much tension in modern America. Occasionally the emergence of a new sect may create tension because it may threaten the common core of beliefs. The Jesus Movement of the early 1970s is an example of this. However, it did not threaten the religious mainstream and ultimately presented no disruptions.

Another aspect of denominational pluralism is intrareligious pluralism, or the phenomenon of small groups breaking away from a denomination because of theological or life-style differences. Although these differences seldom receive much attention nationally, they may be more intense than those between denominations. It has often been observed that there are more hostile feelings between two distinct Baptist groups, for example, than between any given Baptist group and an Episcopalian group. Denominational pluralism continues to exist quite comfortably in America, testifying to an America that has dealt with religious pluralism in actuality. However, there are other aspects of pluralism that have not been actualized yet.

Modern pluralism that has developed as a result of both increased exposure to world religions and increased encounters with nontheistic worldviews has become a theological issue, and it forces the individual to choose between a competing number of gods. Peter Berger summarizes his assessment of modern pluralism when he says that "the premodern individual was linked to his gods in the same inexorable destiny that dominated most of the rest of his existence; modern man is faced with the necessity of choosing between gods, a plurality of which are socially available to him."[9] Destiny does not place many limits on the modern American, particularly in religious matters. In ancient times the location of one's birth, one's family, and one's roots had much more influence in determining which gods one would serve than those same factors do today. The numerous religious alternatives undoubtedly have led many individuals toward choosing a syncretized approach to religious faith both in everyday life and in theoretical religious discussion.

Ted Peters has suggested that external pluralism has lended itself to an internalized pluralism in many situations; that is, instead of aligning ourselves with one major world tradition to the exclusion of all others, we may choose from the various traditions and combine our choices into our own personalized and privatized syncretistic religion.[10] First-century Christianity attempted just this when it encountered Gnosticism, the mystery religions, and emperor worship; however, several New Testament letters made a point of saying that such syncretization was not to be pursued if one were following the earliest Christian traditions.

To some extent Harvey Cox's book *Turning East* is an example of America's strong interest in a syncretistic approach to religion. Cox refers to the turn toward eastern religions as "neo-Oriental" because he believes what has happened in America represents a turn not toward the great eastern traditions themselves, but rather toward the American versions of these religions, which encompass both western and eastern values.[11] Syncretism's root problem is that it denies the integrity of a given religious tradition. It tends to add to a tradition without gaining the strength that an authentic tradition has within itself. Religious thoughts then become like a cluttered attic; much is lying around but no unifying center exists from which one can gain meaning.

The study of universal theology is another manifestation of the depth of religious syncretism in the modern world. The work in this area is not limited to America or American theologians. It is nevertheless a current topic in theological circles in America and it serves both to reflect current trends in religious thinking and to make an impact on future religious trends. Even though it is not possible to present a full analysis of universal theology here, it is important to understand what the issue is and how it relates to religious pluralism in America.

In its simplest form, universal theology is an effort to establish common ground among the world's great religious systems. The British theologian John Hick, one of the many proponents of universal theology, like many others begins with the belief in a transcendent divine reality. Most universal theologians also would affirm that within each world faith there is a belief in and a process of salvation and liberation. The method and language used in each system is different but the end desire for salvation and liberation is very similar.

For the traditional Christian believer efforts to syncretize and universalize are interesting to consider, but their acceptance is based on the presupposition that all truth is relative and determined by its time and place in history. In the past, religious pluralism has worked well in America because of the "common ground" in its Judeo-Christian roots and its individual rights guaranteed by the Constitution. In modern times religious pluralism in America must include the major world

traditions, and yet such pluralism inevitably challenges the strong
Judeo-Christian belief that ultimate truth and the way to ultimate salvation lie only within its theological structures, however diverse.

The primary difficulty many Christian theologians have with universal theology is how to interpret New Testament passages that seem
to imply that the Christian system is superior because of Jesus Christ.
Much interfaith dialogue struggles to deal with this traditional view of
Jesus as God incarnate. The reinterpretations take various forms but the
goal is to develop an alternative that will allow Christianity to be a part
of the religiously diverse world, without asserting its superiority to any
other faith system.

Religious pluralism poses no problem to the nation politically because we are legally bound to it by the Constitution. From the theological perspective, it is also advantageous to be pluralistic. James E.
Woods states this ideal well when he says:

> A truly religiously pluralistic society is not only one in which there is a
> multiplicity of religious communities which claim freedom for them-
> selves, but also one in which each religious faith affirms equal freedom
> for other faiths, whatever these beliefs may be—Buddhist, Christian,
> Hindu, Jewish, Muslim, or even atheist or secularist. Religious plural-
> ism, when it enjoys the protection of the state, protects the rights of in-
> dividuals to believe, to doubt, or to reject any or all religious traditions.
> Thomas Jefferson argued in a manner that is distinctly American when
> he wrote, "Difference of opinion is advantageous in religion." There is
> ample evidence to suggest that America's religious pluralism has been
> and remains a creative force in American life, both for religion and for
> the state, more so than in countries where one religion enjoys state sup-
> port, protection and special privileges.[12]

Pluralism not only may be a positive creative force, it may also
serve as a means of authenticating one's own theological beliefs and
experiences. Proponents of universal theology believe that when diver-
gent religious worldviews encounter each other, the result will lead to
"cross-fertilization" and increased "spiritual wisdom."[13] Religious
ideas, like all other ideas, tend to flourish when challenged and to stag-
nate when not exposed to diverse thought. It also is important to recognize that even though universal theology and religious pluralism are
closely related, universal theology as a means of coming to religious
pluralism is somewhat of a contradiction of terms. A truly pluralistic
outlook recognizes intrinsic religious differences and chooses to affirm,
accept, and live with those differences, whereas universal theology at-

tempts to minimize the differences and to move toward uniformity. The eventual outcome of such dialogue is hard to predict. At this point, Ann Marie Bahr's conclusions seem appropriate:

> A "universal theology of religion" is an enterprise whose ultimate goal of universality can never be achieved and should not be achieved but nevertheless needs to be attempted . . . both for an individual discipline and for social cooperation and harmony.[14]

Religious pluralism's third face is secular and holds no particular beliefs in any transcendent reality. Peter Berger has written that modernity forced religion into a crisis that has been characterized by both secularity and pluralism.[15] Berger goes on to say that "in the pluralistic situation . . . the authority of all religious traditions tends to be undermined,"[16] resulting in relativism with regard to all worldviews.

Theoretically, pluralism seems to work for the good of a democratic society, both politically and theologically; but in actuality tension continues in the American situation because of Christianity's claim to uniqueness. Lucien Richard raises this issue when he asks:

> Can Christianity accept other religious traditions as valid ways to salvation without giving up its fundamental conviction about the absoluteness and uniqueness of Jesus Christ? Is it possible to believe simultaneously that God has acted decisively and for the salvation of all in the person of Jesus Christ and that Jews, Hindus, Muslims and Buddhists are warranted in remaining who they are and in following their own different ways to salvation?[17]

Christian believers attempt to resolve this problem in different ways. But despite their efforts, the ordinary Christian in the United States continues to believe in the absoluteness of Jesus Christ as God's divine son. Therein lies the dilemma. If the Christian populus believes in the absoluteness of Christianity, then ultimately skirmishes will continue whenever and however pluralism seems to threaten Christian absolutes. This tension will exist regardless of the Christian's belief in the theoretical goodness of religious pluralism. Politically, the Christian community can accept pluralism as long as it does not threaten directly the common Christian beliefs. Theologically, its acceptance is much more difficult.

Realizing and accepting this tension, we must then ask what are the theoretical and practical implications of continued religious pluralism? The implications seem to be mixed; some may decrease the sacred dimension and others may result in heightened spiritual awareness.

One major implication of religious pluralism for the traditional Christian is that he/she must, like everyone else, deal with a large number of choices. Os Guinness has suggested that increased choice leads to decreased commitment.[18] One can grow accustomed to disposing of beliefs as easily as one can dispose of insignificant market items. Commitment tends to lose meaning when the choices are regarded as inconsequential and easily eliminated. An example of this is a new college student who on one given day makes a commitment to Jesus Christ in a dorm Bible study, and the next evening joins the International Society of Krishna Consciousness after being invited to a free dinner. Increased choices may diminish the quality of commitment and one's understanding of what lasting commitment involves. It also treats beliefs as commodities, which are easily exchanged or returned from one day to the next.

Another dilemma created by a large number of choices is that choosing may no longer be necessary[19]—a common criticism of liberalism in Christian thought. Liberalism presented the believer with too many possibilities and not enough absolutes. Thus, the believer was left with little to be committed to. When beliefs are exposed to numerous alternatives, the result may be an evasion of or even a withdrawal from belief.[20]

A second implication of religious pluralism is its inherent relativism, which Ronald Thiemann contends is a genuine threat to Christians' beliefs.[21] In the past the American society reinforced the values and beliefs of Christianity, but this is not necessarily true now. He illustrates this by discussing an issue in medical ethics. The Judeo-Christian belief in regard to human life is that each life is sacred and of equal worth because each human being has been created in the image of God. However, when an ethical issue arises, such as keeping alive a newborn infant who has Down's Syndrome and a blocked digestive system, some ethicists would say that rather than give the same life-preserving care to this infant as they would a normal infant, it would be better to abandon the Judeo-Christian belief that all life is of equal worth. In this situation Judeo-Christian beliefs would be just one system among many. Thiemann then concludes: "Insofar as our public institutions begin to reflect those alien values, and insofar as we ourselves become influenced and formed by them, we run a risk of a crisis of Christian identity."[22] Thiemann is suggesting that Christian beliefs and the moral values of the nation have paralleled each other throughout most of America's history. However, a possible consequence of pluralism is a greater difference between the two, which may lead to a crisis for one who seeks identity from both the nation and the religious institutions.

Christianity in modern America has struggled with relativism in ethical norms, but authentic religious pluralism implies relativism in regard to the worldview itself. In such a society, all Christianity's doctrinal and moral beliefs become one alternative among many. Such all-encompassing religious pluralism will inevitably affect every foundation of our Judeo-Christian-rooted nation.

A third implication of religious pluralism is that the discipline of theology itself has been altered. Theologians who are primarily interested in making theology a scientific discipline, or who are interested in universalizing theology, lose its higher purpose. Both Thiemann and Berger would urge Christians to remember that theology's primary purpose is to enhance and nurture one's faith commitment.[23] To the extent that it does so, theology also serves a very practical function. Through the enhancement of faith, theology cannot become isolated from the faith community to which it speaks nor can it become a purely intellectual enterprise.

Despite the problems religious pluralism raises for the Christian community, it does have some positive implications. Increased exposure to various world religions does lead potentially to a greater understanding of one's own faith commitment. Insights gained from other traditions may also aid one in dealing with the problems presented by modernity and relativism. Faith can be revitalized by other faith statements and by observing acts of faith in other traditions. Tolerance, as a principle, does not demand that the Christian community abandon its belief system. Christian history has shown repeatedly that Christian faith has not diminished when challenged by competing worldviews. Rather, in such situations Christian beliefs have tended to thrive. In ancient Rome Christianity not only maintained its beliefs but also became the legal religion of the Empire. A more recent example is the United States in the 1960s, when, in the midst of great religious and civil disagreement a lot of new religious groups emerged, many of which were Christian. Despite a declining church membership among mainline churches, many individuals seemed to be relocating, often in a Christian group. Berger's analysis of Christian history and faith provides an appropriate summary statement:

The history of Christianity is not the history of Christian theology. Rather, it is the history of a particular kind of religious experience and religious faith . . . if Christianity has a future, it will be in the resurgence of Christian experience and faith in the lives of people who have never read a theological book. . . . For the Christian, history is in the hands of God.[24]

The Christian must remain open to the universe and learn what is to be learned from other religions.

To be open and tolerant and also to be somewhat closed and committed to only one belief system is a paradoxical task. Nevertheless, the combination of the Judeo-Christian worldview and the directive of the First Amendment has created an ideal tension in America that provides the society with a solid foundation. In addition, it directs the nation toward a greater understanding of itself and its neighbors.

NOTES

1. Robert T. Handy, *A Christian America* (New York: Oxford Univ. Press, 1984), 23.

2. See James H. Smylie, "Protestant Clergy, the First Amendment and Beginnings of a Constitutional Debate, 1781–91," in Elwyn A. Smith, ed., *The Religion of the Republic* (Philadelphia: Fortress Press, 1971), 116-53.

3. Ibid., 152.

4. John E. Smith, "Tolerance as Principle and as Necessity," *Union Quarterly Seminary Review* 38 (1984): 290.

5. Ibid., 295.

6. John Murray Cudihhy, *No Offense: Civil Religion and Protestant Taste* (New York: Seabury Press, 1978), 164.

7. Catherine L. Albanese, "Dominant and Public Center: Reflections on the 'One' Religion of the United States," *American Journal of Theology and Philosophy* 4 (1983): 83.

8. See Wade Clark Roof and William McKinney, "Denominational America and the New Religious Pluralism," *Annals of the American Academy of Political and Social Sciences* (July 1985): 24-38. The authors estimate that 4 percent of the population has a faith commitment outside of Judaism, Catholicism, and Protestantism, which is an increase of 3 percent since the early 1950s.

9. Peter L. Berger, *The Heretical Imperative* (New York: Doubleday, Anchor Press, 1980), 24.

10. Ted Peters, "Pluralism as a Theological Problem," *The Christian Century*, 28 Sept. 1983, 844.

11. Harvey Cox, *Turning East* (New York: Simon & Schuster, 1977), 20.

12. James E. Wood, "Religious Encounter in a Religiously Plural World," editorial, *Journal of Church and State* 25 (1983): 9.

13. Harold Coward, *Pluralism* (New York: Orbis Books, 1985), 13.

14. Ann Marie Bahr, "Toward a Universal Theology of Religion," *Journal of Ecumenical Studies* 22 (1985): 198.

15. Berger, *Heretical Imperative*, xi.

16. Ibid.

17. Lucien Richard, *What are They Saying About Christ and World Religions?* (New York: Paulist Press, 1981), 3.

18. Os Guinness, *The Gravedigger File* (Downers Grove, Ill.: InterVarsity Press, 1983), 96.

19. Ibid., 103.

20. Ibid.

21. Ronald Thiemann, "From Twilight to Darkness: Theology and the New Pluralism," *Trinity* 6 (1984): 17.

22. Ibid., 18.

23. Ibid., 20.

24. Berger, *Heretical Imperative*, 171.

Recovering the Mind
of the Constitution

Ronald A. Wells

A nniversaries invite those celebrating an event to reflect on the past and look to the future. The asking of "whither and whence," however, often causes divisions and distresses to come to the surface. Holidays are often very disappointing because it is during the celebration that the participants become more deeply aware of their differing views of reality. The bicentennial of the American Constitution is such an occasion in which the grasping for "the meaning" of that event will reveal deep divisions among the American people. In this chapter I will attempt to discover the "mentality" of the American people in respect of their frame of government. As one looks within and without the academic community one notes a sense of crisis, with persons along the entire ideological continuum lamenting the state of things and insisting that "we can't go on like this." In family therapy, counselors know that the most creative moment in attempting to resolve dysfunction is when all parties agree that "we can't go on like this." The bicentennial of the Constitution offers such a creative moment for the American people. In this chapter we will attempt to listen emphatically to those who deplore the current national malaise. Then we will inquire into how Americans arrived at this condition. Finally we will listen to some commentators who see a way forward. The essential question throughout will be this: Is there any way to restate hope in American government and law as we begin the republic's third century?

Commentators on the left and especially on the "new Christian right" agree that we are in a state of crisis in American society and law. While other examples might be chosen, for purposes of the present argument let us listen to Christopher Lasch, the *enfant terrible* of secular radicalism, and to Francis Schaeffer, the *guru* of politicized evangelicalism. First Lasch:

> The international dimensions of the current malaise indicate that it cannot be attributed to an American failure of nerve. Bourgeois society

seems everywhere to have used up its store of constructive ideas. It has lost both the capacity and the will to confront the difficulties that threaten to overwhelm it. The political crisis of capitalism reflects a general crisis of western culture, which reveals itself in a pervasive despair of understanding the course of modern history or of subjecting it to rational direction. Liberalism, the political theory of the ascendant bourgeoisie, long ago lost the capacity to explain events in the world of the welfare state and the multinational corporation; nothing has taken its place. Politically bankrupt, liberalism is morally bankrupt as well.

From the other end of the ideological spectrum we hear from Francis A. Schaeffer:

The basic problem of the Christians in this country in the last eighty years or so, in regard to society and in regard to government, is that they have seen things in bits and pieces instead of totals.

They have very gradually become disturbed over permissiveness, pornography, the public schools, the breakdown of the family, and finally abortion. But they have not seen this as a totality—each thing being a part, a symptom, of a much larger problem. They have failed to see that all of this has come about due to a shift in world view—that is, through a fundamental change in the overall way people think and view the world and life as a whole. This shift has been *away from* a world view that was at least vaguely Christian in people's memory (even if they were not individually Christian) *toward* something completely different—toward a world view based upon the idea that the final reality is impersonal matter or energy shaped into its present form by impersonal chance. They have not seen that this world view has taken the place of the one that had previously dominated Northern European culture, including the United States, which was at least Christian in memory, even if the individuals were not individually Christian. . . . We have been utterly foolish in our concentration on bits and pieces, and in our complete failure to face the total world view that is rooted in a false view of reality. And we have not understood that this view of reality inevitably brings forth totally different and wrong and inhuman results in all of life. This is nowhere more certain than in law and government— *where law and government are used by this false view of reality as a tool to force this false view and its results on everyone.*[2]

Both Lasch and Schaeffer wrote the above within two years of each other (1979 and 1981, respectively) and both books were called "jeremiads for our time."

When those of the radical left and Christian right lament the state of things, we might reply "what's new about that? They've been alienated for years." But when respected and sober commentators from the liberal center agree that malaise and alienation are the proper terms with which to understand our age, it is time to take notice. For example, Richard John Neuhaus wrote in 1984 that "ours is indeed a period of crisis throwing into severe jeopardy the future of religion and democracy in America."[3] And, in 1985, Robert Bellah and his associates, in a book to which we shall return, follow in the intellectual trail of Alexis de Tocqueville in worrying about the corrosive effects of individual liberty: "We are concerned that this individualism may have grown cancerous—that it may be destroying those social integuments that Tocqueville saw as moderating its more destructive potentialities, that it may be threatening the survival of freedom itself."[4]

What apparently is shared across the ideological continuum is the insistence that it wasn't always like this, that there is a world we have lost. There was once a time when there was human community (Lasch), when religious affirmation was not eclipsed (Schaeffer), when the public square was not naked (Neuhaus), when people could assume a consensus of the habits of the heart (Bellah). While Lasch, Schaeffer, Neuhaus, and Bellah might not agree on much else, they would agree that something has happened to a culture that, as Lasch writes, has replaced "Goodbye," that is, God be with you, with "Have a nice day," and "enjoy." While linguistic shifts in popular parlance may be superficial, they nevertheless parallel substantial shifts elsewhere in the culture.

As we turn specifically to government and law we can identify a constellation of views that undergirded the work of the framers of the American Constitution. As Richard Hofstadter pointed out a generation ago, in a memorable phrase, "the Constitution of the United States was based on the philosophy of Hobbes and the religion of Calvin."[5] While the Constitution was not intended to be an exercise in abstract reasoning but a practical document to govern a nation, it was, nevertheless, a major event in the intellectual history of the West. As Hofstadter writes, "The men who drew up the Constitution in Philadelphia during the summer of 1787 had a vivid Calvinistic sense of human evil and damnation, and believed with Hobbes that men are selfish and contentious."[6] In view of the conviction that "natural" man is oriented toward vice, the Founders believed that a government of virtue could emerge only when vice checked vice in a balanced institutionalization of countervailing forces.

James Madison, properly regarded as the philosopher of the Constitution, explained this view in his now-famous *Federalist*, number 51:

Ambition must be made to counteract ambition. . . . It may be a reflec-
tion on human nature that such devices should be necessary to control
the abuses of government. But what is government itself, but the
greatest of all reflections on human nature? If men were angels, no
government would be necessary. . . . In framing a government which is
to be administered by men over men, the great difficulty lies in this: you
must first enable the government to control the governed; and in the next
place oblige it to control itself.[7]

This, surely, was not an extremely idealistic basis on which to
found the American government. But, some argue, won't such a strong
dose of realism disillusion the idealism of Americans, especially the
young people? Madison was asked the same question by a mocking
delegate at the Constitutional Convention: Was he saying that "the frail-
ties of human nature are the proper elements of good government?"
Madison replied, "I know no other." As Alistair Cooke has commented,
"That simple sentence, which reflects Madison's unsleeping sense of
reality and his ability to get the Convention to set up a system that hopes
for the best in human nature, but is always on guard against the worst,
is what—I believe—has guaranteed the survival of the Constitution as
a hardy and practical instrument of government."[8]

So, it would seem possible for us to identify a fundamental aspect
of the worldview of the Founders. One supposes it could be restored if
the relatively monist, Protestant (even Calvinist) worldview of the
eighteenth century were reasserted. But in our more pluralist times that
does not seem possible. While Americans are free to accept a Calvinist
worldview, those who call for a reassertion of the "Judeo-Christian
heritage" cannot realistically expect American belief and behavior to
change that radically, at least in a deeply religious sense.

Shifting now from ideology to social behavior, we inquire into how
Americans have behaved and do behave. Undergirding the work of the
Founders was an unspoken but deeply felt conviction that there was
such a thing as the public good, or, as they often called it, the commonweal. While the Founders cherished and guaranteed individual liberty,
it was assumed that liberty would always be referenced against what
Daniel Boorstin has called "the givens" of the social order, based on the
Protestant notion of covenant or contract.[9] Judicially, this is repeatedly
reaffirmed during the Federalist ascendancy on the courts, especially in
such landmark cases as *Marbury vs. Madison, McCulloch vs. Maryland,* and *Gibbons vs. Ogden.*

What broke apart the context that formed this unspoken consensus? The answer is complex. A shorthand version would go something like this: The consensus about "the common good" (what the classically educated called "virtue") was broken by no less than the experience of the American people in the nineteenth century, in short, the history of liberty. The history of liberty has always been the history of attempts to negate restraints. Freedom has typically been seen as "freedom from," and as the American people moved west and as they built cities, a new ideology arose to describe their actual and hoped-for experiences. The given of a commonweal in an organic social order was replaced by an ideology that was individualistic and atomistic, which is at the heart of the mythos of American liberalism, and a central cultural theme in American history. Stephan Thernstrom has called this "the mobility ideology."

> According to this complex of ideas, American society was a collection of mobile, freely competing atoms; divisions between rich and poor could not produce destructive social conflict because the status rich and poor was not permanent. If society was in a state of constant circulation, if every man had an opportunity to rise to the top, all would be well.[10]

For a time, indeed, it seemed like all might be well in the land of the free. Powered by a "Transportation Revolution" across the frontier, the "common man" was supposedly liberated during the era of Andrew Jackson. To what extent this actually occurred is a matter of some doubt, but there is no doubt that capitalism was liberated. And with the liberation of capitalism came the rejection of the Federalist culture (and its worldview about human nature) that had given America both the Hamiltonian financial system and the Constitution.[11]

During the middle third of the nineteenth century, many Americans began to wonder just where an ever-expanding liberty would lead. With increasingly fewer common bonds some citizens began to object to the behavior of others, as witness the attempts to "reform" social behavior first through persuasion, then through attempts at social control. The "ferment of reform" was part of the general ferment of American society—a society without national institutions. As Stanley Elkins and C. S. Griffin have shown, reform was largely a failure in the antebellum period: despite the campaign against slavery, the cotton kingdom flourished; despite the campaign against drink, the whiskey flowed; despite the campaign against Catholic immigration, Ireland and Germany gave forth its huddled masses. Reform was a failure precisely because a society dedicated to liberty had no core values upon which all

citizens could rely. The frustration and anger of reformers and those re-
sisting their attempted controls resulted in social violence in the growing cities and, finally, in the Civil War itself.[12]

While it is difficult to assign precisely a time when America became a "modern" society, surely after the Civil War Americans felt the
pressures of modernity more deeply. As the nation began its second century, industrialization transformed American society and created a large
urban middle class and working class. Cities grew rapidly, swelled both
by internal migration and the "new" immigration from southern and
eastern Europe. A mass market emerged, tied to a national economy.
Businesses, separating ownership from control, became large through
horizontal and vertical integration. Business leaders were opposed to
the rise of the "administrative state," which itself was a structural reply
to the nature of rationalized behavior begun by the business community.[13] As Glenn Porter writes, "The nation remade itself to accommodate to the requirements of the modern corporation."[14] It was not easy
for Americans to understand the nature of the emerging society, and
they groped for new principles of social order in a nationalized, mech-
anized, urbanized, and industrialized set of institutions. In an excellent
summary paragraph, Robert Wiebe suggests the paradoxical nature of
the modern state:

> Yet to almost all the people who created them, these themes meant only
> dislocation and bewilderment. America in the late nineteenth century
> was a society without a core. It lacked those national centers of author-
> ity and information which might have given order to such swift changes.
> American institutions were still oriented toward a community life where
> family and church, education and press, professions and government, all
> largely found their meaning by the way they fit one with another inside
> a town or a detached portion of a city. As men ranged farther and farther
> from their communities, they tried desperately to understand the larger
> world in terms of their small, familiar environment. They tried, in other
> words, to impose the known upon the unknown, to master an impersonal
> world through the customs of a personal society. They failed, usually
> without recognizing why; and that failure to comprehend a society they
> were helping to make contained the essence of the nation's story.[15]

In a context of social upheaval, conservative judges and lawyers
thought America to be in a state of crisis, and they worried deeply about
the stability of society and the rule of law. At the same time Populists
and Progressives were appealing to the state for intervention on behalf
of those victimized by the same changes. Both sides were looking to

law for the purpose of social control and stability, but their respective visions of that stability varied markedly.[16] There was a "psychic crisis" in the 1890s centered on no less than two levels of consciousness about the very meaning of America itself. "In the eyes of those farmers, laborers and radicals who joined in the People's Party of the 1890s, America incorporated represented a misappropriation of the name. To the Republican Party, swept to victory in 1896 under William McKinley, it represented the exact fulfillment of the name."[17] In short, as Alan Trachtenberg asks, was the new America represented by the World's Columbian Exposition in Chicago in 1893—called "The White City"— or was it represented by the blood and fire of the great railroad strike of 1894? Both visions of American reality could not be simultaneously true.

The 1890s saw concerted attempts to enact legislation of social order and control. As Morton Keller writes:

> The definition of social status in the late nineteenth century was intimately linked to the control of social behavior. . . . Social and economic change gave new force to old concerns over the threat to public order. . . . The conflict between freedom and constraint of course predated industrialism; the coming of a new economic and social order heightened rather than resolved that tension.[18]

Both legislation and legal decisions in the period 1890–1910 attempted to define, or redefine, the status of persons. Some of these attempts were more successful than others, but it is the concerted attempt that is interesting. First the nation attempted to restrict immigration, initially against Chinese and Japanese, then against southern and eastern Europeans, in the belief that "unmeltable" people would be a threat to social stability.[19] In the same context, legislation, mostly by state governments but reinforced by national judicial decisions, restricted and defined narrowly the scope of black participation in American life. Buttressed by a new ideology of scientific racism, the Supreme Court endorsed the Louisiana separate accommodations laws (*Plessy vs. Ferguson,* 1898) not mainly out of overt racism but out of a desire "to avoid social conflict and to preserve public order."[20] The American government also attempted to define "the place" of Native Americans. The Dawes Act (1887), while helpful in giving some manner of guarantees to Indians, nevertheless sprang from similar beliefs as those expressed toward blacks. The exclusion of Indians from American life was based on the similar assumption of the racial and cultural superiority of white civilization.

Family relations typically were viewed as the private concerns of the persons involved. But the general climate that demanded a definition of status for immigrants, blacks, and Indians also sought definition for children, parents, wives, and husbands. As to the common law, children had no rights, and the parents held property rights in the children's work and service. But by 1900 every state held child support to be a moral obligation of parents, and many regarded it as a legal one. Concerning adoption, Massachusetts passed the first law governing it in 1851, and by 1870 most states outside the South had laws defining the rights of the adopted child. As to sexual intercourse, most states adhered to the common-law rule that the minimum age of consent was ten, although Delaware's was, incredibly, age seven. By 1900, most states, again outside the South, had raised the minimum age to fourteen. The same held in marriage. The common-law rule (fourteen for males, twelve for females) was raised in most states, as the requirements of an urban-industrial society found less socially desirable the early marriages that had typified agrarian America. And, in the establishment of "reform schools" after 1880, the states tried to institutionalize the teaching of working-class skills and middle-class values. This reflects the mix of Christian moral benevolence and the protection of a threatened social order.

Relations between men and women also underwent great change at the end of the nineteenth century. The common-law understanding of marriage ("husband and wife are one person, and that one is the husband") assumed a fixed status for women. But marriage moved from ascribed status to contract, and by 1900 women enjoyed wide powers to contract and to control property independent of their husbands. But there were limits, based on the broadly shared cultural assumption that women needed a social guardianship, both because of their supposedly inherent incapacity to deal in the real world and because of the felt need of a moral guardianship over sexuality.

The belief in the importance of marriage and family as guarantors of social order was so deeply felt that areas hitherto untouched by law, and even unmentioned in public discourse, were now to be regulated, as witness the anti-abortion laws passed in most states by 1900. Anti-abortion policy cannot be seen apart from the general institutional history of the late nineteenth century.[21] In a generally "free" society before the coming of the administrative state, Americans had used their liberty very widely indeed. Throughout the nineteenth century abortions were performed, on a national average, on 25 percent of all pregnancies. Michigan had a national high of 34 percent. In the population history of the United States, a massive shift took place during the nineteenth century. In 1810 there were 1,058 children under the age of five for every 1,000 white women of child-bearing age. By 1890, this figure had dropped to 685 per 1,000. In other words, whereas the average family at the beginning of the century had seven children, by the end of century it had three or four. Contraception alone cannot account for the steep decline because birth-control information was haphazardly distributed and its methods were marginally effective at best. It seems that abortion was the main means of American birth control.

By 1900, most states had some form of anti-abortion law in place. The crusaders for these laws were physicians, not clergy or other moral reformers, and their crusade can be understood more in institutional terms than in moral ones. University-trained doctors, calling themselves "regulars," banded together in a new organization, the American Medical Association, founded in 1847. They campaigned against the irregularly trained persons posing as doctors and against home-remedy-type "folk healers," the latter of which performed most abortions. The "regulars" believed, rightly as it turned out, that if they were successful in criminalizing abortions, they would deprive the "competition" from a considerable part of its business and income. As James Mohr notes, in a most incisive book on the subject, two factors emerged after 1870 that allowed the AMA and its indefatigable leader, Boston doctor Horatio Storer, to succeed in the campaign to enact anti-abortion legislation. Amid the general professionalization of America doctors were increasingly seen as the only credible group to deal with health issues. The rise of the Republican party, moreover, "whose members were willing to use the powers of the state, were predisposed to rationalizing and bureaucratizing public policies of all sorts, and were very open to the influence and the advice of professionals and experts."[22] While anti-abortion policy never became a politically partisan issue, it was supported by persons who were worried about the general threat to social order, and who supported both legislation and judicial decisions that brought social stability. It is in this sense that historian Gabriel Kolko could assert that the triumph of "progressive" legislation was, in a certain sense, "the triumph of conservatism."[23]

In constitutional and legal terms the "psychic crisis" of the nineties and its result can be seen best in the transition on the Supreme Court from a kind of legal formalism to a new kind of law called "sociological law." Formalism in law seeks to perpetuate the law as immune from social influence, while sociological law accepts social influence. This transition has vexed and exercised such contemporary writers on the new "Christian right" as John Whitehead and Rousas Rushdooney, and the popularizer of their viewpoints, Francis A. Schaeffer.

Schaeffer finds it intolerable that a legal scholar like Oliver Wendell Holmes should write that "the life of the law has not been logic: it has been experience," and that former Chief Justice Frederick Vinson should state: "Nothing is more certain in modern societies than the principle that there should be no absolutes."[24] Schaeffer's insight is valuable, but in offering it he loses sight of the fact that the common law itself was changing. The best (or worst) example of formal legal thinking gone mad is the Supreme Court case of *Santa Clara County vs. Southern Pacific Railway Company* (1886), the famous case that allowed large corporations to be declared "persons" under the meaning of the "due process" clauses of the Fifth and Fourteenth amendments, thereby largely freeing them from restraint by the "Administrative State." This doctrine was developed and formalized in *Smyth vs. Ames,* in 1898. It would seem to be the height of legal formalism, untouched by reality, if the Supreme Court cannot distinguish between a "person" who is a freed slave who needs protection of his civil rights and a "person" who is Carnegie Steel Corporation. In fact, even in "formal" legal thinking there had already been an adaptation to social change, as noted above, when law and the administrative state moved to create a new pattern of social order in the face of perceived threat. Indeed, the advent of "sociological law" does not run to the logical antithesis of formal law. The acceptance of materials other than pure legal precedents in making judicial decisions does not imply that precedents are no longer important but that courts and bureaus must also bring sociological, economic, medical, or other social-scientific materials into the decision-making process.

The first major break in formal legal decisions came in *Muller vs. Oregon* in 1908. Louis D. Brandeis, then still in private practice, presented a brief that was accepted by the court in which both social information and precedent were heard. Indeed, this did open the way for a new understanding of law, in which legal formalism was balanced with extralegal information. Under this new style of thinking many Congressional acts were now deemed constitutional that in prior times would probably have been unconstitutional. In the Pure Food and Drug

Act, the Meat Inspection Act, and even the morals-related Mann Act, the court listened to, and partly based it decision on, extralegal information. Under the influence of such law professors as Roscoe Pound, Oliver Wendell Holmes, Thomas Powell, and Felix Frankfurter, legal formalism was devalued in the education of lawyers, and by the mid-twentieth century sociological law was widely accepted. The most memorable recent example was the landmark Supreme Court case, *Brown vs. The Board of Education of Topeka Kansas* (1954), on school segregation. The lawyers for the board thought they had the case won in citing prior precedents, especially the "separate but equal" doctrine of *Plessy vs. Ferguson* (1896). In the end, the Supreme Court made its decision more on the basis of the social-psychological information on the effects of segregation on children than on prior legal precedent. Despite one's personal views on whether or not the court did right in banning segregation from any legal standing, it surely allowed the question to be raised that John Adams voiced long ago: "Is this a government of laws or of men?"

These two conceptions of law have always been present in American history, although it is clear that sociological law has been more widely taught and practiced for at least two generations. The writing of Daniel J. Boorstin, one of the least hysterical observers of the American scene, can help us to identify some of the problems in this shift of legal thinking and perhaps to suggest a possible way forward. In answering John Adams's question about a government of laws or of men, Boorstin inquires into the realities of American history, in which laws are thought to be both immanent and instrumental. He writes:

> We wish to believe both that our laws came from a necessity beyond our reach, and that they are our own instruments shaping our community to our chosen ends. We wish to believe that our laws are both changeless and changeable, divine and secular, permanent and temporary, transcendental and pragmatic.[25]

The discovery that man could make his own laws could be considered a burden. If laws were seen to be "given," then men could obey or object, but if laws are extensions of our own creation it places a burden of responsibility on society hitherto unfelt. Boorstin asks the most serious question possible in this context: "How retain any belief in the immanence of law, in its superiority to our individual, temporal needs, after we have adopted a wholehearted belief in its instrumentality. . . ? How believe that in some sense the basic laws of society are given by

God, after we have become convinced that we have given them to ourselves?"[26]

Part of the American difficulty in thinking about law is that Americans bore no struggle in bringing forth the common law. It was one of
"the givens" of America at its creation. Since there was no national,
self-conscious act of adopting the sum of British legal experience,
Americans came to assume a certain inevitability to the whole system
of law. As Boorstin writes, "We embraced the Blackstonian view
(which in England even by the time of our Revolution was coming to
seem obsolete) that the common law was providential embodiment of
Reason and Nature."[27] As a result, Americans gave little attention to
legislation as an instrument for social change because of their devotion
to a Constitution that would govern the nature of that change, or constitutional law would be immanent in "the American way of life." Law
as immanent force, however, can become sterile if unchanging, and, as
noted above, especially in the cases regarding the anti-abortion laws,
instrumental law—as vehicle for social change—had to have been
enacted when the common law proved to be unaccommodating to the
changing needs of society. The task facing Americans in the last quarter of the twentieth century is to regain that sense of balance between
implicit and explicit law, between the immanent and the instrumental.
It is, however, difficult to recover that balance when the social context
for balance—a consensus—either no longer is seen to exist or is
severely eroded. It is the task of rebuilding that American social consensus to which we now turn in conclusion.

As stated at the beginning of this chapter, all parties in the contemporary debate about the future of America are agreed that an essential
social consensus no longer exists. Conservative commentators insist
that the only way forward is to admit fully and frankly that we have lost
the mentality that undergirded the work of the Constitution writers, that
is, that there is such a thing as the commonweal, and that the whole discussion of public virtue must take place in a context in which religious
values are formative, as they were then. My essential thesis is to affirm
that view, but proceeding further, we must see how and why the mind
of the Constitution was lost. In short, that mind was lost because of the
history of liberty in America. Community in America was not lost because elite groups began to think differently but because the American
people, as a whole, began to behave differently. So, before conservative commentators too quickly savor their intellectual victory, they
should be aware of what that victory will cost them. Most contemporary

conservatives, of course, are really radical liberals, in that they have a foundational belief in individual liberty and a distrust of a government that would shape the exercise of that liberty. Only in America could radical liberals get away with calling themselves conservatives!

One of the most telling examples of the contemporary confusion about "liberal" and "conservative" viewpoints is that about "Right to Choose" and "Right to Life." Pro-abortionists believe in liberty, an individual's right to choose, and, in doing so, they stand squarely in the mainline tradition of the American people who celebrate a good society as one that gave scope for an ever-expanding liberty. Anti-abortionists do not believe in liberty because they deplore the result of the individual's free choice. They say that community is violated by such liberty, that the virtue necessary for a commonweal does not exist. In taking these positions for "choice" and for "life," many commentators argue at philosophical cross-purposes, apparently unaware of the paradoxes and ironies involved. For example, Jerry Falwell, a noted anti-abortionist, founded a university he insists on calling "Liberty." I take it that Falwell means to assert community, so he really should have named his school "Solidarity University." It is a functional nonsense for someone to look out on the disarray of contemporary America and say "liberty has failed, give us more liberty." Similarly, Francis Schaeffer, who did more than any other person to make anti-abortion a Christian issue, is confused about law and liberty.[28] He believes that the reason for the abortion crisis is the prior acceptance of sociological law. The irony here is that under immanent law throughout the nineteenth century there were millions of abortions, but it is only through instrumental law that states criminalized abortion in a desire for social control. To be sure, he is correct in believing that the recriminalizing of abortion in our time would restore the foundational beliefs of the founding, constitutional generation of Americans, but it would do so in self-conscious rejection of the main American cultural belief— in an ever-expanding liberty.

It would seem that we need some new ways of talking about our current problems because the words in the extant lexicon (liberal, conservative, left, right) are not only not useful, they are essentially secular distinctions that should not define the work of Christian writers, such as those in this volume. Richard John Neuhaus helps form a new basis for discussion by speaking of the arena for the commonweal as "the public square."[29] The public square, the forum for public discourse and the place where the American consensus was formed, was once "clothed" with the conviction that public attitudes and policies were, and ought to be, informed by religious values. In Neuhaus's view, that public square has, in the past half-century, become "naked," both because a "new class" of elite thinkers has asserted and assumed that American society is now secular and because the courts have pressed relentlessly the constitutional requirement of the separation of church and state to ends that the writers of the Constitution and the majority of the American people never intended. In putting the argument in this ingenious way, Neuhaus caused his readers to rise above the conventional-wisdom positions of left and right. He is critical of "main-line-liberalism" and of the politicized "sectarianism" of fundamentalist-evangelicalism. Very much in the Niebuhrian mold of "Christian realism," he calls for a new "third way" that equally rejects the vacuousness of religious liberalism's embrace of modernity and the absolutism of the moral majoritarians' desperate clinging to a monist culture of a white Protestant hegemony.

A. James Reichley further expands our new ways of talking about the subject we all want to redefine, the role of religion in American life. Reichley insists on what, by now, must be seen as a starting place for redefinition: that whatever Americans might mean by the establishment clause in the Constitution, the founding generation and the majority of Americans since then have believed that the functional separation of church and state in no way excludes the notion that religious values should guide and support government in the American republic.[30] He calls his prescription for good government "theistic humanism," which indicates a commitment to the ordering of human life in accountability to transcendent truth.

Robert Bellah and his associates have written what I believe to be both the best analysis of the American malaise and the best prescription for recovering the lost consensus. In the quotation cited earlier, they invoke the analysis of Alexis de Tocqueville, whose *Democracy in America* (1835, 1840) may be the best and most enduring work about America. Tocqueville hoped that America would succeed, both for itself but also as an example to the world. Yet he warned that the race was on between the vitality of liberty's possibilities and the decadence of liberty's excess. He believed that Americans need not go all the way to the anarchy toward which the logic of their liberty tended. Rather, liberty would be safeguarded by certain "givens"—most notably "the equality of condition"—in the context of a consensual community. As noted, Bellah and his associates see decadence winning over vitality.

A decadent America is not so much reprehensible as pitiable. The Americans to be pitied in Bellah's work are not the oppressed and outgroups, but the winners and holders of the "American Dream." The people who form the basis for Bellah's study are those who, in one definition or another, are successful. They are winners but they are not fulfilled. The American ideal of liberty has propelled them on their way. But where has it brought, or left, them? (Here one thinks of Whitman in "Facing West from California's Shores," saying, "Where is what I started for so long ago, and why is it yet unfound?")

The main reason that Americans are unfulfilled, even in their success, is they have lost even the way of expressing themselves in culture, with a language to disclose real human needs.[31] Bellah et al. make the very important point about the "two languages" Americans speak. The first language reflects the prevailing ideology of individualism, of which there are two types: utilitarian individualism, related to jobs and consumption; and expressive individualism, related to psychological fulfillment, spoken in the jargon of psychotherapy. The prevailing American ideology says that the most fulfilled person is the unencumbered, autonomous self, but down deep in the unspoken affective people know, or feel, that that just is not so. Bellah reminds us that there is a second language, deep in cultural memory, now nearly lost, in which Americans express themselves in terms of their callings and commitments, both for the self and for society. Bellah calls these older patterns of discourse republican and biblical. The authentic self, in this language, sees itself as anchored in a "community of memory," related to much more than our jobs, leisure, or the pursuit of the "unencumbered self." Bellah and his associates believe that it is only in the recovery of biblical and republican language that Americans can recover a sense of what to say in "the public square," to use Neuhaus's phrase.

So the message, afer all, is recovery of the lost heritage. One might ask: "Isn't this just an academically respectable version of what the moral majoritarians are calling for in a less articulate way?" No, it is not. Bellah recognizes, as we all must, that the world we have lost is lost indeed. There is no way to "return to religion" in the manner advocated by reconstructionists. That world is unrecoverable because the structures that brought our modern world into being cannot now be unstructured. And a restoration of the monist world of the Protestant "righteous empire" would be worse still. We must, somehow, make do with the modern nature of our society and especially with its pluralistic character. But just because we cannot see the way to restore the former community, it does not mean that we can do nothing at all. Re-covering the mind behind biblical and republican language can help us to reachieve that lost balance between the dual imperatives of society—in short, the one and the many—that was present in the American con-sensus before liberty broke it apart. It is with this reestablished consen-sus that Americans might see the way forward, that they can go on. They would recover the habits of the heart, a deep conviction in the unspoken affective, that causes them to walk with confidence into the future be-cause they remember how far they have come together in those two hundred years since the Founders gave them a document that would endow them with the blessings of liberty.

NOTES

1. Christopher Lasch, *The Culture of Narcissism: American Life in an Age of Diminishing Expectations* (New York: W. W. Norton, 1979), 8.

2. Francis A. Schaeffer, *A Christian Manifesto* (Westchester, Ill.: Crossway, 1981), 17-18, 131.

3. Richard John Neuhaus, *The Naked Public Square* (Grand Rapids: Wm. B. Eerdmans, 1984), viii.

4. Robert Bellah et al., *Habits of the Heart: Individualism and Commitment in American Life* (Berkeley: Univ. of California Press, 1985), viii.

5. Richard Hofstadter, *The American Political Tradition* (New York: Alfred A. Knopf, 1948), 3.

6. Ibid.

7. A good and inexpensive edition is *The Federalist Papers,* ed. Lester DeKoster (Grand Rapids: Wm. B. Eerdmans, 1976).

8. Alistair Cooke, *The Patient Has The Floor* (New York: Alfred A. Knopf, 1985).

9. Daniel Boorstin, *The Genius of American Politics* (Chicago: Univ. of Chicago Press, 1953).

10. Stephan Thernstrom, *Poverty and Progress* (Cambridge, Mass.: Harvard Univ. Press, 1964), 56.

11. George Rogers Taylor, *The Transportation Revolution, 1815–1860* (New York: Rinehart, 1951); Douglass North, *The Economic Growth of the United States* (Englewood Cliffs, N.J.: Prentice-Hall, 1961); Edward Pessen, "The Egalitarian Myth and the American Social Reality: Wealth, Mobility and Equality in the 'Era of the Common Man,'" *American Historical Review* 76 (Oct. 1971): 989-1034; Bray Hammond, *Banks and Politics in America from the Revolution to the Civil War* (Princeton, N.J.: Princeton Univ. Press, 1970); Richard D. Brown, *Modernization: The Transformation of American Life* (New York: Hill and Wang, 1976).

12. C. S. Griffin, *The Ferment of Reform, 1830–1860* (New York: Crowell, 1967); Stanley Elkins, *Slavery: A Problem in American Institutional and Intellectual Life* (Chicago: Univ. of Chicago Press, 1959); Michael Feldberg, *The Turbulent Era: Riot and Disorder in Jacksonian America* (New York: Oxford Univ. Press, 1980).

13. Alan Trachtenberg, *The Incorporation of America: Culture and Society in the Gilded Age* (New York: Hill and Wang, 1982).

14. Glenn Porter, *The Rise of Big Business* (New York: Crowell, 1973), 25.

15. Robert H. Wiebe, *The Search for Order, 1877–1920* (New York: Hill and Wang, 1967), 12.

16. William M. Wiecek, *Constitutional Development in a Modernizing Society* (Washington, D.C.: American Historical Association, 1985), 55-74.

17. Trachtenberg, *Incorporation of America,* 7-8.

18. Morton Keller, *Affairs of State: Public Life in Late Nineteenth Century America* (Cambridge, Mass.: Harvard Univ. Press, 1977), 473.

19. Barbara Miller Solomon, *Ancestors and Immigrants* (New York: John Wiley, 1956); John Higham, *Strangers in the Land: Patterns of American Nativism, 1860–1925* (New York: Atheneum, 1970).

20. Keller, *Affairs of State,* 454; C. Vann Woodward, *The Strange Career of Jim Crow* (New York: Oxford Univ. Press, 1974), esp. 67-109, "The capitulation to racism."

21. Most of the following discussion is drawn freely from James C. Mohr, *Abortion in America* (New York: Oxford Univ. Press, 1978).

22. Ibid., 203-4.

23. Gabriel Kolko, *The Triumph of Conservatism* (New York: Free Press, 1977).

24. Schaeffer, *Christian Manifesto,* 26, 41.

25. Daniel Boorstin, *The Decline of American Radicalism* (New York: Random House, 1970), 72-73.

26. Ibid., 75-76.

27. Ibid., 86.

28. The confusion in Schaeffer's thought can be seen in several of his books, but most clearly in *Christian Manifesto,* noted above.

29. Neuhaus, *Naked Public Square.*

30. A. James Reichley, *Religion in American Public Life* (Washington, D.C.: The Brookings Institution, 1985), 112-13.

31. Bellah, *Habits of the Heart,* esp. 27-34.